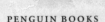

PENGUIN BOOKS

VALUES FOR A GODLESS AGE

Francesca Klug is a senior research fellow at King's College Law School, London, and director of the Human Rights Act Research Unit. She was one of the driving forces behind the 1998 Human Rights Act, for which she was the joint winner of *The Times/ JUSTICE* 1998 award for an outstanding contribution to civil justice. She is a member of the Government's Human Rights Task Force.

Her published work includes *A People's Charter: Liberty's Bill of Rights* (1991), 'A Bill of Rights as Secular Ethics' in *Human Rights in the United Kingdom* (Clarendon Press, 1996), *Reinventing Community: The Rights and Responsibilities Debate* (Charter 88, 1996) and (with Keir Starmer and Stuart Weir) *The Three Pillars of Liberty: Political Rights and Freedoms in the UK* (Routledge, 1996). She writes frequently for legal and political journals and has appeared on radio and television. She lives in London with her husband and daughter.

Helena Kennedy is a leading human rights lawyer and QC. A frequent broadcaster and journalist in law and human rights, her book on women and the British criminal justice system, *Eve was Framed*, was published in 1992. She is Chair of the British Council and the Human Genetics Commission and was made a life Peer in 1997.

...IRE COUNTY COUNCIL

paper

D1353756

Values for a Godless Age

The Story of the UK's New Bill of Rights

FRANCESCA KLUG

Foreword by Helena Kennedy

HAMPSHIRE COUNTY
LIBRARIES
C 003989346
Macaulay 28.06.00
342.41085 7.7.96
0140266X

PENGUIN BOOKS

PENGUIN BOOKS

Published by the Penguin Group
Penguin Books Ltd, 27 Wrights Lane, London w8 5TZ, England
Penguin Putnam Inc., 375 Hudson Street, New York, New York 10014, USA
Penguin Books Australia Ltd, Ringwood, Victoria, Australia
Penguin Books Canada Ltd, 10 Alcorn Avenue, Toronto, Ontario, Canada M4V 3B2
Penguin Books India (P) Ltd, 11, Community Centre, Panchsheel Park, New Delhi – 110 017, India
Penguin Books (NZ) Ltd, Private Bag 102902, NSMC, Auckland, New Zealand
Penguin Books (South Africa) (Pty) Ltd, 5 Watkins Street, Denver Ext 4, Johannesburg 2094, South Africa

Penguin Books Ltd, Registered Offices: Harmondsworth, Middlesex, England

First published 2000
10 9 8 7 6 5 4 3 2 1

Copyright © Francesca Klug, 2000
Foreword copyright © Helena Kennedy, 2000

All rights reserved

The moral right of the authors has been asserted

Set in 9.5/12.5 pt PostScript Linotype Sabon
Typeset by Rowland Phototypesetting Ltd, Bury St Edmunds, Suffolk
Printed in England by Clays Ltd, St Ives plc

Except in the United States of America, this book is sold subject
to the condition that it shall not, by way of trade or otherwise, be lent,
re-sold, hired out, or otherwise circulated without the publisher's
prior consent in any form of binding or cover other than that in
which it is published and without a similar condition including this
condition being imposed on the subsequent purchaser

HAMPSHIRE COUNTY	
LIBRARIES	
C 003898328	
Macaulay	28/09/00
323·40941	£ 7.99
014026678X	

To Adam, Jonathan and Tania: the future is yours.

'A Declaration of Rights is, by reciprocity, a Declaration of Duties also. Whatever is my right as a man, is also the right of another; and it becomes my duty to guarantee, as well as to possess.'

Tom Paine

'I still believe, in spite of everything, that people are truly good at heart.'

Anne Frank

'Men, I think, are not capable of doing nothing, of saying nothing, of not reacting to injustice, of not protesting against oppression, of not striving for the good society and the good life in the way they see it.'

Nelson Mandela

Contents

Foreword

Something is happening: a different *Zeitgeist*, a shift in the legal tectonic plates. The issue of human rights may once have been considered the eccentric preserve of activists monitoring abuses in countries is considered to be less civilized than our own, but all that is now changing. Human rights is becoming the language of diplomacy and peace-keeping and the sea change is being felt not only internationally but also in our domestic jurisdictions.

The Pinochet case was undoubtedly a seminal event in the globalization of human rights. Even if the General did finally avoid extradition and is now turning cartwheels in the streets of Santiago, the Pinochet precedent marks an astonishing advance for global justice. Many of my own generation will remember that one of the student leaders of the 'Evenements' of 1968 was Daniel Cohn Bendit. He reminded us that we all bore responsibility to keep alive the terrible memory of anti-semitism and the concentration camps in the slogan 'We are all German Jews now.' After the Pinochet decision he declared 'We are all English Lords now!'

The factors that have contributed to the current desire to find shared principles by which the human race can coexist are numerous: the slow bedding-down of human rights norms as a result of the Universal Declaration of Human Rights, the end of the Cold War and a loss of faith in the strict ideologies of Right and Left, ethnic conflict and the need for established protections for minorities in a mobile world and, of course, the complex ramifications of the global market. Citizens are also better informed and better educated than ever before and are making greater demands of public authorities.

In Britain the effects of this new climate are manifest in a whole range of ways but most significantly in the early introduction by the Labour government of the Human Rights Act, incorporating the European Convention on Human Rights into the law of the United Kingdom. No more, the long wait before a case can be brought to the court in Strasbourg, now our own judges can consider human rights issues in the cases before them. The legislation will create a novel dynamic in British public life. Nobody is completely sure within obvious limits how the new rights under the Human Rights Act will be interpreted by the courts but some of the decisions could be very far-reaching, with local government, the NHS and all public sector organizations and bodies affected. In the context of healthcare, for example, the right to life article in the convention may demand a reappraisal of the patient's right to resuscitation. Health authorities may be required to provide special cancer drugs without the current geographical lottery. Local authorities may have to consider their responsibilities under Article 8, which protects family life, if an elderly couple are not offered the opportunity of being jointly housed when one requires long-term care.

The government sensibly created a lag time of two years before bringing the Act into operation to enable organizations to review their existing strategies and practice and make appropriate changes so that organizations became human rights aware. However, some of us feel that the dead hand of 'process' could prevent the lively citizen-led debate and release of energy which should accompany this brave new legislation.

I have watched as this book emerged, born out of Francesca Klug's passionate belief that human rights have the power to bring new energy and imagination to the solving of so many problems which now face our world. I had the privilege of participating in discussions with Francesca as the book took shape in her head and hands, and what became clear to me in those months was that few people understand this terrain better than our author. Perhaps the wartime experiences of her own extended family have seeped into her soul and created the huge well of humanity which is the hallmark of her understanding. Her political awareness and intellectual analysis, honed in many different fields, have enabled her to bring a sharp eye to the subject.

Francesca Klug's argument is that unleashing the potential of human rights involves the creation of an all-embracing, human rights culture. The vista she creates is inspirational and challenging. It places justice, tolerance, mutual respect and human dignity at the heart of all our activities. It holds up the best in man and woman and creates not just aspirational principles but a practical code for existence; the possibilities are awe-inspiring. Rightly, this means that lawyers must not command the heights. The risk of a new erudite priesthood, taking the life out of the debates, would devalue the currency. The cultural shift has to include everyone. Once human rights are reduced to the finely argued interpretations of words or cases, or time-consuming meritless arguments in the courts, the huge, embracing possibilities for change will be lost. If human rights are about anything they are about a set of values, whose spirit and philosophy should inform everything from government policy to personal relationships. To travel this new journey we need new words and new methods and all of us have to be engaged.

The language of rights engenders suspicion in many quarters. Law is currently something to be invoked against people rather than used by them. Human rights abuses are still perceived to be the stuff of Third World countries and little to do with post-industrial democracies. The notion of rights is presented as the obvious extension of sixties permissiveness, a selfish egocentric mindset which leads to litigiousness. 'What about responsibilities and duties?' is the rhetorical challenge. Even Jeremy Bentham, the great eighteenth-century philosopher and jurist, displayed scepticism. 'From laws of nature, fancied and invented by poets, rhetoricians, and dealers in moral and intellectual poisons, come imaginary rights, a bastard brood of monsters.'

However, there was nothing ill-conceived or bastard about contemporary human rights law, which had its conception in the aftermath of the Holocaust. The fever of outrage and disgust after the Second World War led to declarations that never again would the world allow such atrocities to take place. International Law had not previously concerned itself with individuals but now in the creation of crimes against humanity it shifted its focus to people; this concept unlocked modern human rights law, which is decidedly intentional in construct, and not organic or pragmatic. What human rights seek to do is articulate an underlying moral consensus. We see this argued most clearly by John Rawls in his book *A Theory of Justice*: 'We do not all agree on whether one should go to church on Sunday but we do agree that everyone should have the right to do so.'

Seeking consensus means emphasizing the non-ideological nature of human rights. Human rights belong neither to the Left nor the Right. It would be too easy for the Left to place a disappointed politics on the back of human rights discourse but doing so undermines the power of human rights ideals. Their strength comes from their distance from ideology. The Right is also at fault in too readily assuming that human rights norms are a liberal conspiracy. No government should be able to declare that they abused human rights in a good cause, as Pinochet supporters have on occasions claimed on his behalf and as supporters of Stalin have maintained for him. Seeking consensus and finding universal values is not without its difficulties but I do believe that there are values to which all people, whatever their background or culture, aspire. There are evils in the presence of which human beings cannot thrive. The reason there are universal values is because there are universal experiences of being degraded, exploited, despised and persecuted on the negative side, and of being valued as a member of a community, having rich personal relationships and belonging to a political organization on the other. The values are embedded in what it means to be human.

The government has sought to woo the 'rights' sceptics by making it clear that rights travel in tandem with responsibilities, which is certainly true. Respect for your rights inevitably creates responsibilities upon me and vice versa. There are also occasions when the rights of groups clash and careful, balancing judgements have to be made. The right to freedom of expression has often collided with the rights of minority communities to live free of fear and loathing. However, what the government must not be tempted to do is see rights as a privilege which can be removed for behaviour which falls short of its idea of the acceptable.

Like Francesca Klug I see the Universal Declaration of Human Rights as the most important and revolutionary document of the last millennium. I am certainly convinced that just as democratic rights – the rights of people to participate in the democratic process – were the driving idea at the beginning of the last century so the notion of human rights will be the dominant idea of the twenty-first century.

For too many people the law has become identified with the state and divorced from the concerns of humanity. The time has come to uncouple the law from the state and give people the sense that the law is theirs. Human rights are the privileged ground where we can bring the law back to the common conversation of humankind.

Helena Kennedy QC

Acknowledgements

This book is the result of an ongoing ten-year conversation with Andrew Puddephatt, formerly Director of Liberty and now of Article 19. Although the responsibility is all mine, it is true to say that many of the themes in this book are a product of this unending dialogue. During this decade we witnessed enormous changes – social, economic, political and technological – in this country and in the wider world. These led us to question many of the preconceived ideas which had motivated like-minded members of our generation all our adult lives.

As the Berlin Wall came tumbling down in 1989 so did the ideological straitjacket of Socialism versus Capitalism or Left versus Right that had coloured the way virtually every major event – domestic or international – was viewed. With this openness to new ideas came a revived interest in an old one, the inalienable rights of every human being. Andrew and I soon became hooked on the potency of this appeal, spending many hours over long dinners debating the meaning of rights, where the idea had come from and how it was likely to develop. It became hard not to ponder how different might the course of history have been had the ideas of Tom Paine and other radicals not been quashed and submerged by the titanic struggles that have defined the last two hundred years. I look forward to continuing this dialogue in the future.

This book could not have been written had others not preceded me and written works from which I have liberally drawn (and fully sourced). These include Keir Starmer's encyclopedic work, *European Human Rights Law, The Human Rights Act 1988 and the European Convention on Human Rights*, which is the most user-friendly book of its genre; Geoffrey Robertson's *tour de force, Crimes Against Humanity: The Struggle for Global Justice*; Paul Sieghart's *The Lawful Rights of Mankind*, which remains the most accessible introduction to international human rights law ever published; Professor Robert Blackburn's unique and invaluable collection of relevant sources and materials in *Towards a Constitutional Bill of Rights for the United Kingdom*; Alan Gerwith's *The Community of Rights*, which is the most ambitious attempt to date to locate modern human rights within three very different traditions: liberalism, Socialism and communitarianism; and Johannes Morsink's beautifully crafted *The Universal Declaration of Human Rights*, which would convince any reader of the profoundly 'moral purpose' of the Declaration. I strongly recommend them all to anyone interested in following up the themes in this book.

I am very grateful, too, to a whole number of people who have helped me in different ways. Helena Kennedy, QC, friend and mentor, has not only written the Foreword but also greatly encouraged me to pursue this project when it was barely a twinkle in my eye. Professor Conor Gearty of King's College Law School, London, likewise inspired and emboldened me to plough my own furrow and not be intimidated from deviating from a more conventional treatment of human rights. Professor Kevin Boyle, Director of the Human Rights Centre at Essex University, shared with me over many years his stimulating ideas, which put me on the road to understanding human rights as a set of ethical values in the first place.

Four very able researchers provided me with invaluable assistance at various stages of the project: Laura Millar, Margot Salomon, Iain Byrne and Mitchell Woolf. Their attention to detail and capacity to 'hit the spot' with the material they provided was unfailing. I expect to see their names on the covers of many publications in future years. My cousin Barry Bluston acted as my informal IT consultant during many technological hitches, demonstrating unfailing good humour throughout and all for no charge!

A number of extremely busy and talented people gave freely of their time to comment on various drafts or chapters with impeccable precision and insight. They are Jonathan Cooper, the highly respected Human Rights Project Director at JUSTICE; Rabinder Singh and Murray Hunt, both eminent barristers at the new human rights chambers Matrix and authors themselves; Veena Vasista, the Director of the Human Rights Programme at the 1990 Trust who has played an inspirational role in bringing together the race and rights movements; Keir Starmer, human rights barrister at Doughty Street Chambers and highly valued colleague at the Human Rights Act Research Unit; Professor Kevin Boyle; and Andrew Puddephatt. My heartfelt thanks to you all.

I must also mention the many people I have worked with over the years lobbying for a bill of rights for the UK, all of whom have helped to shape my own ideas and enthusiasm for this issue. They include Pam Giddy, Director of Charter 88; Anne Owers, Director of JUST-ICE; Nicole Smith and Aisling Reidy, formerly of the Constitution Unit; Sarah Spencer, Director of the Citizenship and Governance Programme at the IPPR; John Wadham, Director of Liberty; and Stuart Weir, Director of the Democratic Audit.

My editors at Penguin, Margaret Bluman and Sarah Coward, both deserve special mention. Margaret's capacity to believe in me as month after month went by with no evidence that I was ever going to deliver defies understanding. I would never have completed this book without her steely confidence that I could do it and her encouragement for the whole project. Sarah's ceaseless sensitivity and patience kept me going to the end. Her brilliant copy-editing skills should be evident on every page of the book!

On a personal level, I am indebted to family and friends for their practical and emotional support when I despaired whether the book would ever be completed on time as one domestic crisis followed another. I am blessed with an array of people in my life who can always make me laugh just when I think I will keel over. Special thanks must go to the 'caravan crowd': Alison, Jill, Nony, John, Neil and Philip.

My strongest personal thanks are for Michael (or Mick) and our daughter Tania, both of whom encouraged me enormously in this project at considerable cost to themselves in terms of time and tranquillity! As head teacher of a comprehensive school Mick was quite busy enough without having to supply me with supper trays on endless evenings as I worked into the night. He became father and mother over several critical weeks and was equally brilliant in both roles. Tania, amazingly, put up with it all with barely a complaint, only eager for me to finish so that I could type her first story, *The Teddy Who Flew up in the Air*.

Finally, I cannot conclude without mentioning the ghosts who have hovered over this project from its inception. The tens of thousands of people down the ages and throughout the world who developed the human rights ideal and fought for it to the end. I grew up with some of these ghosts – distant relatives murdered in the Nazi Holocaust, black people lynched in the Southern States of America, people dehumanized and murdered in Apartheid South Africa – my parents and brothers introduced me to their struggles and never let me forget them throughout my growing years. These men, women and children may or may not have agreed with the ideas in this book but the spirit in which it was written owes everything to them.

Francesca Klug
April 2000

Table: Three Waves* of Human Rights – Major Features

First Wave
Defining feature: Liberty
Era: Late eighteenth century
Political context: Totalitarianism and lack of religious freedom
Underlying values: liberty, justice, equality before the law
Characterization of rights:

1. Individual versus abuse of State and Church power. State mainly to refrain from abusing rights; plays only small role in protecting rights.

2. Anti-democratic; protection of minorities from will of majority.

Enforcement strategy:

1. Domestic bills of rights and declarations.

2. Evolving role for domestic courts.

Second Wave
*Defining **new** feature*: Community
Era: Post-Second World War
Political context: Brutalization of civil society as well as states; establishment of United Nations and evolving international human rights law
New underlying values: dignity, equality and community
Characterization of rights:

1. Evolving duty on states to protect rights as well as refrain from abusing them.

2. Responsibilities and limitations combine with rights to forge vision of 'decent society'.

---

* These waves overlap in part with some countries still exhibiting more of a first-wave approach to rights (for example, the US) than a third-wave one (for example, the UK).

Enforcement strategy:
   1. International human rights treaties and declarations; domestic
   bills of rights.
   2. International and domestic courts and monitoring bodies.

Third Wave
Defining new feature: Mutuality
Era: Post-Cold War
Political context: Globalization and abuse of private power; millennial search for common values
New underlying values: Participation and mutuality
Characterization of rights:
   1. Positive obligations on corporations, private bodies and even
   individuals to protect and promote rights alongside public
   sector.
   2. Rights presented as set of progressive values in era of failed
   ideologies; evolving human rights ethic.
Enforcement strategy:
   1. International and domestic courts and monitoring bodies.
   2. Codes of practice, trade agreements, human rights commissions, parliamentary committees, education and public
   debate.

List of Abbreviations

Treaties and Acts

ECHR	European Convention for the Protection of Human Rights and Fundamental Freedoms, otherwise known as the European Convention on Human Rights (1950)
ESC	European Social Charter (1961)
HRA	Human Rights Act (1998)
ICCPR	International Covenant on Civil and Political Rights (1966)
ICESCR	International Covenant on Economic Social and Cultural Rights (1966)
UDHR	Universal Declaration of Human Rights (1948)

Institutions and Countries

CSCE	Conference on Security and Co-operation in Europe
EU	European Union
ILO	International Labour Organization
OAS	Organization of American States
UK	United Kingdom
UN	United Nations
UNESCO	United Nations Educational, Scientific and Cultural Organization
US	United States of America

Human Rights:
An Idea Whose Time Has Come

The world has turned on its axis in the last decade and with it the face of modern Britain. The end of the Cold War, creeping globalization, the revolution in new technology, the comatose state of Socialism, the emergence of New Labour and the search for a 'third way' in domestic politics, have all contributed to the sense of a new era in British political and social life.[1] Everyone is talking about it. Newspaper editorials, magazine articles, television chat shows, radio phone-ins and websites are all awash with comments about how few traditional patterns we can take for granted at the start of a new millennium.

The decline of the traditional nuclear family, changes in gender roles, widespread job insecurity, the lowest number of strikes on record, the questioning about what it means to be British as the effects of devolution hit home, a growing recognition that diversity is part of our heritage, are all cited as evidence of this brave new world.

The old maps which helped us navigate the contours of political life are now hopelessly out of date. The ideological faultlines which characterized this country, and much of the rest of the world, for more than a century can no longer be relied upon to guide us through unchartered waters. The bitter battles between Socialism and Capitalism have been fought to a point of exhaustion with the classical model of both systems utterly discredited in many people's eyes. There is a widely acknowledged yearning for a gentler, less polarized approach to political life than that which characterized previous eras. The old certainties are fading away but the shape of what is to replace them is still far from clear.

This search for new political values has coincided with a quest for new moral values by a number of commentators, politicians, educators and religious leaders over recent years. Much of this has centred on debates around the teaching of sex education and 'spiritual and moral' education in schools.[2] There is a view that in an era where deference has declined and no single dominant religion or other world-view binds the vast majority of individuals in the UK, we have lost the basis we once had for shared moral values.

Enter human rights; an idea whose time has come. It is not an ideology, or a belief system, in the generally understood meaning of the terms. It has little to say about many of the issues which preoccupy modern Britain. But new life has been breathed into the idea of human rights. It has never before occupied such a prominent position either domestically or internationally. This has barely been remarked upon by the chroniclers of change other than by a few political commentators.[3] This book seeks to redress the balance.

From Kosovo to Pinochet

On the international stage, the 1999 Kosovan conflict can fairly claim to have been the first war initiated in the name of human rights.[4] However history might judge the war, and whatever the merits of the case for and against it, there can be no dispute that the leading political figures of the day judged that popular support for the conflict could best be maintained by depicting it as a humanitarian initiative, whatever other motives might have been involved.

This was no Falklands conflict with its jingoist overtones. It was not even Iraq, where the safety of the world – not to mention the West's oil supplies – was said to be in peril if Saddam Hussein's military and nuclear capability was not kept in check. From the outset, the British Prime Minister, Tony Blair, and the US President, Bill Clinton, sought to convince their electorates that their motivation was entirely humanitarian. Delivering his broadcast to the nation in March 1999, Blair used repetition to stress the point that ethnic Albanians are 'our fellow human beings'.

Liberal journalists generally backed this presentation of the war. 'Not for self-interest did we go to war,' wrote the political columnist Andrew Marr. 'Rather we went to answer the call of our moral imagination, fuelled by the stories of Hitler's horror, now repeated in Kosovo.'[5]

The contrast with the Second World War was forcibly made by a number of commentators. Writing in the *Observer* Reverend Dr Paul Ostreicher, former Chair of Amnesty International, UK, maintained that:

The Second World War was certainly not fought to save the Jews. Indeed their plight was played down by the Allies. Neither during nor after that war were human rights high on any political agenda ... the term ethnic cleansing had not been invented. There was no law to impede it. Human Rights Conventions are of a recent date ... Ethnic cleansing is now recognized as a crime justifying foreign intervention.[6]

In the time that has elapsed since the end of the Kosovan War, the perception has grown that 'national self-interest' remains the driving force of British foreign policy, subjecting the Foreign Secretary Robin Cook's once-vaunted 'ethical dimension' to foreign policy to mockery in the press and elsewhere. But even if this were to turn out to be the last, as well as the first, war fought in the name of human rights, there are signs that the Kosovan precedent has strengthened the hand of those who pursue an alternative approach to international affairs.

As if designed to add to a new appreciation that the obligation to uphold human rights trumps the former hegemonic doctrine of national sovereignty – or non-interference with what governments do to their own citizens within their own borders – new precedents were struck in international law while the Kosovo War was still raging. The British Law Lords, the nearest we have to a Supreme Court, made history when they declared, in a celebrated case in 1999 concerning the ex-dictator of Chile, General Pinochet, that former heads of state can no longer claim immunity from prosecution in another country for acts of torture carried out by the security forces in their home territory.[7]

This judgment, which may prove to be one of the most momentous ever given by a UK High Court, has set a precedent in international law. It gives substance to the post-war international human rights treaties whose purpose was to establish the principle that crimes against humanity know no borders and that heads of state must be held to account for gross crimes like torture, much as ordinary criminals are brought to justice for far lesser offences.[8] In the end, Pinochet escaped prosecution on the grounds that expert medical opinion led the Home Secretary, Jack Straw, to believe that he was unfit to stand trial. Although this was a blow for the victims of Pinochet's regime, it may ironically have served to strengthen the general understanding of the human rights approach as one that shows respect for *everyone*'s fundamental rights.[9] Giving his reasons for not proceeding with the extradition of the ex-dictator to Spain, Jack Straw presented his decision in such terms:

The trial of an accused in the condition diagnosed in Senator Pinochet, on the charges which have been made against him in this case, could not be fair in any country and would violate Article 6 of the European Convention on Human Rights . . . He was accused of torture and of conspiracy to torture of a very extreme kind. These were, and remain, crimes that should have been the subject of international judicial process, but for the fact that this man was unfit to stand trial.[10]

Only weeks after the landmark Pinochet case, Slobodan Milošević, President of Yugoslavia, became the first *serving* head of state ever to be indicted for war crimes while still in office. This indictment was by The Hague Tribunal established by the Security Council of the UN in 1993 to try crimes arising out of the Balkans conflict, most notably the 'ethnic cleansing' of Bosnian Muslims, by mainly Serb forces.[11]

More recently still, Tharcisse Muvunyi, a former Rwandan army commander accused of complicity in the slaughter of tens of thousands of people in his homeland in 1994, was arrested in South London in February 2000 on a warrant issued by the UN international tribunal for Rwanda.[12] A spokesperson for Amnesty International was quoted as saying that Muvunyi's arrest 'seems to be the Pinochet effect in action'.[13]

From civil liberties to human rights in the UK

But the focus of this book is on developments within this country. It is unashamedly orientated towards a domestic perspective of a universal phenomenon because this has been under-explored in the past. Even in the UK, human rights is an idea whose time has come.

This country has traditionally had a somewhat remote relationship with the idea of human rights as it has evolved and developed over the last two hundred years. While earliest British governments played an active role in drafting international human rights treaties and bequeathing bills of rights to former colonies when they received independence, the broad assumption has been that the culture of liberty is so strong in the UK that similar human rights protection is not needed here.

Ask most people in this country and they would probably say that human rights are something that foreigners lack. They are about torture, disappearances, arbitrary detentions, unfair trials and so forth; outrages which are not within the personal experience of the vast majority of people in a country like the UK. A number of politicians actively perpetuate this perception. Virtually every time the European Court of Human Rights delivers a judgment which goes against the UK government, for example, an MP or political commentator is guaranteed to respond with the retort that the issue in question is not what the framers of the European Convention on Human Rights[14] had in mind when they drafted it.[15] In other words, they seem to be saying, human rights have got nothing to do with what goes on in the courts or police stations of the UK, let alone in classrooms or residential homes. Yet the jurisprudence, or case law, of the European Court of Human Rights is entirely consistent with a growing trend in international human rights thinking that human rights principles can be meaningfully applied to situations that face us all in our everyday lives.

In so far as there has been a broad understanding of what the idea of fundamental human rights is all about in the UK, it has tended to be mediated through the notion of freedom, which has had such a strong grip on British identity for generations. In this way the unique characteristics of a human rights approach are lost on all but a tiny minority. Not even many lawyers tend to appreciate the crucial distinction between our legal system characterized by unwritten liberties and others based on written rights. The terms 'human rights' and 'civil liberties' have been used interchangeably over the years. There has been little awareness of the increasing weight given to the values of dignity, community and equality in post-war human rights thinking, for example.

But this stand-offishness is starting to crumble. In the decade following the collapse of the Berlin Wall and the end of the Cold War the phrase 'human rights' has come to eclipse the term 'civil liberties' in everyday discourse in the UK. For the legal commentator Marcel Berlins, human rights have become 'the fashion of the day, and probably of the next decade'. His specific example is the way members of the legal profession now tend to describe themselves. Those who once adopted the label 'radical' are now more likely to identify themselves as 'human rights lawyers' or as working in 'human rights chambers'.[16]

But this shift extends way beyond the legal profession. Even the civil liberties lobby only occasionally calls itself that any more. Liberty has repositioned itself as a human rights body in recent years, adopting the slogan 'Protecting civil liberties, promoting human rights.'[17] The Scottish Council for Civil Liberties has changed its name to the Scottish Human Rights Centre. JUSTICE has broadened its brief from miscarriages of justice to describe itself as a national human rights organization.

While not wishing to overstate its significance, this change in orientation is more profound than it seems. It is not just a question of semantics. By renaming themselves human rights organizations, a whole range of groups are conceding that we have entered a new era. The name-switch signposts a new *Zeitgeist*, or spirit of the age, in which the individualism which had to some extent become associated with the term 'civil liberties' no longer fits as comfortably as it once did. Preoccupations with issues like freedom to party or to buy pornography, characteristic of organizations like Liberty just a few years ago, have been overtaken by a concern to strike the appropriate balance between the rights of individuals and the protection of the wider society.[18]

Single-issue race, disability, women's, children's and gay rights groups increasingly express their demands in the language of human rights with all that implies for a more inclusive approach. The national black organization, the 1990 Trust, has established a human rights programme which, in the words of the Trust's Director, Lee Jasper, aims to universalize the particular. Peter Tatchell, the spokesman for the radical gay rights group Outrage, wrote a long article in June 1999 calling on the movement to embrace the idea of human rights and reject 'divisive, selfish attitudes' which do not appreciate the needs of other groups:

The time has come to abandon gay rights campaigning in favour of a broader human rights agenda. Instead of promoting separate, exclusively gay equality legislation, homosexuals should push for comprehensive human rights law to protect everyone.[19]

Most significantly of all, after two hundred years of resisting the idea, the UK has gone the way of most of the rest of the world and introduced a Bill of Rights, whose story is the subject of this book. With intentional symbolism the government chose the year 2000 to bring the 1998 Human Rights Act (HRA) fully into force, incorporating the European Convention on Human Rights (ECHR) into UK law. For the first time in history we have on the statute books a 'higher law';[20] an overarching set of principles with which all other laws and policies, practices and procedures – past, present and future – must comply. Jack Straw, the Home Secretary, has repeatedly gone on record to declare the significance of the Act:

These are new rights for the new millennium. The Human Rights Act is a cornerstone of our work to modernize the constitution. It is one of the most important pieces of constitutional legislation the UK has seen.[21]

The new influence of human rights on domestic policy does not end there. There are many other examples. Chief among them is the Belfast Agreement on peace in Northern Ireland.[22] The document is infused with human rights sentiments. It has led to the establishment of a Human Rights Commission and consultation on a separate Bill of Rights for Northern Ireland.

Under the 1998 Northern Ireland Act, which was passed to devolve powers from Westminster to Northern Ireland, the new Assembly must comply with the ECHR. A special committee can be appointed by the Assembly to scrutinize proposed legislation for its adherence with human rights and equalities principles.[23]

Admittedly there has always been a strong civil rights element to the conflict in Northern Ireland, particularly among the nationalist community. However, similar measures are included in the Welsh and Scottish devolution legislation. The 1998 Government of Wales Act confers a duty on the Welsh National Assembly to act compatibly with Convention rights.[24] Under the 1998 Scotland Act any Act of the Scottish Parliament which is incompatible with the ECHR is deemed unlawful.[25]

For the first time in modern constitutional history, the courts in Scotland – unlike their counterparts in England and Wales – can actually strike down Acts of Parliament.[26] Members of the Scottish executive, such as ministers and law officers, are also prevented from taking decisions or exercising their discretion in a way which breaches fundamental rights.[27] It has been under-remarked that in addition to all the other ways in which the devolution statutes overturn centuries of tradition, they introduce a system for upholding individual rights which is close to the continental and American approaches that this country has spent the last two centuries distancing itself from.

Yet the government that has introduced these changes is one whose mantra is 'No rights without responsibilities.' It is a government which claims that one of the hallmarks of the failed Old Labour Party, as it sees it, was its emphasis on rights rather than duties. A government, one of whose defining slogans – 'Tough on crime and tough on the causes of crime' – intentionally sought to create an association in the public mind between New Labour, law and order, and victims. This is a world away from the criminals and defendants whose protection bills of rights are generally presumed to champion.

The three waves of rights

This book sets out to make sense of this conundrum. To this end it seeks to explain the values that define human rights, which include, but far exceed, the principle of liberty. The central claim of the book is that to properly appreciate the idea of human rights it is necessary to understand that it has evolved over time, passing through what can be described as three distinct 'waves' characterized by different, but overlapping, sets of values (see Table). These in turn are shaped by social and political factors which contribute to the way rights are conceived in a given era.

This categorization differs from the more commonly made distinction between three generations of rights: first, 'negative' civil and political liberties; second, 'positive' social, economic and cultural rights; and third, environmental rights.[28] The problem with this latter characterization is threefold. First, it creates too rigid a distinction between rights. It has often been pointed out that a number of first-generation so-called 'negative civil liberties' do not simply require governments to leave people alone. Some inevitably require the state to take positive steps, and spend money in the process, to uphold rights such as the right to life or to a fair trial, blurring the distinction with so-called second-generation rights in the process.[29]

Second, this characterization implies a sequential order which is somewhat misleading. The civil and political liberties which gained recognition two hundred years ago at the time of the American War of Independence and French Revolution were further developed, and in some sense transformed, by the international human rights treaties drafted after the Second World War. This was at the same time that so-called second-generation social and economic rights were first given international recognition. Conversely, Tom Paine, the British proponent of the 'natural rights' tradition in the late eighteenth century, developed a complex scheme for securing individuals' social and economic rights.[30]

Third, the classification of rights according to their external characteristics leaves largely unexplained the question how or why rights have evolved. It is as if they came down from on high as tablets of stone; a successor to the Ten Commandments. The people and events who shaped them do not even hover as ghosts in the background.

By way of contrast, the word 'wave' is specifically adopted in this book to highlight the dynamic aspect of rights evolution. The idea of rights has changed over time because people have acted together to claim rights in different circumstances and with varying goals in mind. Implicit in the term 'wave' is a recognition that there have been distinct periods when the idea of rights has come to prominence as a force for change. The analogy with the sea also suggests that the distinctions between the different waves are not rigid but that ideas flow between them. Judicial interpretations of a first-wave bill of rights like America's, for example, could in theory be influenced by the jurisprudence of a second-wave human rights treaty like the ECHR, which was in turn inspired by first-wave charters.

The term 'wave' is unashamedly borrowed from chroniclers of the women's movement who have successfully established the idea of first- and second-wave feminism to encapsulate a movement that ebbs and flows in strength but whose ideas have evolved over time.[31] The defining features of the three waves of rights, I suggest somewhat controversially, are liberty, community and mutuality respectively.

First came the libertarian wave, which burst on the scene in the period known as the Enlightenment. Ideas like the 'natural rights of man' gave intellectual coherence to a generalized discontent with despotic rulers and Church leaders. Together with the suppression of religious and intellectual freedom in parts of Europe and the New World, these factors helped to fuel the French and American uprisings at the end of the eighteenth century. Although the philosophical basis of the movement for 'inalienable rights' has roots which go back much further, it was only in this period that this idea became sufficiently popular to bring about widespread change.

The second wave of rights was a response to the horrors of the Second World War. This was the era when the international human rights movement as we now know it was born. While the plethora of human rights declarations and treaties which emerged at this time still sought to protect individual freedoms and liberty, this was in a new context. For it was not only states that were implicated in the persecution and genocide that had disfigured the world. Thousands if not millions of men and women of various European nationalities had played their part.

Values like dignity, equality and community drove the characterization of rights in this period. There was now an explicit recognition that if the old Enlightenment values of liberty and justice were to become a reality, it was insufficient to rely on states to refrain from tyrannizing their people. Governments had to be required to take positive actions to secure rights – social and economic as well as civil and political – and individuals had to be brought to understand their responsibilities to others and to the wider community if the human rights vision was to materialize.

No issue was considered to be more relevant to this approach than discrimination, and racial discrimination in particular. The Nazi Holocaust against the Jews and other minorities influenced every aspect of the deliberations of the drafters of the 1948 Universal Declaration of Human Rights, leading to a new emphasis on the value of equality. This was no longer to mean only formal equality before the law but a requirement that states take action to root out racial hatred and discrimination of all kinds, including between private individuals. This approach was to change the way that human rights defenders viewed the principle of liberty. Once people are told they cannot be free to choose who to let their house to or who to hire and fire if their choice is based on racial or sexual discrimination, for example, then freedom takes on a new and more complex meaning.

Now, it is possible to make out the contours of a third wave in the evolution of rights. You will not find this development named or clearly identified in any international law book. But in retrospect the post-Cold War era will probably be seen as marking a new wave in human rights thinking. It may not be as decisive a break with what has gone before as the Enlightenment or post-war periods were; nothing like it. Nevertheless, a new trend can be discerned which is worthy of description. Widespread disillusionment with the false dawns of the twentieth century has set in. This is particularly strongly felt on the Left and among those intent on developing a new progressive politics. The idea of fundamental rights as a motor for change is once again undergoing a renaissance.

While there is still the same recognition of the values of liberty and community as in the second wave, there is now a growing emphasis on participation and mutuality. In legal terms the net of liability is spreading ever wider. Corporations, charities and even private individuals in some circumstances are increasingly held responsible for upholding the rights of others (even if, under international law, this is indirectly through their governments).[32] More definitively than at the dawn of the second wave, it is now established that states are not the only, or always the main, abusers of power.

As significantly, there is a new emphasis on seeking change through trade agreements, education and persuasion as well as through litigation. A cross-cultural dialogue on human rights is developing which involves a far wider set of participants than the jurists and standard-setters who dominated the second wave. In essence this fledgling third wave does not so much involve a change in the characterization of rights as an evolution in the place of rights within society.

This new participatory trend is likely to gain in strength. For if the idea of human rights is to live up to the claims that are increasingly made for it in this era of failed utopias, then it has no future as the sole preserve of judges, lawyers and human rights pressure groups. The idea of human rights is relatively simple (especially if compared to the great ideologies of the last century like Capitalism and Socialism). It is based on an appreciation of the inherent dignity of each individual. If this idea is to hold dictators to account, encourage public officials to act fairly, politicians to rule wisely and all people to behave conscientiously, then rights have to come out from the closet or the law court and be understood and even contributed to by a growing circle of people.

While the three waves largely correspond to different historical periods this is emphatically not a history book. Others have chronicled the history of international human rights.[33] The equivalent British story has yet to be adequately told (although a stab at it is made in Chapters 3 and 6). But that is for another book.

This book's main goals

Through this book I hope to achieve three related goals. First, to introduce the UK's new Bill of Rights to a wider audience than that which is attracted to the excellent legal textbooks on the 1998 Human Rights Act.[34] This includes an attempted analysis of how the Act came to be adopted when it did; the degree to which it does or does not chime with the rights and responsibilities agenda of the New Labour Party which gave birth to it; and what changes it might bring to legal, political and cultural life in the UK.

My second purpose is to clarify what I believe the human rights message in its modern incarnation to be. Without this, I suggest, it is not possible for anyone – from judges to ordinary punters – to fully understand the likely long-term effects of our new Bill of Rights.

Given the absence, to date, of human rights education in schools, most people glean their understanding of bills of rights from American movies and news reports that gun control cannot be introduced into the US as a result of this albatross. There is confusion between human rights, bills of rights and international or regional human rights treaties.

This general lack of clarity tends to result in one of two repeated misconceptions. First, that all bills of rights are presumed to be in the image of the liberal, American model with its Supreme Court that can overturn all legislation. Second, that every time the European Court of Human Rights makes an adverse judgment against the UK it is assumed that this is part of a plot hatched in Brussels to undermine British sovereignty. In fact, of course, the ECHR has nothing whatsoever to do with the European Union, which is currently in the process of drafting its own Charter of Fundamental Rights.[35]

In so far as rights are discussed at all in the domestic context, there has in recent years been a significant backlash in this country against 'rights talk'. It is presented as a route to selfishness and a cause of general social dislocation.[36] There is a view that there is too much concentration on rights and that to restore the balance we need to inject some responsibilities and duties into our thinking[37] (even though we were, until now, one of the only liberal democracies in the world without a bill of rights). This backlash has involved a profound caricature of human rights as irredeemably egotistic and individualistic, with no capacity to recognize the common good. By tracing the evolution of the three waves of rights I try to demonstrate how profoundly misguided that conception is.

My third goal in writing the book is this: in the process of explaining what I understand to be the forces that have shaped the modern idea of rights, I hope that my enthusiasm for the possibility of human rights informing a new progressive politics will rub off. Human rights are not a substitute for a fully fledged political ideology. Should they ever become one, that would probably destroy them completely. But if a better understanding of the human rights message and its implications for action had been more widely shared, then the story of the last blood-soaked century might have been very different.

The chapters of this book

The book is divided into six chapters. The first acts as a backdrop to the rest of the book. It seeks to explain what a bill of rights is and provides a simple introduction to the Human Rights Act 1998, which came fully into force on 2 October 2000. Changes to the law and to our legal culture brought about by the Act are explored. The first chapter also describes some of the measures taken by Whitehall and other public bodies to prepare for the cultural shift that the Act is supposed to generate, and suggests reasons why these might fall short of expectations.

For readers who want to know more about human rights debates and less about the Human Rights Act they could start at Chapter 2, which attempts to locate the place of human rights within modern British politics. It explores a growing backlash against rights from two, sometimes overlapping, sources.

First, religious and political commentators from the Archbishop of Canterbury to senior educationalists, who lament what they perceive to be a lack of shared ethical values in a society no longer bound by a common faith or one moral authority. From this perspective there is already a rights culture in this country reflected in increased license and selfishness. Second, a range of thinkers and politicians – including some central figures in the present government – who are concerned to find a 'third way' between the old Left and new Right and who blame both political tendencies (in different ways) for over-emphasizing individual rights at the expense of values like responsibility and community.

The rest of the book is an attempt to show how misguided this backlash is, based as it is on an outdated representation of human rights thinking which has never, in truth, more than loosely conformed to the caricature drawn of it by the 'anti-rightists'. In seeking to counter this misconception I hope to shed greater light on what it means to have adopted a bill of rights based on an international human rights treaty (the ECHR) than that provided by the more formal treatment necessarily given to the Human Rights Act in Chapter 1.

In Chapters 3 to 5 I explore what I mean by first-, second- and third-wave rights respectively, and compare them with each other. Chapter 5, on a new third wave of rights, is inevitably sketchier than the other two in that it is only now possible to begin to make out its shape.

In telling some of the stories of the French and American revolutionary struggles; of the eclipsing of the idea of 'natural rights' by the titanic battles between Capitalism and Socialism; of the ambitious enterprise to draft the Universal Declaration of Human Rights after the Second World War by delegates representing a range of different viewpoints and religions; of the forces which shaped the European Convention on Human Rights; and of some of the consequences of globalization and the end of the Cold War, I suggest what the defining features of each wave are. My argument is that many current debates about rights take place as if this evolution has barely occurred. They are still struck in the first wave.

A straight line is frequently drawn between the Magna Carta, the American Bill of Rights, the Universal Declaration of Human Rights and our own incorporation of the European Convention on Human

Rights with little appreciation of the twists and turns along the way. This contributes to some of the common misunderstandings and false pictures that bedevil current rights discourse. By understanding the way rights have evolved to include values like community and mutuality it is easier to see how it has come to pass that New Labour has turned its back on two hundred years of resistance from nearly all political quarters in this country and adopted a Bill of Rights. An international human rights ethic is developing that could fairly be said to chime with aspects of the world-view of the New Labour government.

But there is also a sense in which the new Human Rights Act poses a significant challenge to New Labour's 'third way'. Chapter 6 tells the story of how the Labour Party changed its mind and came to support the incorporation of the ECHR into UK law. It connects some central themes in the previous chapters by relating the special features of the Human Rights Act to the main characteristics of the emerging third wave of rights and by seeking to locate the significance of the Act to New Labour politics. The argument is advanced that the UK's Bill of Rights both reflects aspects of New Labour's 'third way' approach and stands as a potential rebuke to it. This chapter suggests areas where the Act might challenge key aspects of New Labour's legislative programme as well as fundamental tenets of its philosophy.

The Conclusion tries to tie together some of the sub themes of the book. It explores whether human rights values, were they to be better understood, have the potential to inform (but not more than that) a progressive politics of the future. One which might owe more allegiance to Tom Paine than Karl Marx. It muses on whether, now the century of failed utopias has drawn to a close, the idea of human rights might become one of the central motifs of modern political life.

This can happen only if lessons are learnt from the mistakes of the past and the champions of the idea of human rights do not let it become the new dogma of the new century. Too often the case for human rights is presented as self-evident rather than one that has to be continually made. But the fact is that while every culture will accept that certain basics, like murder, are plain wrong, human rights values have never been universally accepted. It is not only dictators and despots who challenge them. The Conclusion makes an attempt to address some of the key criticisms that have been levelled at the idea of human rights over the years, including an apparent refusal to acknowledge group rights; an alleged preoccupation with public life at the expense of private abuses; and the adoption of the term 'universal rights' to describe what are really Western liberal values or a new form of cultural imperialism.[38]

A debate without end

To successfully engage in such debates without end, human rights advocates not only need to develop an understanding of the human rights message. They need also to be confident enough to open the message up to challenge and allow it to be influenced by current debates, provided this process does not obliterate the very essence of the human rights idea. The evolution in rights thinking which has taken place over the last two centuries is powerful evidence that it is possible to hold on to the fundamental principles behind an idea while allowing it to grow and develop with changing circumstances. As the famous American judge Leonard Hand once said: 'The spirit of liberty is the spirit which is not too sure it is right.'[39]

This book is presented in that spirit. It is an attempt to further the debate on the meaning of human rights. It is not presented as a definitive text. The hope is that some of the themes explored in this book will help to open the frontiers of human rights to a wider group than the lawyers and activists who currently monopolize it.

The nub of my argument throughout the book is that to be fully appreciated, the modern idea of human rights has to be understood as a quest for common values in an era of failed ideologies and multiple (including non-existent) faiths.[40] Of course, human rights values are a particular kind of values in that they have claims attached to them which, as Geoffrey Robertson, QC, has amply documented, are honoured more in the breach than anything else.[41] But their importance as an idea must be judged by more than their legal standing and judicial enforcement.

Human rights are best understood as part law, part philosophy and part political movement. The values which drive the idea of human rights owe almost as much to poetry and music as they do to legal principles. They owe nearly as much to the spirituality of all the great religions and to the eternal quest for righteousness as they do to revolution and the demand for freedom from state tyranny.

Human rights are now probably as significant as the Bible has been in shaping modern, Western values. With the coming into force of the Human Rights Act their influence in Britain is set to expand significantly. In a country where there is no one unifying religious or ethical world-view, human rights values have an as yet untapped potential to bind and cement a diverse society. They are, I suggest, values for a 'godless age'.[42] It is in these terms that they must be understood and judged.

Francesca Klug
March 2000

CHAPTER I

The Quiet Revolution:
The UK's New Bill of Rights

The events of 2 October 2000 will go down as one of the most extraordinary in British history. On that day the British government voluntarily relinquished a whole chunk of its power without any coercion from another force. It hadn't lost an election. It hadn't been forced to cede power to a foreign government or even to bow to a directive from the European Union. It merely brought fully into force an Act of Parliament passed two years previously: the Human Rights Act 1998.[1] To mark this event, a major launch was held at the Queen Elizabeth Hall in Central London hosted by ministers, and over a million pounds was spent promoting the new Act.

Nothing will ever be quite the same again. From now on governments will no longer be able to pass any legislation they like regardless of its effect on the fundamental rights of the people who elect them. They will no longer be secure in the knowledge that the courts are constitutionally bound to enforce all Acts in the manner that Parliament intended. Instead, judges will be required to interpret every law so that it complies with human rights principles wherever possible. Where this is not possible, then for the first time they are empowered to formally declare that our politicians have breached our fundamental rights.

We the people are now entitled to take any official or minister, however high or humble, to court if we believe that our rights enshrined in the Human Rights Act have been breached. Our formal citizenship-status is irrelevant (although our purse-strings are not necessarily[2]). Any of us living on UK soil, however briefly, can now hold all public bodies, and many private ones, to account in ways that have been denied to us in the past.

What has happened is that the European Convention on Human Rights (ECHR) has finally been incorporated into UK law. The ECHR was drafted in 1950 in response to the traumatic events of the Second World War and as part of a new wave of human rights thinking which emerged at that time. It is a regional human rights instrument intended to give legal force within Europe to many of the principles in the United Nation's Universal Declaration of Human Rights (UDHR), adopted two years earlier.[3] The European Convention is often described as the greatest achievement of the Council of Europe. This is an inter-governmental body set up in 1949 to promote peace, democracy and human rights after two wars had embroiled the whole world in conflict. It is currently composed of forty-one member states spanning from Eastern to Western Europe.[4]

Although the ECHR was ratified by the UK government in 1951 and came into force two years later, it has not, until now, been part of UK law, directly enforceable in the domestic courts. This has meant that anyone living in the UK who needed to exercise their rights under the European Convention has had to undertake a long and expensive journey to Strasbourg to take the British government to the European Court of Human Rights.[5] Since individuals gained the right to petition the Strasbourg organs directly in 1966 there have been over 6,000 applications against the UK. Of the decided cases, sixty-eight have involved at least one violation of a Convention right.[6]

But the Human Rights Act is more than just the incorporation of a regional human rights treaty into UK law, which on the face of it could be a relatively minor, technical development. The people of these islands have finally got a bill of rights.

Although the ECHR, as we shall see in subsequent chapters, can be criticized as limited and outdated, the Human Rights Act is of enormous significance in that it has bestowed 'higher law' status on most Convention rights.[7] These are now set to influence all other legislation and policy in the UK in ways that cannot yet be fully predicted. If the Act works as intended, its values should infuse the whole of public life and aspects of private relations too. In the words of Lord Steyn, one of the senior judges who will be responsible for interpreting the Act, it has given rights like free expression 'a constitutional or higher legal order foundation'.[8]

UK judges, although required to take into account ECHR case law (or jurisprudence) when interpreting the new Act, will not be bound by it. This means that while the courts will be guided by the decisions and judgments of the Strasbourg organs, they are empowered to go further. ECHR jurisprudence will provide a floor below which UK judges cannot go without risking a challenge at the European Court of Human Rights. But it will not be a ceiling. Law professor Keith Ewing explains:

what we have incorporated is not the European Convention on Human Rights, but a number of principles which happen to be included in the Convention. We have something much closer to a distinctively British Bill of Rights than is sometimes imagined: not perhaps in terms of the structure of the rights themselves; but certainly in terms of their interpretation and application, with British judges having the same unfettered ... discretion as their counterparts in Canada and elsewhere[9]

The government itself has been increasingly willing to acknowledge the momentous implications of the way they have incorporated the ECHR into UK law. In the words of Jack Straw, the Home Secretary, the new Human Rights Act amounts to:

the first written Bill of Rights this country has seen for three centuries.[10]

He might have added that the last one, passed in 1689, was the only bill of rights in history to give more rights to parliamentarians than to the people.[11]

Bills of rights and political contexts

But bills of rights are strange creatures. They are not like any other pieces of legislation. Part symbolism, part aspiration and part law, they are fundamentally a set of broadly expressed entitlements and values. As a result they are open to wide and varied interpretations by their enforcers. Their impact, therefore, depends on many factors outside the formal terms in which they are written.

In some regimes – the former Soviet Union comes to mind – bills of rights, particularly if they are contained in a written constitution, are little more than a fig-leaf behind which an entirely different reality unfolds. They mean very little even as a symbolic statement of a country's values, these being embodied in other events like a revolution or independence struggle.

In other cases, most notably the United States, bills of rights have come to be recognized the world over as an emblem for everything the country likes to believe it stands for. Despite this, until the twentieth century, the American Bill of Rights was barely acknowledged, let alone enforced, by the courts in the terms we recognize today. Before 1917 the Supreme Court rarely considered civil liberties issues at all. But as the century wore on civil rights campaigners and lawyers were increasingly successful in persuading liberal-minded judges to apply the Bill of Rights in a new spirit and to extend its reach to the individual states of America.[12]

Even then there were 'emperors' clothes' hiatuses. For example, during the Cold War McCarthy era, freedom of expression was routinely suppressed in the name of fighting Communism. It was not until 1954 that the Supreme Court, under the leadership of Chief Justice, Earl Warren, began to dismantle the system of apartheid which operated in many Southern states, beginning with the famous ruling in *Brown* v. *Board of Education* which led to the desegregation of state schools.[13] Notwithstanding the effectiveness of the civil rights movement, it is arguable whether legalized discrimination would have been overturned in this period in the US had there been no Bill of Rights to evoke. But it took more than one and a half centuries before the American Bill of Rights achieved the reputation it has today of protecting the rights of minorities against majorities and carving out new liberties from old ones.

Even in recent years the interpretation of the Bill of Rights by the courts appears sensitive to wider political and social currents in America. Despite the rejection of the death penalty as a legitimate punishment, particularly against juveniles, by a number of international human rights treaties, America can boast one of the highest rates of capital punishment in the world. Since 1976, when a Supreme Court ruling that the death penalty in itself was not unconstitutional led to its reinstatement, over six hundred people have been executed, of which a hugely disproportionate number have been African American and a significant number were juveniles at the time of their offence.[14]

While the American Bill of Rights does not directly prohibit capital punishment, it does provide protection against 'cruel and unusual punishment'.[15] Yet the Supreme Court has in recent years refused to intervene to any significant extent against the broad principle of using the death penalty as a punishment, even on 'equal protection' grounds.[16] In 1987 the Court rejected an application by a black man convicted of murdering a white man, despite a statistical study revealing significant disparities in imposing the death sentence based on the race of the murderer and victim. The Court balked at endorsing 'wide-ranging arguments that basically challenge the validity of capital punishment in our multi-racial society'.[17]

The effectiveness of bills of rights, therefore, and the way they are interpreted, depend greatly on the political and cultural climate in which they operate. Their star can rise and wane over time. Provided the courts are given a role in enforcing them, the precise terms of this role can be less important than other factors in predicting their performance. These range from the manner and extent to which human rights campaigners and lawyers seek to use bills of rights, to the way they are introduced and the degree to which they are seen as part of a national heritage or as an alien imposition.[18]

In Canada, for example, the 1960 Bill of Rights proved to be a damp squib with almost no lasting effect on law or practice. The common explanation for this is that the enforcement mechanisms and scope of the Bill were weak and narrow.[19] While there is some truth to this, particularly in the restrictive application of the Bill to federal laws, in fact the Canadian Bill of Rights gave considerable powers to the courts to strike down legislation which did not comply with its terms. The fact that they did this only once was more to do with the lacklustre way the Bill was introduced and received than the terms of the legislation as such.

The 1982 Charter of Rights and Freedoms, the successor to the 1960 Bill, was introduced in a much more auspicious manner. It was inserted into the Canadian Constitution as part of a wider process of constitutional reform.[20] It was also greeted with much more publicity and fanfare than its predecessor. A huge consultation process heralded its introduction and, although it was not received with universal support, the courts could be under no illusion about its *gravitas*. Consequentially it has had a significant impact on Canadian law, particularly in the field of criminal justice and equality.

Even so, with the passage of time the Charter of Rights has gone out of favour in some quarters. The courts, as ever, appear sensitive to the broader context. There has been criticism in the press and elsewhere about the 'legalization of politics' and concerns that the Charter of Rights represents an unacceptable shift in power from elected representatives to an élitist judiciary.[21] Anecdotal evidence suggests that the courts have exercised greater caution than they might have done in some of their more recent judgments as a consequence of this partial backlash.

Preparations for the Human Rights Act

The climate which greets the UK's new Bill of Rights is a mixed one. Obviously there has been no major national upheaval to precipitate its introduction. There has been no revolution or freedom struggle, as experienced in many former colonies which adopted a written constitution and bill of rights on achieving independence. There has not even been a sustained period of consultation on its terms, as occurred in Canada or post-Apartheid South Africa. Instead our Bill of Rights has been delivered to us wholesale from on high. Nor has there been any attempt to set down the core values of the Human Rights Act in an appropriately worded Preamble, as is customary elsewhere. The Preamble to the South African Bill of Rights, for example, expresses the fundamental values of the new nation:

This Bill of Rights is a cornerstone of democracy in South Africa. It enshrines the rights of all people in our country and affirms the democratic values of human dignity, equality and freedom.[22]

The adoption of a bill of rights in the UK seems almost prosaic by comparison. It is a development which appears to spring from nowhere.[23] But it is starting to be noticed in countries with long experiences of bills of rights. An article in *The New York Times* in October 1999, for example, titled 'Britain Quietly Says It's Time to Adopt a Bill of Rights', announced to an unsuspecting American public that:

Quietly, doggedly, somewhat nervously, Britain is preparing itself for a constitutional revolution that will profoundly alter its citizens' relationship to the state and to the rule of law. A year from now, when Britain incorporates the European Convention on Human Rights into domestic law, ordinary Britons will for the first time have a set of fundamental rights that can be enforced in British courts, similar to those guaranteed by the Bill of Rights in the United States.[24]

The weight given to the Human Rights Act by the government that introduced it has varied over time, ranging from embarrassed silence to wholehearted support and encouragement.[25] This also sends out mixed messages.

On the one hand the government has refused to date to create any kind of Human Rights Commission to promote the Act, let alone one with comparable supervisory functions to the Commission for Racial Equality, Equal Opportunities Commission or Disability Rights Commission responsible for race, sex and disability discrimination legislation respectively. The government's case is that the need for such a commission has yet to be proved and raises unresolved issues about the role of the existing commissions.[26] However, the Home Secretary has pointedly not turned his back on the idea.[27] A Human Rights Commission is now up and running in Northern Ireland but this owes more to the Belfast Agreement on peace in Northern Ireland than to the Human Rights Act. Similarly, extensive human rights scrutiny of legislation and allied training of public officials in Scotland and Wales flowed from the devolution legislation in the first instance.[28] A Human Rights Commission for Scotland is now on the cards.

On the other hand, recent preparations for the introduction of the Human Rights Act nation-wide, co-ordinated by the Home Office with judicial training organized through the Lord Chancellor's Department (LCD), have been impressive in their quality, if somewhat limited in their scope. A Human Rights Task Force charged with overseeing implementation of the Human Rights Act was appointed by the Home Secretary in January 1999. It was composed of three ministers, senior officials from the Home Office, the LCD and Cabinet Office, professional interest groups (like the Association of Chief Police Officers and the Local Government Association) and representatives from a number of key human rights non-governmental organizations (NGOs).

The Task Force was given two terms of reference. First, to help public authorities, including Whitehall, prepare for the coming into force of the Human Rights Act. Second, to increase public awareness of the rights and responsibilities in the European Convention on Human Rights 'and thus to help build a human rights culture in the United Kingdom'.[29] In other words, the overall goal of the Human Rights Task Force was to ensure that this new Bill of Rights led to a cultural shift way beyond the law courts.

The government obviously had an interest in limiting the extent to which the Act became a litigants' charter, and the rest of the Task Force were happy to oblige on the grounds that 'prevention is better than cure'. The broad goal was to shift the mind-set of officials from one where, in most circumstances, they are trained only to ask themselves whether law and policy permit or require them to take a specific action, to one where they also query whether an individual's fundamental human rights are at stake whatever the law might technically say.

The Task Force received briefings from major Whitehall departments and agencies on progress towards reviewing legislation and policy for compliance with the Act over an eighteen-month period. Using a variously coloured dove as a logo, it prepared material on the Act for the public and private sectors and for the general public. All the information had a consistent core message of cultural, as well as legal, change. Number 10 Downing Street put its weight behind this exercise. In a Foreword to a leaflet on the Act, aimed at every public official, the Prime Minister, Tony Blair, wrote:

The Act gives every citizen a clear statement of rights and responsibilities. And it requires all of us in public service to respect human rights in everything we do.[30]

At the time of writing it is far too early to say with any certainty whether public officials will take this appeal seriously once the reality of the Act has set in. It is hard to envisage how, without a permanent successor body to the Human Rights Task Force, the momentum created by it will be sustained. With the best will in the world, it is difficult to see how the professionalism of the Home Office's Human Rights Unit or the equivalent structures in other government departments can substitute for a Human Rights Commission or equivalent, once the Act starts to affect people's everyday lives. Where will individuals go to find out about the Act? Which body will be responsible for keeping public (and relevant private) bodies regularly updated as the case law under the Act starts to develop? Who will monitor the press on a daily basis to rebut the predictably lurid media coverage the Act is likely to attract should court decisions protecting life prisoners or paedophiles, for example, start to hit the headlines?

The initial impact of the Human Rights Act on the courts is almost bound to be significant but its overall effect long term is less easy to predict. It will depend as much on peoples' perceptions of it and the extent to which it finds favour among successive governments as on how the Act is received in the courtroom. If the Act genuinely seems to offer something to most of the people most of the time (if, inevitably, not to all of the people all of the time), and if politicians and human rights advocates promote it in these terms, then public authorities and the courts are likely to give the Act the green light.

If, on the other hand, the Act goes out of political favour and is perceived, however unfairly, as a 'criminals' charter' of little relevance to the bulk of the population (as anecdotal evidence suggests happened to some extent in Canada), then it is likely that all but a minority of committed officials would be affected by this climate. Compliance with the Act would probably be viewed as a defence against legal action rather than as a shift in public service norms. Even the courts would be more likely to give it a wide berth under such circumstances.

But one thing is clear. Bills of rights have a reputation for longevity. No government is keen to be seen repealing them, even if they are introduced without any special protective measures, as is the case with this one. Even if – after an initial burst of energy – the UK's Bill of Rights should lie low for ten or twenty years or more, this would not last. As long as human rights advocates do not give up on it, then it is safe to say that it will get up and bite one day.

The new Bill of Rights as a set of core values

But bills of rights, as we have seen, are more than legal documents. They can help to shape a country's national identity by expressing the fundamental values of a nation. Historian Linda Colley emphasized this point in a highly regarded presentation she made at 10 Downing Street in December 1999. Apparently oblivious of the Human Rights Act, or unconvinced of its potential outside the law courts, Colley sought to persuade the Prime Minister and assembled guests that:

... we badly need more inspiring and more accessible definitions of citizenship ... What is indispensable, it seems to me, is a new millennium charter or contract of citizens' rights[31]

She might have added that the process of passing a bill of rights, as much as its contents, can, in providing a space for national reflection, alter the way a country sees itself, or at least the way it has been presented over centuries by politicians and constitutional historians. The adoption of a bill of rights at the beginning of a new millennium, for example, itself has symbolic significance.

In the absence, until now, of any defining document to express the values of the UK, there are a number of competing versions of what this country stands for. One traditional but highly contested narrative, that anyone brought up in this country will recognize, tends to run as follows: This is a country that never needed revolutions to adapt and change. Other than one civil war, one or two beheaded monarchs and skirmishes between the different nations that inhabit these islands, changes have taken place mainly through peaceful means.[32] Responding to wave after wave of popular protests – from groups as varied as the barons, the propertied classes, the Chartists and the Suffragettes – successive élites learnt to accept the tide of history and share power with an ever-expanding section of society until democracy as we know it was born. Recent moves to devolve power to Scotland, Wales and Northern Ireland and to reform the House of Lords are further examples of this capacity for evolutionary change. We do not need grand documents like constitutions to count as one of the freest countries in the world. Nor is it of any major significance to us that until now we were one of the only democracies in the world without some kind of bill of rights.

Like all national narratives, this one is partly based on a version of reality and partly based on myth. But given its potency it is difficult to imagine what most British people will make of learning that they have suddenly been presented with a Bill of Rights; assuming that they get to hear of it at all. Until now the European Convention on Human Rights and the Court which enforces it have largely been presented by the press as yet another manifestation of interference from Brussels,[33] even though, as we have seen, they have nothing to do with the European Union.

Despite the boast, not altogether unfair, that this is a country which cherishes abstract ideas like civil liberties and freedom, the symbols which until now have emerged as representative of the UK have tended to reside elsewhere. As heritage we have the Monarchy, the Anglican Church and the Empire; more recent candidates are Britpop and football. The problem is that, to varying degrees, the older and more enduring symbols have always been highly disputed emblems, to say the least, in the bits of the Kingdom which were never united. As the country becomes ever more diverse and fluid in terms of lifestyle and culture, these are less suitable than ever as candidates for unifying the peoples of this country. While the loss of Empire, for example, is still routinely portrayed as a trauma the UK has only just recovered from, the reality is that for about a third of the population of London this loss was their liberation.

Now suddenly we are being presented with a set of values which has the potential to provide a minimum definition of what we stand for. Values which are written down and which will be taught in schools. Other countries have had this for generations, of course. In the words of Ronald Dworkin, the renowned law professor:

Most contemporary constitutions declare individual rights against the government in very broad and abstract ways . . . the moral reading proposes that we all – judges, lawyers, citizens – interpret and apply these abstract clauses on the understanding that they invoke moral principles about political decency and justice.[34]

The values in the ECHR

The values reflected in the European Convention on Human Rights, although limited, are now part of our law. In Dworkin's terms, and as the rest of this book hopefully demonstrates, they do indeed strive to invoke moral principles of decency and justice.

Principles like: the right not to be subject to inhuman or degrading treatment; to have one's dignity, lifestyle and privacy respected; to be free to listen to one's conscience; to speak freely and to protest, demonstrate and join a trade union without hindrance; to marry and found a family; to receive an education and to the peaceful enjoyment of possessions; to free and fair elections and not to be discriminated against in the exercise of these rights. Together these paint a picture of what a fair and tolerant society should look like. Rights to life, liberty, security and a fair trial; prohibitions on slavery, forced labour, torture and capital punishment; and the principle of no retrospective or inhuman punishment, all point to a vision of what a just society might be.[35]

Taken as a whole, the rights and limitations set down in the Convention are described by the European Court of Human Rights as the 'values of a democratic society',[36] which are 'pluralism, tolerance and broadmindedness'.[37] But in case there is any misunderstanding, '. . . democracy does not simply mean that the views of a majority must always prevail; a balance must be achieved which ensures the fair and proper treatment of minorities and avoids any abuse of a dominant position'.[38]

Some Convention rights are expressed in absolute terms, like the right not to be subject to torture or slavery. But most of the rights are qualified or limited in some way, usually to protect the rights of others or the needs of the community as a whole. The requirement that no individuals destroy the rights of others and that the right to free expression entails reciprocal duties,[39] together with the grounds on which rights can be legitimately limited, brings individual responsibilities squarely within a vision of society which is primarily addressed to governments.[40]

It is fair to say that many Convention rights are already well recognized in the UK. Indeed, the origin of some of these rights can be traced back to these shores,[41] although others, as we shall see, were not well recognized in English law before the Human Rights Act came into force. But they have never before been written down in an accessible form or presented as a defining statement of what this country stands for.

Whether our new bill of rights can in fact provide the symbolic role performed by its equivalents in other countries, like America or South Africa, has yet to be tested. Some scepticism about its potential to do this is inevitable, given the manner of its birth. It was presented fully formed from on high without consultation and minus many of the social and economic rights that are most cherished in the UK, like the right to health care based on need. Likewise, whether in years to come the Human Rights Act provides the catalyst for a 'home-grown' bill of rights, much as the Canadian Bill of Rights was the midwife to the Charter of Rights, is impossible to predict at this stage.

Nevertheless, incorporation of the European Convention is what we have at the moment and it provides a rare opportunity for this society to take stock and consider whether there is indeed a set of basic, coherent values which we can share regardless of ethnic origin or gender; regardless of whether we ascribe to any particular religion or to none. It also provides an opportunity to distinguish in law between fundamental rights which are internationally recognized as such and everyday claims – like the unrestricted use of mobile phones in public places – presented in rights clothing to give them greater weight.

The human rights values in our new Bill of Rights should not, however, be misrepresented as a set of strictures. They are not a Ten Commandments for the twenty-first century. Nor do they represent a clear ideology on a par with Socialism or free-market economics. Instead, they set a framework in which to debate the difficult issues of our age.

Anyone can join in this debate once they appreciate its terms. Inherent in the whole of the European Convention is the need to find a fair balance between the protection of individual rights and the interests of the wider community.[42] The case law developed by the European Court of Human Rights has established that the principle of 'proportionality' is pivotal in finding this balance. This concept is as central to human rights thinking as any of the substantive rights. It means – on a strict interpretation of the principle – that any limitations on individual rights must not only be necessary to pursue a legitimate goal, like protecting the wider community from a public health scare, but must also not go beyond what is strictly necessary to achieve that purpose. Encouraging and persuading parents to vaccinate their children against mumps, measles and rubella, yes. Imprisoning them for not doing so, no.

So instead, for example, of having to choose between the civil liberties of suspects or the rights of victims – as many people feel polarized into doing – we are encouraged to think of a new way of approaching both issues in human rights terms. Do new laws designed to crack down on juvenile crime involving curfews and bans sufficiently protect the rights of young people to be presumed innocent until proven guilty and to associate with their peers? Are such measures disproportionately harsh and liable to criminalize the innocent or those guilty of trivial misdemeanours? Or are such infringements of liberty the minimum necessary to achieve the legitimate aim of, for example, protecting Asian shopkeepers who up and down the country suffer from persistent racial abuse? Is there evidence that elderly people are in fact freer to leave their homes without fear of harassment because of such new laws?

The way questions are framed affects the answers given. Adopting a human rights framework within which to approach contentious and difficult issues helps to guard against the knee-jerk reactions and rampant prejudices which lurk within us all when faced with fear or anxiety. This approach is especially important if it can help influence the way power is exercised in our society. If our new Bill of Rights succeeds in introducing a new culture of rights and responsibilities this should affect decision-making at all levels. Officials will be duty-bound to consider the human rights implications of all their discretionary acts. Even if only on pragmatic grounds, civil servants and ministers will hesitate before subjecting themselves to the indignity of having their laws declared a violation of human rights by the highest court in the land.

It is not impossible that the values in the Human Rights Act may even prompt the odd politician to remember the idealism that drove him or her into politics in the first place. It could even help insulate beleaguered backbenchers from the pressure to think only of the next headline or call on their pager when deciding whether to support or oppose legislation which obviously violates human rights. The government is under no illusion that these are the likely consequences of incorporation of the European Convention. The Human Rights Act, said Lord Irvine, the Lord Chancellor, 'will create a more explicitly moral approach to decisions and decision-making'.[43]

A new legal culture for protecting rights[44]

The government has just spent £4.5 million training judges to rethink the way they approach whole swathes of the law in preparation for the Human Rights Act. This is the largest programme in the history of the official training body, the Judicial Studies Body. Magistrates and tribunal members have also received training on the Act by well-respected human rights lawyers, including from the human rights organizations Liberty and JUSTICE.

Lord Hope, giving judgment in a key case in October 1999 that considered some of the likely effects of the Human Rights Act before it was fully enforced, indicated how seriously the judiciary viewed its implications. He stated that:

although the 1998 Act is not yet in force, the vigorous public debate which accompanied its passage through Parliament had a profound influence on thinking about issues of human rights. It is now plain that the incorporation of the European Convention on Human Rights into our domestic law will subject the entire legal system to a fundamental process of review and, where necessary, reform by the judiciary[45]

The intention behind the judicial training on the new Act is to change not only the way the law is interpreted, but also the culture in which judges and their colleagues operate. In Jack Straw's words:

By and large, our legal culture is about finding the true meaning of the law. In the case of statute, what matters is what Parliament intended. Moral norms and ethical principles don't normally come into it. The Human Rights Act requires us to look for *possible* meanings, not the *true* meaning. And the ambition of the Human Rights Act is that possible meanings that fit with the Convention principles and norms are always to be preferred. Deciding day-to-day legal questions on the basis of such fundamental ethical principles, set out in statute, is a new departure.[46]

Speaking at a symposium on the challenges of incorporating the ECHR into UK law, in October 1997, Lord Browne-Wilkinson, a senior Law Lord,[47] drew on his extensive experience as a judge to declare that, 'it is going to make an enormous difference to the way that judges perform the law'. Up until now, he maintained, there has been nothing to stop judges operating on the 'dirty dog principle'. In other words, 'Dirty dogs don't win.' Now, he continued, an entirely different approach will be needed:

If statements of general principle are going to be applied by the courts you are going to stop going from the particular to the general, and start with the general principles in the ECHR.[48]

At a conference hosted by the City solicitors' firm Clifford Chance the following month, Lord Browne-Wilkinson elaborated on this point. Describing the European Convention as a code of 'moral principles' he predicted that one of the effects of incorporation will be that the moral judgments involved will not only be those of individual judges. There should emerge, he said, a

code of morals reflecting the input of many different viewpoints and not merely the prejudices of the individual. This will, I hope, put an end to the most extreme versions of the dirty dog principle ... that because an individual is guilty of a serious crime he has lost all his rights to fair treatment[49]

Defects in the English legal system

Until now, the rights of the people of the UK could be summed up in one phrase – the right to be left alone. This principle was amplified by Lord Donaldson in the famous *Spycatcher* case, which followed the Thatcher government's attempt in 1986 to ban publication of the memoirs of the former MI5 agent Peter Wright. Donaldson clarified what he meant with the classical formulation that:

the starting-point of our domestic law is that every citizen has the right to do what he likes, unless restrained by the common law or statute[50]

Drawing on the thesis most famously expounded by the nineteenth-century constitutional theorist A. V. Dicey, Donaldson was describing the basic approach to rights and liberties in the English legal tradition – that liberties are expressed as 'negative rights' left over after all prohibitions are accounted for. Dicey maintained that individual liberties were more effectively protected by the English legal system than by its continental counterparts. The common (or judge-made) law, in particular, has an advantage over declarations and bills of rights, he argued, both because it provides effective remedies when liberties are violated and because it is harder for governments to suspend rights which are not written down but emanate from court decisions.[51]

The problem with this thesis, in a nutshell, is that the idea of fundamental human rights is almost entirely alien to this tradition. English common law is basically concerned with remedies rather than rights. It recognizes what could be termed 'basic interests' rather than fundamental rights.[52] Where these interests happen to coincide with internationally recognized human rights then it can be said that the common law provides something like the same protection. Fair trial rights, personal freedom, reputation and property rights are the 'basic interests' which the common law has historically protected very well, probably better than in many countries with bills of rights.

Other internationally recognized rights, however, have until now received little or no protection under the English system. The right to privacy, for example, is barely recognized by the common law. There are remedies for related issues like trespass, defamation or breach of confidence. But although the courts have edged closer in developing a general right to privacy over the years they have still not succeeded in doing so. Were that leap to be made the judges would no doubt be criticized, not entirely unfairly, for usurping their powers in the absence of a parliamentary green light.[53]

Most citizens of the UK have lived in blissful ignorance of this situation. They have had little idea that until now they were barred from claiming in the domestic courts the fundamental human rights available to the citizens of nearly all other democracies. Few people would have been aware of which liberties are and which are not recognized by the common law, or that those which are could be taken away at the stroke of a parliamentary pen.

Sally McLeod was one such unsuspecting victim when her estranged husband, his siblings, his solicitor's clerk and the police entered her house without her permission in October 1989. They had come to remove some furniture as part of the former couple's separation agreement, three days before Ms McLeod was required to hand the property over. To her amazement Ms McLeod discovered that although she could sue her husband, his siblings and his solicitor's clerk for trespass, in the absence of any general right to privacy, she had no remedy against the police. They claimed they were acting to prevent a breach of the peace even though only Ms McLeod's elderly mother was present when they arrived at the scene. In the end Ms McLeod had to wait nine years to go to Strasbourg to hear the European Court of Human Rights declare that her right to respect for her private life and home, under Article 8 of the ECHR, had been violated.[54]

Similarly, the common law failed to provide any meaningful protection against discrimination. Putting innkeepers under a duty to accept all travellers 'in a reasonably fit condition to be received'[55] was about as far as it went. The English courts certainly gave recognition to the principle of the 'rule of law' and established that the law applies equally to everyone from princes to paupers. This was a progressive principle in its day but 'equality before the law' proved completely inadequate in the face of widespread discrimination in everyday life.

Parliament partially remedied this failure with a series of race and sex discrimination Acts in the 1960s and 1970s and more recently with the 1995 Disability Discrimination Act. Even these had significant gaps, particularly in relation to discrimination by public authorities,[56] and until the Human Rights Act came into force there was no protection against discrimination on grounds of sexual orientation or age, for example.[57] The point being that specific pieces of legislation, while essential to amplify the generalized entitlements provided by bills of rights, are no substitute for them. They are inevitably limited to the particular terms of the Act in question and often fail to keep up with new developments.

In any case what Parliament gives it can take away. So, going back to Donaldson's formulation, in an era where an increasing amount of public and private life is controlled by legislation, it does not sound like a major guarantee to be told that you are free to do whatever is not forbidden. The right to freedom of assembly, for example – that is to march, to protest or demonstrate – is 'one of the oldest common law rights' according to a government report to the United Nations

Human Rights Committee.[58] This may be so, but the common law provided little or no defence against a range of legislation which regulated that 'right', from Acts controlling public order to regulations and byelaws on the use of public spaces and parks.

It was not until the Human Rights Act was already on the statute book, although not in force, that what could be described as a positive right to assembly resembling Article 11 of the ECHR – which could be used to limit the effects of restrictive legislation – was recognized by the courts.[59] It may be relevant that the case in question was heard by Lord Irvine, among others, who introduced the Human Rights Act into the House of Lords and who drew upon the ECHR in his judgment.

Changes to the judges' role

The effects that the Human Rights Act (HRA) should have on the way that judges perform their role can be summarized in three parts.[60] First, judges who develop the common law must no longer be primarily guided by past judgments or precedents in determining the outcome of a case when the rights in the ECHR are involved. This is a crucial change. The common law must be developed so as to give effect to Convention rights.

Second, when interpreting legislation, judges need to be equipped with the equivalent of invisible ink, 'writing in' fundamental rights or 'writing out' rights abuses whenever they can. Their aim must be to make the Act in question comply with the ECHR so far as is possible. With a similar, but weaker, 'interpretation clause' the New Zealand courts have effectively used invisible ink to rewrite legislation so that it conforms with their 1990 Bill of Rights. In one case the judges 'read in' the right of individuals to consult a lawyer when breathalysed, at least over the phone, even though not a word of this was contained in the 1962 Transport Act which had preceded the New Zealand Bill of Rights by nearly twenty years.[61]

As we have seen, judges in the UK higher courts can also, for the first time, declare that Acts are in breach of Convention rights where it is not possible to reconcile them.[62] And what is known as subordinate legislation, like Immigration or Prison Rules, must be overturned if judges determine that they breach the Human Rights Act and that they cannot be interpreted to comply with it.

Third, the HRA has made significant changes to the way that judges review the discretionary powers of ministers or officials. These are the kinds of cases that often hit the headlines when ministers are told they have acted illegally by the courts, for example, in ordering the deportation of an asylum seeker without properly examining the facts.[63] In addition to the common law and Acts of Parliament, 'judicial review' has increasingly been presented as another route to the protection of individual rights under the UK legal system.

There is no doubt that judges have significantly extended the degree to which they have held ministers and officials to account through this route over the last few decades. But it is only since the Human Rights Act has come into force that they have properly been able to intervene on human rights grounds. Now individuals need only demonstrate that a Convention right has been interfered with and the 'burden of proof' passes to the authority in question to justify the interference as both 'necessary' and 'proportionate' to protect the wider community (in line with the principle of proportionality described above).

This is a very different approach to judicial review to that developed by the courts before we had a bill of rights, even where fundamental human rights were at stake. This old approach was known as the Wednesbury principles of judicial review (after a case dating back to 1948 involving Sunday cinema performances and the Wednesbury Corporation[64]). In a nutshell, it meant that a decision could be overturned only on substantive (rather than procedural) grounds where it was unreasonable 'in the sense that it was beyond the range of responses open to a reasonable decision-maker'.[65] The 'burden of proof' on an individual pitted against a minister or official to show that he or she had acted 'unreasonably' was very high.

The more that an interference with fundamental human rights was at stake the more the courts would require by way of justification before they were satisfied that the decision was reasonable.[66] Nevertheless, they doggedly refused to alter the threshold for judicial intervention beyond 'unreasonableness'.

The human rights barrister Rabinder Singh has argued that it is a 'myth' to claim that 'adequate protection was given to human rights through the doctrine of *Wednesbury* unreasonableness' or that it was equivalent to the European Court of Human Rights' doctrine of proportionality.[67] That an interference with a fundamental right is 'necessary' requires much more justification than whether it is 'reasonable'. In any case, Wednesbury is now dead, at least for the judicial review of fundamental human rights issues. The birth of the 1998 Human Rights Act killed it off. As a consequence a whole range of issues which have never been properly reviewed before should now come before the courts.

Some illustrations of how our right to challenge authority will be strengthened

So what practical difference will our new Bill of Rights make to us? In one sense it comes down to accountability; to the capacity to hold authorities to account when our fundamental rights or freedoms are threatened in ways that were blocked to us under the old system.

The plight of Richard Young provides a good illustration. He was sacked from the Royal Navy in September 1999. Richard was a full-time chef, aged twenty-five. He had not committed any criminal offence. He had not been found incompetent in his work. He had not been rude to his superiors. He simply acknowledged to his employers that he was gay. It did not matter if he had a gay relationship or not. As with approximately two thousand former armed forces personnel before him, it was the fact of his being gay that lost him his job.

Only a few days later the European Court of Human Rights ruled that the ban to prevent gay men and lesbians from working in the UK armed forces was a breach of fundamental human rights. It took a group of three gay men and a lesbian five years for the European human rights court to find in their favour. The judges found that not only had the UK government breached the four applicants' right to a private life in upholding the ban (under Article 8) but also that the sacked armed forces personnel had no effective remedy for their grievances before a British court. The ruling came close to damning the whole British judicial system for protecting human rights prior to incorporation of the European Convention. The judges said that the system:

effectively excluded any consideration by the domestic courts of the question of whether the interference with the applicants' rights answered a pressing social need or was proportionate to the national security and public order aims pursued, principles which lie at the heart of the Court's analysis of complaints under Article 8 of the Convention[68]

This lack of an effective remedy was evident when the ban on gays in the military case was heard in this country a few years earlier. The judges in the Court of Appeal were straining to overturn the ban on human rights grounds. But they were simply unable to consider the fundamental principles at stake. Constitutional tradition barred them from doing so. (Indeed, if the ban had been required by a lawful Act of Parliament instead of military rules the courts could not have reviewed it at all.) Sir Thomas Bingham, the then Master of the Rolls, recognized that there might be room for argument about whether the interference in question met the 'proportionality' test and:

'answers a pressing social need and in particular is proportionate to the legitimate aim pursued' [but] these are not, however, questions to which answers may properly or usefully be proffered by this court[69]

The only issues the courts could properly consider were the procedural ones about whether the ban was itself against the law, which it clearly wasn't, and whether it had been carried out in a procedurally improper way, which it hadn't. As far as the substantive issue of whether the ban was just or not, all the judges could decide on was whether it was so irrational that no sensible person could have arrived at it. Many might argue that the policy of banning men and women, who are eager to serve in the army, navy or air force, purely on the grounds of their sexual orientation, regardless of their conduct, is extremely irrational. But, as we have seen, prior to the Human Rights Act, the threshold of irrationality had to be very high before a ministerial decision could be overturned.

Regarding the status of the European Convention on Human Rights under UK law, Lord Bingham summed up what is now the *ancien régime* of human rights enforcement in the UK:

It is, inevitably, common ground that the United Kingdom's obligation, binding in international law, to respect and ensure compliance with [the Convention] is not one that is enforceable by the domestic courts. The relevance of the Convention in the present context is as background to the complaint of irrationality. The fact that a decision-maker failed to take account of Convention obligations when exercising an administrative discretion is not of itself a ground for impugning the exercise of that discretion.[70]

Now our courts will be *required* to consider whether a ban by a public body, like the armed services, affecting a particular section of the community, is a breach of fundamental rights. This is an entirely different question from asking whether it was 'reasonable' or not. Perhaps, if the Human Rights Act had been in force at the time, the case would not have come to court in the first place. A new code of service conduct covering all personal relationships in the armed forces was issued in January 2000. If the Ministry of Defence had been advised that it was likely to face the ignominy of having its policy overturned by the domestic courts, it might well have taken such sensible, pre-emptive action earlier.

Stop and search

The police's stop-and-search policy provides another illustration of how the Human Rights Act should, in time, force the authorities to justify actions for which they previously remained largely unaccountable. It is no good telling many black people that the common law protects their personal freedom when they are six times more likely to be stopped by the police than any other group. In some areas, like Liverpool or London, many young black men feel themselves to be effectively living in a police state. The 1981 riots in Brixton and Toxteth were sparked off by massive police 'fishing expeditions'. But the practice of routinely stopping black youths on the street or in their cars continued. This was an issue addressed by the Macpherson

Inquiry into the death of Stephen Lawrence, a young black man killed in a vicious racist street murder in April 1993. Because his alleged killers were never properly brought to trial (other than in a failed private prosecution), the Home Secretary, Jack Straw, ordered an inquiry. It received testimony from black communities around the country about their major grievances, recording that:

If there was one area of complaint which was universal it was the issue of 'stop and search' . . . It is pointless for the police service to try to justify the disparity in these [stop-and-search] figures purely or mainly in terms of the other factors which are identified. The majority of police officers who testified before us accepted that an element of the disparity was the result of discrimination.[71]

The Inquiry Report recommended that a full record be made by police officers of each stop and search, including the reason and outcome, with a copy given to the person stopped. The Metropolitan Police subsequently piloted a more targeted approach to stop and search on seven London sites, adopting some of the recommendations of the Macpherson Report. This both increased the proportion of searches leading to arrests from 10 to 18 per cent and reduced the ratio of black to white people searched from 4.4 : 1 to 3.3 : 1.[72]

On the face of it the disparity between the pilot and non-pilot areas provides a case for maintaining that discrimination is involved in the selection of who to stop. At the very least it is far from clear that there are always the 'reasonable grounds for suspicion' required by law before someone is stopped.[73] It would be interesting to know, for example, on what 'reasonable suspicion' the police stopped Neville Lawrence, the murdered teenager's father, or John Sentamu, an Anglican Bishop and only black member of the Inquiry group, in two separate incidents in January 2000.

Under the old regime it was extremely difficult to successfully challenge most stops or searches on discrimination or other grounds. Until an amendment was introduced to the Race Relations Act following the Macpherson Inquiry,[74] most aspects of policing were not covered by the Act. Under judicial review procedures the police would undoubtedly have referred to crime statistics to defend themselves against charges of irrationality in accordance with the old Wednesbury principles.[75]

One 27-year-old man, disc jockey and butcher Carl Josephs, was stopped while driving his car thirty-four times in two years. In 1999 he tried to sue the West Midlands Police Force for racial harassment. He was unsuccessful. Nothing changed. After being stopped four more times following the court case he handed his vehicle documents to the Force's headquarters to hold them 'to save time and hassle'.[76]

Now, through a combination of the amended Race Relations Act and the Human Rights Act, it is probable that the policy of stop and search will come under the scrutiny of the courts in ways that were not possible before. Provided the courts accept that one of the rights under the Convention is at issue,[77] the police will need to establish that any stop or search is 'necessary' and 'proportionate' and that it did not take place on discriminatory grounds.[78] Even if the first or second or third stop-and-search case is lost, the days when such policies are virtually immune from legal challenge should now be over.

There are also some grounds for optimism that the Human Rights Act may encourage the police to change their approach to stop and search without litigation. Police National Training, responsible for ensuring that all police personnel are prepared for the Act, are providing training on the exercise of police powers in the light of the HRA. Referring to stop and search (among other issues), the training materials advise using 'the minimum action that can reasonably be expected to achieve the legitimate lawful aim pursued'.[79] In the same vein, Assistant Metropolitan Police Commissioner Denis O'Conner has commented:

The Human Rights Act ... itself enshrines a new concept of proportionality which will require increased vigilance on the part of the police but which may yet prove to be a useful basis for achieving fairness.[80]

New 'positive obligations' on public authorities to respect human rights

Peoples' lives will be changed in other ways too. The Human Rights Act does not just put limits on the exercise of unaccountable power but also requires the government or other public authorities to take preventative or corrective action in certain circumstances. Because of the wide definition of 'public authority' under the Act, this requirement can apply even when it is charities or private companies that are abusing peoples' fundamental rights.[81] Whole categories of people who have had nowhere to turn to until now may be helped as a result.

Despite the common association between human rights and the protection of suspects or perpetrators of crime, one of the groups that is set to benefit most by this change is the victims of serious crime. In particular, those who feel that they did not receive adequate protection from the state in the face of serious threats to their life or well-being will now have recourse to the law in the UK.

One such family, the Osmans, lived in Hackney in East London. Ahmet Osman was a pupil at Homerton House School in the mid-1980s when one of his teachers, Paul Paget-Lewis, developed a crush on him, a situation noted by the Head of the school. As the situation deteriorated, with Paget-Lewis even changing his name by deed poll to Paul Ahmet Yildirim Osman, the police were informed of the Head's concern that harm could come to his pupil.

In 1987 a number of violent incidents were reported to the police, including a brick thrown through the Osmans' window and paraffin poured outside their house. Finally, on 7 March 1988, Paget-Lewis seriously wounded Ahmet and shot and killed his father. On his arrest the next morning Paget-Lewis said: 'Why didn't you stop me before I did it, I gave you all the warning signs?' Later that year he was convicted of manslaughter, having pleaded guilty on grounds of diminished responsibility, and was detained indefinitely in a secure mental hospital.

The Osman family decided to sue the police for negligence, arguing

45

that although they were aware of the situation they had failed to arrest Paget-Lewis, search his home or charge him until it was too late. All they had done over the long period of harassment was to 'invite' Paget-Lewis to the police station for an interview.

The Court of Appeal threw out the case. The judges held that under English law 'public policy' demanded that the police be immune from prosecution for negligence in the way they investigate a crime. The exception would be where there was a close enough relationship between the police and the affected party to argue that the police had a 'special duty of care'; for example, where the police failed to warn the prison authorities that they had detained someone who was recognizably suicidal. But this, the Court ruled, could not be said to apply in these circumstances.[82] Whatever the merits of this particular case, the courts would not review the police action.

The Osman family felt they had received no justice at all. Their only recourse was through the European Convention on Human Rights but it was not yet part of English law. In 1998 the case finally came before the European Court of Human Rights in Strasbourg. The judges ruled that the fundamental human rights of the Osman family had been violated. By throwing out their case without any consideration of the particular facts, the English courts had breached Article 6 of the ECHR, the right to a fair trial. Although the right of access to a court under Article 6 is not absolute, there should have been a review of the merits of this case, the European Court of Human Rights ruled, especially given that the life of a child was at stake rather than minor acts of incompetence.[83]

The Court also decided that as the police did not know that the Osman family were at 'real and immediate risk' from Paget-Lewis their right to life was not breached. But in a significant statement, which affirmed the doctrine of 'positive obligations', the Court ruled that Article 2 of the Convention, the right to life, requires the state:

not only to refrain from the intentional and unlawful taking of life, but also to take appropriate steps to safeguard the lives of those within its jurisdiction ... [there is] in certain well-defined circumstances a *positive obligation* on the authorities to take preventive operational measures to protect an individual whose life is at risk from the criminal acts of another individual[84]

Now the Osman family, like any other victims who consider they have not received sufficient protection from the police when their life is threatened, should be able to hold the police to account in the UK courts in similar circumstances. This would also apply where death or ill treatment occurs while a detainee is in the custody of the police themselves. There have been five hundred such deaths in the last decade. The police will probably be required to demonstrate that they have taken action to prevent death and injury, not just refrained from killing someone. The doctrine of 'positive obligations' could also lead to new investigations where no one has been charged over a death in custody and there are complaints that the initial investigation was inadequate.

A shift in the culture of public life

Whether individuals win their particular case or not usually depends on the facts. But most people never enter a court in their lifetime. Any changes that occur will be most keenly felt on the ground. And in many instances it will be the positive steps taken by public (and some private) authorities to promote and protect human rights that will have the greatest impact on people. In time, the Human Rights Act could lead to a huge change in the culture of public life.

There is a reasonable analogy here with the race relations and sex discrimination legislation. They have been legitimately criticized for the narrowness of their scope. The Acts have been fairly accused of failing to protect individuals against institutional discrimination by a range of bodies. Yet they have punched above their weight in effecting changes that are not strictly required by law.[85]

There is no requirement in the Race Relations Act, for example, that employers take the positive step of drawing up equal opportunities policies for their recruitment procedures. No requirement that they advertise themselves as equal opportunities employers. No requirement that they monitor the ethnic origin of their workforce. Yet these practices, with varying effects, have been introduced by local authorities and some major companies up and down the country. No doubt the advice that such procedures could defend them against charges of discrimination has concentrated the mind. But these developments are evidence of a cultural shift which has taken decades to begin to take hold. Lord Williams, the Attorney-General and former Home Office minister, made this point when the Human Rights Bill was introduced to the House of Lords:

It is exactly the same ... following the introduction of, for example, race relations legislation and equal opportunities legislation. Every significant body, public or private, thereafter had to ask itself with great seriousness and concern, 'Have we equipped ourselves to meet our legal obligations?' That has caused ... a transformation in certain areas of human rights. The same is likely to follow when this Bill becomes law.[86]

If the Human Rights Act works as intended, then governments, public bodies and even private bodies where they carry out 'public functions' will have 'positive obligations' to secure peoples' rights in a range of circumstances. Public officials of all kinds will no longer be bound only by the letter of the law, nor will they be prohibited just from infringing fundamental rights. There will be pressure on them to respect the rights of the people in the everyday decisions they make as they go about their work.

Some of this pressure will come from the case law of the European Court of Human Rights. Some will come from the domestic courts. But over time the most significant pressure could come from the users of services, local communities and interest groups. Human rights values, like equal opportunities principles, should start to become part of the national dialogue, helping to frame the demands people make on bodies which have power over their lives.

Health authorities may find that they are required to be more explicit about their rationing policies, particularly if there are discrepancies between different regions, when decisions about new medicines like cancer drugs are taken. They will probably be called upon to demonstrate that they are sufficiently protecting patients' right to life. Public health bodies will need to consider whether they are providing enough information about the risks of certain treatments or new agricultural developments. Individuals should be able to hold the authorities to account for threats to their life in situations like the BSE in cattle crisis and the genetically modified food scare.

Housing authorities, as well as the police, might need to justify any lack of positive action to protect old people from harassment, women from domestic violence or black families from racial violence on their estates, particularly where lives are put at risk.[87] Environmental agencies will be held liable if they fail to take appropriate steps to inform the relevant communities of 'severe environmental pollution [that] may affect individuals' well-being so that their family and private life is affected adversely, even if it cannot be established that their health is'.[88] The police will not only have to refrain from preventing marches and demonstrations but will also have to ensure that demonstrators are given sufficient protection to carry out their protests.[89]

When the Paddington rail crash took place in October 1999 there was even speculation among lawyers that, had it been in force, the Human Rights Act could have established a 'positive obligation' on Railtrack to demonstrate that they were adequately protecting the right to life of their passengers. As a private company carrying out the public function of rail safety, their refusal to invest in the latest train protection technology could have made them subject to judicial scrutiny under the Act.

It may take several years yet for these various implications to strike home. But this is surely the revolution which dares not speak its name. Jack Straw came close to this conclusion as the Human Rights Bill completed its passage through Parliament:

Over time the Bill will bring about the creation of a human rights culture in Britain. In future years historians may regard the Bill as one of the most important measures of this Parliament.[90]

One day, when stories about spin doctors and loans for homes have faded from memory,[91] the new Bill of Rights may turn out to be one of the most enduring legacies of the Blair government.

CHAPTER 2

A Curious Mixture:
Rights, Responsibilities and the Third Way?

The Human Rights Act marks a widely recognized departure from the past. A modernization, if you like, to beat all modernizations. This far there is no surprise. For the New Labour government that has introduced it has elevated the idea of modernization to a virtue in itself.

What may seem more surprising, given this government's reputation – fair or otherwise – are the checks and balances created by the Act and the rights culture it heralds. This is an administration more commonly associated with being tough on crime than soft on rights. 'Napoleonic tendencies' and 'control freakery' are labels frequently hurled at the government; labels which have to a certain degree stuck, perhaps because they have been pasted by some government supporters as well as critics.[1] Yet the new Cabinet decided to incorporate the European Convention on Human Rights, and thereby restrict its room to manoeuvre on rights issues, immediately after Labour's 1997 election victory. A better example of unilateral disempowerment by a government it would be hard to find.

Hugo Young, the respected *Guardian* journalist, singled out the new Bill of Rights as the one shining light in a dismal record on 'libertarian questions' by the Blair government in its first thousand days. Berating the lack of a 'liberal instinct' among government ministers, Young stated that 'the only offsetting credit was the passage of the Human Rights Act.'[2]

The determination of some ministers to press ahead with this legislation cannot be explained in the usual terms. There were virtually no opinion polls, focus groups or tabloid leader writers urging them on.[3] There was not even the same level of popular demand for a bill of rights as there was for Scottish or (minimally) Welsh devolution.

The politics of rights

Being in favour of granting people more rights has, in fact, become almost a term of abuse in some circles in recent years. Perhaps, in part, because there has been no real tradition of fundamental rights in this country (as opposed to common law liberties) the term 'right' has become associated with license and excessive individualism in the minds of many commentators and political leaders.

An almost schizophrenic distinction is routinely made between abroad – where support for human rights is generally perceived as a good and noble thing – and home, where an overemphasis on rights, at the expense of responsibilities, is said to be one of the causes of social disintegration in modern Britain. Reverend Lord Habgood, for example, argued in a lecture at Westminster Abbey in 1998 that:

I have claimed that the indiscriminate use of the concept of rights can undermine morality at its very core by focusing attention on what the world owes us, rather than on the network of mutual obligations and shared assumptions which compose the fabric of a healthy society.[4]

The recent identification of rights with selfishness and permissiveness took off during the years of the Thatcher government. The double whammy routinely employed by the Conservative Party in the 1980s was to paint the Left as having Janus-like qualities. On the one hand Labour was said to be an enemy of individual freedom in its support for state control of the economy and collectivist bodies like trade unions. On the other hand it was presented as a threat to social cohesion with its emphasis on rights rather than responsibilities and its lax attitudes to sex, crime and the family. As a mirror image to this, the Left would accuse the Tories of being too authoritarian in their social attitudes and too libertarian in their economic policies.[5]

Throughout this period the Conservatives were able, not always unfairly, to caricature Labour as a party with a confused and confusing agenda on civil liberties and rights. One that was concerned about miscarriages of justice but not about crime unless it was domestic or racial violence. One that avidly defended the rights of suspects or perpetrators of crime unless they were racist skinheads or violent husbands, in which case there were calls to reduce their liberties.[6]

The capacity to portray the Left as concerned about rights but not usually about victims' rights, or the responsibilities people should have to each other, played a role in the repositioning of the Labour Party as New Labour. Tony Blair's most famous saying as Shadow Home Secretary, that Labour would be 'Tough on crime and tough on the causes of crime,' came out of a concern to counter this portrayal.

Presenting a formula that was to be repeated many times, Peter Mandelson, now Secretary of State for Northern Ireland, and Roger Liddle, now a Downing Street adviser, wrote in 1996, in a book aimed at explaining the Blair project, that:

Whereas the Left appeared to argue for rights without responsibilities and that one was responsible for oneself alone, New Labour stresses the importance of mutual obligations.[7]

Rights and morality

This presentation of rights as a route to indifference towards others was not only co-opted into a party political battle but became central to a wider debate on the moral fabric of society.[8]

In July 1996 the Archbishop of Canterbury, Lord Carey, initiated what *The Times* newspaper described as an unprecedented debate on morality. Speaking on behalf of the then Tory government, Viscount Cranborne traced the breakdown of society's 'traditional Christian values' to the late 1960s. Since that time, he lamented, moral censure could no longer be relied upon to shame wayward individuals into conforming with the broad consensus.[9]

For Lord Ashbourne, speaking in the same debate, the rot had set in as early as 1951 when the prohibition on witchcraft was ended. It was further entrenched in the 1960s with the abolition of capital punishment and the introduction of libertarian legislation decriminalizing homosexuality and abortion.

New permissive legislation has weakened the traditional family structure ... the concept of the stable, two-parent family as the basic unit in society is fast disappearing.[10]

Lord Jakobovits, the late Chief Rabbi, appeared to capture the tenor of the debate when he asserted that a common factor underlying their various concerns was an overemphasis on the idea of rights:

could it be that the greatest moral failure of our time is the stress on our rights, on what we can claim from others – human rights, women's rights, workers' rights, gay rights and so on – and not on our duties, on what we owe to others? In our common tradition, the catalogue of fundamentals on which our civilization is based is not a bill of rights, but a set of Ten Commandments, not claims but debts.[11]

Interestingly, Jakobovits did not simply disagree with what he saw as an excessive emphasis on rights, but he described this as 'the greatest moral failure of our time'. He was in good company here. David Selbourne, a political philosopher quoted approvingly by Home Secretary Jack Straw on a number of occasions, has coined a new phrase: 'dutiless rights'. He has warned that:

the ethics and politics of dutiless right, demand-satisfaction and self-realization through unimpeded freedom of action have been a costly moral failure in the corrupted liberal orders[12]

The newspaper columnist Melanie Phillips, formerly of the *Guardian* and *Observer* but now at the *Sunday Times*, has been pushing this approach for years. One of many assertions she has recently made is that 'In our culture of rights what we desire is elevated to an entitlement regardless of the consequences for others.'[13] It is no defence, according to Phillips, to claim that rights imply responsibilities, because from her point of view they tend to obliterate them. If, she has argued, rights were to form the basis of a new moral order, as human rights activists propose:

This would mean replacing the network of duties on which Western civilization is based by the apotheosis of individual self-gratification in the mistaken belief that rights and duties are mirrors of each other's virtues.[14]

On a related theme, Baroness O'Neill, a renowned moral philosopher and Principal of Newnham College, Cambridge, has warned against the consequences of focusing on rights rather than obligations when justifying universal human rights norms. In a lecture at King's College, London, in January 2000 she said: 'To focus on rights to the exclusion of the counterpart of obligations is dangerous as no one is there to uphold them.' The alternative, she maintained, 'is to focus on obligations and see if there are any universal bases for them'.[15]

The current Chief Rabbi, Jonathan Sacks, has written a book devoted to the search for a new politics based on the idea of responsibility. This new politics would:

think more expansively about the citizen as a bearer of duties, sharing responsibility for the civic order and not merely as a voter, consumer of services and bearer of rights. It would campaign vigorously for a richer language of public discourse than one confined to the defence of autonomy, the advocacy of sectional interests and the unargued pursuit of claims-as-rights.[16]

All these commentators might be surprised to learn that they share their exception to championing rights without duties with Karl Marx and Friedrich Engels. The latter, when critiquing the draft Erfurt Programme of 1891, complained that it included a statement on rights:

Instead of 'everyone shall have equal rights,' we would suggest 'everyone shall have equal rights and duties'.[17]

Similarly, the 'Statutes of Organization of the International Federation of Labour', drawn up by Marx and adopted in 1871, stated that:

The Federation recognizes that there shall be no rights without duties and no duties without rights.[18]

Coming back to the present, Dr Nicholas Tate, Chief Executive of the Qualifications and Curriculum Authority, has tried to make the theme of rights versus responsibilities central to the current education debate. Concerned that 'there are no absolute and enduring values that are true to all of us', Tate established a 'National Forum for School and Community Values', which reported in May 1999.[19] Speaking at a conference organized by the Institute of Public Policy Research in June 1999 he maintained that the new curriculum entitlement to citizenship education should emphasize duties over rights:

citizenship education is not just about rights. It is also, and principally, about duties. Rights are important . . . rights often need to be strengthened; but we have heard so much about them in recent years that we have sometimes come to forget that at the other side of the coin are duties. We have somehow developed a public image of human life which is all about self-creation, self-satisfaction, the pursuit of pleasure, doing one's own thing – the 'me society' – . . . We need to redress the balance[20]

Communitarianism and the new politics

This rediscovery of the theme of responsibilities by opinion formers, educationalists and religious leaders is not just a random event with a few individuals expressing their own personal prejudices. The rights/duties nexus has become a central feature of modern political discourse. In particular, it has been absorbed into the landscape of a new kind of politics which has come to be described under the heading of the 'third way'.[21]

This label, though in fact not new,[22] has been adopted by supporters of the 'new politics' to distinguish themselves from both the old Left and the new Right. In UK terms, this means trying to furrow a path between the traditional Labour Party (all wings) and Thatcherism. One of the stated aims of this new politics is to revitalize the idea of duty as a driving force in British culture, although in a less socially repressed form than its Victorian ancestor. To turn the 'me generation' into the 'we generation.'

At a private seminar on third-way politics hosted by the US President, Bill Clinton, involving four European leaders, Tony Blair expressed the goal of the new politics in these terms:

I'll tell you what my generation wants, I believe. We went through a period in the sixties where, if you like, people just sort of said, well, do your own thing. I think what my generation and younger wants is a society that is free from prejudice, but not free from rules. So they want to make sure that there's sexual and racial equality, that there isn't discrimination against people – they don't actually believe that it's tolerable that old ladies are beaten up by young thugs. Neither do they believe that it's tolerable that someone simply takes money off the welfare state and feels no sense of responsibility towards the society in which they live . . .[23]

His answer to problems of injustice and social dislocation?

I think . . . these problems can best be addressed and governed through a concept of active community . . . if you live in a community that's broken apart, if you don't actually have a society in which there is opportunity for everyone, we all lose as a result of that. So that's why I think this new political approach is so important . . .[24]

This pinpointing of community as a central political idea can be traced to a group of thinkers known as communitarians. For decades a debate has raged in the US between academic communitarians like Michael Sandel and liberal philosophers like John Rawls.[25] The communitarians have, if you like, posited a 'third way' between the idea of justice as fairness, promoted by Rawls in answer to his question 'What makes a just society possible?'[26], and the idea of justice as minimal state interference, supported by free-market philosophers like Robert Nozick.[27]

The communitarians quarrelled with the idea that states should provide a neutral framework of rights and freedoms within which individuals can pursue their private ideals. For communitarians, good government involves recognizing and conserving the networks that individuals belong to. Rights entail a responsibility to participate in these networks and to care about the moral tone of society as a whole.[28]

These ideas entered the political realm in the early 1990s when philosophers-cum-activists, led by American sociology professor Amitai Etzioni, tried to spawn a movement aimed at 'shoring up the moral, social and political environment'.[29] With their quarterly magazine *The Responsive Community*, subtitled 'Rights *and* Responsibilities', the communitarians can fairly claim some success in influencing the new politics of the American Democratic Party, Britain's Labour Party and Germany's Social Democratic Party, at least in the earlier phases of their recent developments.

President Bill Clinton, Vice-President Al Gore and Germany's former Chancellor, Helmut Köhl, have all publicly acknowledged their debt to Etzioni.[30] When he visited the UK in March 1995, Cabinet ministers of the then Conservative government attended a dinner in his honour; he was received by the leaders of both the main opposition parties; and tickets for his public lecture sold out. His ideas have been strongly promoted by Geoff Mulgan, formerly Director of the think-tank Demos and now a Downing Street adviser,[31] as well as by commentators and writers like Melanie Phillips and David Selbourne. Pamphlets strongly influenced by the communitarian debate have been published by think-tanks across the political spectrum, including Demos, the Social Market Foundation and Politeia.[32]

The essence of Etzioni's approach can be found in his four-point agenda:

a moratorium on the minting of most, if not all, new rights; re-establishing the link between rights and responsibilities; recognizing that some responsibilities do not entail rights and, most carefully, adjusting some rights to the changed circumstances[33]

At the heart of Etzioni's thinking lies the idea that the notion of duty needs to be restored to its former hegemonic position. He proclaims a 'new golden rule' which:

requires that the tension between one's preferences and one's social commitments be reduced by increasing the realm of duties one affirms as moral responsibilities – not the realm of duties that are forcibly imposed but the realm of responsibilities one believes one should discharge and that one believes one is fairly called upon to assume[34]

The point he is making is that to achieve a cohesive society, responsibilities and duties have by and large to be voluntary. Etzioni cites Tony Blair approvingly as someone who realizes that the law has its limits in this regard and that the law itself must 'be limited largely to that which is supported by the moral voice'.[35] What is required is that:

most members of the society, most of the time, *share a commitment to a set of core values* and that most members, most of the time, will abide by [them] because they believe in them, rather than being *forced* to comply with them[36]

Etzioni insists he is not at all against the idea of fundamental rights. However, he asserts that rights and responsibilities are mutually enhancing only 'up to a point'.[37] Historically, governments that provided a list of rights to their citizens got into trouble not when they demanded that rights entail the exercise of responsibilities, but when they failed to make that demand, he claims. If you don't attend to peoples' basic safety, for example, then you will get calls for stronger and stronger police powers.

However, if a society legitimizes the minting of ever more individual rights or imposes ever more social responsibilities, there comes a point when these two start to undercut rather than reinforce one another. This is reflected, for instance, when as a result of bestowing ever more legal rights on a people, individuals move from attempting to resolve conflicts through negotiations . . . to a high reliance on courts, a phenomenon often referred to as 'litigiousness'.[38]

The exact point at which 'mutually enhancing' relationships between rights and responsibilities 'turn antagonistic', in Etzioni's terms, is not clear. He insists, however, that 'we do know when we have passed from one zone to another'.[39] When large numbers of people rebel or emigrate, he says, it is clear we have reached that point.

New Labour and the ascendancy of duties

By the time that Etzioni's communitarian movement was making its mark on these shores Tony Blair was Leader of the Labour Party and New Labour was born. It is not difficult to detect Etzioni's direct influence in this birth. Many of his ideas on rights, responsibilities and community appear pretty much undiluted in a number of New Labour speeches and pamphlets.

A major speech by Blair in 1996 could well have been penned by Etzioni. Ignoring the strong tradition of collectivism on the Left which had formed part of the Thatcherite critique of Labour, Blair maintained that:

in the 1960s the pendulum swung towards a more individualistic ethos. For a generation or more, the dominant model of behaviour on Left and Right was highly individualistic. This was true in the liberation of private life and in intellectual debate. The Left was captivated by the elegance and power of Professor John Rawls's *Theory of Justice* ... it is derived from a highly individualistic view of the world[40]

On the Right, Blair continued, collectivism became discredited as inefficient and doomed to fail. But, he said, an alternative perspective is taking root.

People increasingly recognize that to move forward as individuals we need to move forward as a community ... We are social beings, nurtured in families and communities and human only because we develop the moral power of personal responsibility for ourselves and each other. Britain is simply stronger as a team than as a collection of selfish players.[41]

Within this overall communitarian perspective Blair gives special emphasis to the idea of duties. 'No rights without responsibilities' has become a mantra of New Labour as closely identified with Tony Blair's 'third-way politics' as social inclusion, or modernized public services. Blair was categorical on the centrality of this idea in what was spun as a keynote pre-election speech in Cape Town in October 1996:

At the heart of everything New Labour stands for is the theme of rights and responsibilities. For every right we enjoy, we owe responsibilities. This is the most basic family value of all. You can take but you can give too. That basic value informs New Labour policy.[42]

The nub of his argument was that both Left and Right have overemphasized rights and duties respectively while New Labour is striking a new, more appropriate, balance. Blair made this case in a pamphlet on the 'third way' published by the Labour Party's think-tank the Fabian Society in 1998, which he subtitled *New Politics for the New Century*:

In recent decades, responsibility and duty were the preserve of the Right. They are no longer; and it was a mistake for them ever to become so, for they were powerful forces in the growth of the Labour movement in Britain and beyond. For too long, the demand for rights from the state was separated from the duties of the individual and institutions. Unemployment benefits were often paid without strong reciprocal obligations; children were unsupported by absent parents. This issue persists ... The politics of 'us' rather than 'me' demands an ethic of responsibility as well as rights.[43]

From a third-way perspective, the legal enforcement of individual rights is presented not so much as a necessary protection of vulnerable people from a powerful state but as part of a contract between citizens and government. As Mandelson and Liddle put it, if individuals want to be given more rights under a Labour government they should expect to be held to account for them:

rights carry with them obligations. Yes, young people have rights to a much wider range of opportunity [*sic*], but with the backing of the wider community goes an obligation to the wider community. Yes, companies should enjoy the freedom to compete in a dynamic market, but along with that freedom goes responsibility to all their stakeholders – workers, shareholders, bankers, long-term subcontractors and customers. All these relationships should involve mutual obligations. The government itself cannot ensure this everywhere but it can show the way and set the standard[44]

But the argument does not rest here. Increasingly, New Labour ministers do not just emphasize the mutuality between rights and responsibilities. In many ways they go further than Etzioni's communitarianism in insisting that rights flow from duties and not vice versa. Writing in September 1998 the Prime Minister declared:

The rights we enjoy reflect the duties we owe; rights and opportunity without responsibility are engines of selfishness and greed.[45]

This reflects the precise wording of the revised Clause IV to the Labour Party's constitution, which Jack Straw has described as the most succinct expression of 'third way' political theory there is.[46] In the stated view of the Prime Minister, it is the idea of duties, not rights, on which a decent society is built:

we need to bring a change to the way we treat each other as citizens of our society. A decent society is not actually based on rights. It is based on duty. Our duty to each other[47]

The Human Rights Act and the third way

This prioritization of duties over rights has left the government with a difficult presentational problem with regard to domestic human rights in general and the Human Rights Act in particular. The promotion of human rights in the UK is, despite the emphasis on duties, still occasionally presented as of value in its own terms. Separate to the reference to rights reflecting duties in the revised Clause IV of Labour's constitution, is a pledge to work for:

an open democracy . . . where fundamental human rights are guaranteed

Likewise the Foreign Secretary, Robin Cook, has presented the pursuit of human rights in the domestic sphere as a goal in its own terms when seeking to explain his so-called 'ethical dimension to foreign policy'. In a speech to the Lord Mayor's Banquet in 1998 he suggested that the reason why his Department's 'mission statement' includes spreading 'the values of human rights, civil liberties and democracy' is because:

Ours is a government that believes that the values which inform our domestic policy must also inform our foreign policy.[48]

But generally speaking it is hard to find a reference to the idea of rights in the UK by a government spokesperson without the words 'responsibilities' or 'duties' following close behind, if not in front.

The Human Rights Act itself has been presented in at least three different ways over time. In the first phase, incorporation of the European Convention on Human Rights into UK law was said by the then Leader of the Opposition, Tony Blair, to be aimed at ending 'the cumbersome practice of forcing people to go to Strasbourg to hold their government to account'.[49] It was not about giving people new rights but making the rights they already had more accessible through the courts. Moreover, as the title of the Labour Party's consultation paper on incorporation, *Bringing Rights Home*,[50] sought to suggest, in making it possible to claim ECHR rights in UK courts Labour was effectively 'repatriating' a document which the government was anyway legally bound to uphold but whose enforcement was in the hands of foreign judges. In Tony Blair's words:

This would make clear that the protection afforded by the Convention was not some foreign import but that it had been accepted by successive British governments and that it should apply throughout the United Kingdom. Some people have said that this system takes power away from Parliament and places it in the hands of judges. In reality, since we are already signatories to the Convention it means allowing British judges rather than European judges to pass judgment.[51]

In the second phase, which has overlapped with the third, what was then the Human Rights Bill was presented as a crucial plank in the government's democracy and constitutional reform programme. Introducing the Bill to Parliament in February 1998 Jack Straw placed it firmly in that context:

Our manifesto commits us to a comprehensive programme of constitutional reform ... The Bill falls squarely within that constitutional programme. It is a key component of our drive to modernize our society and refresh our democracy.[52]

Likewise, in introducing the Bill to the House of Lords, Lord Irvine, the Lord Chancellor, affirmed that it 'occupies a central position in our integrated programme of constitutional change'.[53] The Act has even been described as 'the cornerstone of our work to modernize the constitution' and as 'one of the most important pieces of constitutional legislation the UK has seen'.[54]

But increasingly, support for a bill of rights has been promoted as part of the communitarian vision of the government. Jack Straw, who was the first to place it in that context, sought to tie the constitutional and communitarian agendas together when he said:

Intellectually we all know that rights cannot exist without responsibilities, freedoms without obligations, liberties without duties. But it is crucially important that we spell this out ... Putting rights and responsibilities together brings our constitutional agenda down to earth, gives it real relevance to Britain's families and communities.[55]

So from the communitarian perspective the new Bill of Rights is not primarily about protecting individuals from arbitrary or unfair state action, although it can involve that. It is mainly about inculcating a sense of mutual rights and obligations among everyone in society. In winding up the debate on the Human Rights Bill in Parliament, Jack Straw went further than this. He tried to align the Bill with the 'third way' proposition that rights flow from duties and not the other way round.

I talk about a human rights culture. One of the problems which has arisen in Britain in recent years is that people have failed to understand from where rights come. The philosopher David Selbourne has commented on the generation of an idea of dutiless rights, where people see rights as consumer products which they can take, but for nothing. The truth is that rights have to be offset by responsibilities and obligations. There can and should be no rights without responsibilities and *our responsibilities should precede our rights.*[56]

Home Office minister Mike O'Brien, who subsequently became Chair of the Government's Human Rights Task Force,[57] developed this theme at a major conference for local government officers on the

Human Rights Act in May 1999. Acknowledging that, 'as a nation' we failed 'to develop a human rights culture', he said the purpose of the Act is to build that culture:

It is about weaving the Convention rights and responsibilities deep into the fabric of our legal tradition. And . . . into the public service ethos. Note that I say 'rights and responsibilities'. I make no apology for that. The Home Secretary puts it this way: the Human Rights Act, he says, like the Convention, is a two-way street. One person's freedom is another person's responsibility. *And rights flow from duties – not the other way.*[58]

The interesting thing about this changing emphasis in presentation is that the more the government talked up the value of the Act, the greater was the concentration on its intended cultural, rather than legal, effects. So before the 1997 general election, the stated goal of incorporating the European Convention into UK law was the relatively technical one of 'bringing rights home' and allowing people access to them in their national courts.[59] But by the time the Bill was introduced in the House of Lords, Home Office minister Lord Williams was playing down this aspect:

This is not, as the Lord Chancellor has pointed out, simply, 'You will be able to get your rights enforced quickly and cheaply because you will not have to make the journey to Strasbourg.' It is much more important than that. Every public authority will know that its behaviour, its structure, its conclusions and its executive actions will be subject to this culture.[60]

In the year running up to full implementation of the Act in October 2000 virtually every government reference to it emphasized the rights and responsibilities nexus. What the government was obviously anxious to avoid was any impression that the introduction of a bill of rights somehow stood to contradict its broad policy agenda. That it was a libertarian rather than communitarian measure. That it was a lawyer's charter rather than a peoples' charter. That it was a route to make all those so-called 'fat cat' lawyers the government had pilloried even fatter. Jack Straw was almost explicit about this when announcing that 2 October 2000 was the date that the Human Rights Act would come into force:

Human Rights Day – 2 October 2000 – should not be seen as a field-day for lawyers. It will mark instead a major step-change in the creation of a culture of rights and responsibilities in our society. The Human Rights Act is a two-way street.[61]

The Home Secretary became more determined to stamp on any perception that the new Bill of Rights was inherently a threat to a 'third-way agenda' when it became apparent that local authorities were reluctant to apply for new orders aimed at curtailing antisocial behaviour (ASBOs) because they had been advised that they might breach the Human Rights Act.

In a speech to the Police Superintendents' annual conference in September 1999, Jack Straw criticized 'civil liberties lawyers' who complain about the government's new anti-crime measures 'and then get into their BMWs and drive off into areas where they are immune from much crime'.[62] The press had a field-day with this story, tracking down any human rights lawyer they could find who drove a smart car.

The Home Secretary's attack turned out to be a warm-up for the Prime Minister, who continued the theme of criticizing civil libertarians in his speech to the Labour Party Conference the following week:

I saw that what we said on drugs and new powers was attacked by civil liberties groups. I believe in civil liberties too; civil liberty to me means just that: the liberty to live in a civil society founded on rights and responsibilities and in dealing with the drugs menace, that is the society we can help to build.[63]

To further counter the perception that the government had lost its way (if not its mind) in introducing a bill of rights, Jack Straw set out the government's vision for how the Human Rights Act should be received in a major speech to civil servants in December 1999. What he said was entirely at one with a third-way, communitarian agenda. The European Convention on Human Rights, he stated:

recognizes that rights and responsibilities are two sides of the same coin. Rights are the heading you find if you glance through the ECHR. But rights and responsibilities are what it is really about. I have heard people scoff at this. 'Show me the word "responsibilities" in the ECHR' or 'What responsibilities are justiciable?' they ask. Well, the state's are for a start. The fact is that every right entails a responsibility. But the cynics are missing the really big point. It's this: the responsibilities and duties in the ECHR can be shown to flow directly from what is needed to maintain a society based on modern, pluralistic, democratic values

And he continued:

So you get your rights from your duties. And your rights are based on considerations of common humanity.[64]

Is Straw correct? Is this what human rights are essentially about? Are they at heart individualistic or can they accommodate a communitarian perspective as he suggests? Are they fundamentally a bulwark against a powerful state or do they involve obligations by private bodies and individuals as well as states? Do rights flow from duties or is it the other way round?

Has the government introduced a powerful piece of legislation – a 'higher law' – which, with its apparent indifference to the victims of crime, threatens to unravel a major theme of its 'third way' agenda? Or can the Human Rights Act, while clearly a potential challenge to specific measures which breach it, nevertheless be understood as all of a piece with the new politics? To answer these questions we have to flash back to an era of revolution and turmoil, when the idea of rights as a motor for change first began to take root.

CHAPTER 3

The Quest for Freedom:
First-Wave Rights

In May 1787 delegates from all over America gathered together at Pennsylvania State House for a convention which was to produce the American Constitution. The Virginian delegate, George Mason, was aware of the enormity of the event:

The Eyes of the United States are turned upon this Assembly and their Expectations raised to a very anxious Degree.[1]

If Mason were writing this now he would probably have said, 'The Eyes of the world' are on the American Constitution for if that was not entirely true at that time, it is certainly the case now. The American Bill of Rights, initially adopted as ten amendments to the Constitution (see below) is probably the best-known statements of rights in existence. While there cannot be many who can recite the amendments by heart, the ideas conveyed by the American Bill of Rights have resonated on and on, influencing future generations around the globe.

The passages that are most well-known do not in fact come from the Bill of Rights, or even the Constitution. They were drafted by Thomas Jefferson in 1776 as part of the Declaration of Independence from the colonial power of Britain:

We hold these truths to be self-evident, that all men are created equal; that they are endowed by their Creator with certain inalienable Rights; that among these are life, liberty and the pursuit of happiness.

This resounding statement has fused in the popular imagination with the American Bill of Rights to conjure up a heady brew. It is not necessary to know any of the details to get the basic message – human beings are born with certain rights, no one is allowed to take them away and we are all entitled to the freedom necessary to seek our own personal happiness.

It is a similar story with the other great statement of rights from the same era, the 1789 French Declaration of the Rights of Man and Citizen, which in some form has remained a part of the French Constitution to this day. Adopted by members of the National Assembly during the Revolution, phrases like 'the natural, inalienable and sacred rights of man'[2] and 'men are born and remain free and equal in rights' have echoed down the generations.

These ideas have been evoked to challenge authority for two hundred years. Principles like 'liberty' and 'equality', for example, were widely appealed to during the nineteenth-century anti-slavery struggles in Europe and America. Particularly in the United States, these values went on to fuel a 'rights consciousness' which in turn helped to shape the civil rights and women's movements of the last century.[3] Every bill of rights and international or regional human rights treaty that has been drafted in the ensuing years owes something to these original texts. The basic idea that all human beings without distinction are endowed from the moment of their birth with fundamental rights and are entitled to justice and equality before the law remains the founding principle of what we now call human rights.

The evolution of rights

The era in which the idea of inalienable rights burst forth on the world is one whose imprint is still felt strongly today, at least in the West. It is the period generally known as 'the Enlightenment'.[4] This is a term coined to mark Western society's apparent break with the past; a journey into the light of reason, rationality and science after long years in the dim shadows of superstition. It describes a time when the belief took hold in certain circles that the world was governed by rational laws that could be discovered.

For the renowned German philosopher Immanuel Kant, 'Enlightenment is man's release from his self-incurred tutelage.'[5] The term signalled an escape from the stranglehold of unquestioning obedience to the Church and Monarchy. It marked the beginning of what the Western world recognizes as the modern era.

The idea of rights was not unknown in the *ancien régime*. The first Western theories that human beings are 'naturally' imbued with rights can be traced back to medieval Europe and even to Roman and classical law.[6] What distinguished the claims of the revolutionaries were two factors. First, their capacity to popularize the idea of natural rights in a period that was ripe to receive them. Second, their argument that state power must be grounded in the recognition and protection of individual rights, and that governments which do not exist for that purpose forfeit their legitimacy.

The ideas that were born in this period are so compelling and enduring that anyone could be forgiven for thinking that when the case for strengthening human rights is made in the UK today a call is going out for the British people to finally embrace the revolutions of the Enlightenment two hundred years after the event. This is, effectively, what the *Guardian* newspaper columnist Jonathan Freedland did in his recent book *Bring Home the Revolution*. This is a book which is said to have been bedtime reading for a raft of major political figures including Tony Blair and Jack Straw.[7] Appearing to view the European Convention on Human Rights as a more imperfect and weaker model than 'the real thing', Freedland lauds the American Bill of Rights in its entirety, urging us to adopt something similar:

The options are pretty clear. We can stick with our current system of common law traditions and unspoken conventions, which crumble like sandcastles before the onslaught of a determined government. Or we can insist that individuals deserve not entitlements but rights – liberties that cannot be touched.[8]

Whether or not it is the preferred model, the American Bill of Rights is not so much a prototype as a manifestation of the first wave of rights consciousness which has undergone a significant evolutionary process since then. This needs to be appreciated before later human rights charters are dismissed as a paler imitation. It is like those who judge human behaviour by the patterns of chimpanzees without acknowledging the evolutionary process that separates the two species. They have 98 per cent of DNA in common. But that 2 per cent makes a difference.

The way rights are conceived of, at least in part, is as much a product of time and place as any other phenomenon. The factors which led to the idea of rights as a major force for change at different periods have not been the same, so it is not surprising if they have gone through different incarnations.

This proposition should not be confused with the debate between 'foundationalists' and 'non-foundationalists' over whether or not there are 'essential' features that justify human rights, such as human nature or God.[9] Nor should it be jumbled up with the argument between the so-called constructionists like John Rawls and Ronald Dworken and communitarians like Michael Sandel or Alasdair MacIntyre over whether or not it is possible to construct a justification of human rights from basic principles.[10] What preoccupies these debates is not so much whether the quest for human rights has evolved over time but whether or not there are philosophical or even 'natural' foundations to human rights which can be used to explain them, beyond the beliefs and values of human rights supporters. Alasdair MacIntyre, for example, laid down a gauntlet which shall be picked up in the Conclusion to this book when he wrote about fundamental human rights that:

Every attempt to give good reasons for believing that there *are* such rights has failed ... We know that there are no self-evident truths.[11]

The emphasis on the evolutionary development of rights discourse should also be distinguished from the debate, largely conducted in the United States, between those who believe that a given human rights treaty or bill of rights should be interpreted according to the intention of their drafters and those who believe they should be applied dynamically, taking account of developing mores and circumstances.[12] For the judges who sit in the European Court of Human Rights this matter is settled. The European Convention on Human Rights is viewed as a 'living instrument' to be interpreted in the light of changing conditions and values.[13]

What is being suggested here is altogether simpler. It is that whatever the philosophical justifications of human rights, if any, and regardless of how bills of rights and treaties should be interpreted, the forces which led human beings to champion the idea of fundamental rights at particular times have to be appreciated if human rights in their present incarnation are to be understood. Otherwise modern debates about the value or otherwise of the idea of human rights, like the one described in the last chapter, are bound to descend into confusion and cliché.

While there are lasting principles which have driven forward the idea of fundamental rights from the Enlightenment onwards, there are other perceptions which characterize human rights thinking today that were barely conceived of when the American Founding Fathers and French Revolutionaries decided upon their respective rights charters. This should become clearer as the three waves of rights are explored further.

First-wave rights

The defining feature of the first-wave rights movement is unquestionably liberty from state tyranny and religious persecution. Jonathan Freedland puts it very well when he describes the first-wave conception of rights as liberties that cannot be touched. By and large that is exactly what the Enlightenment version of rights amounted to. This is hardly surprising. The motivation for expending hours of time drafting declarations of rights, in the middle of a revolution in the case of France, and at the birth of a precarious new state in the case of America, came from two clear sources.

First, the tyranny and abuse of power of a British and French king respectively. Although one was a colonial ruler and the other an indigenous despot they both relied on notions like duty and obligation, not to mention naked force, to justify why obedience to their rule should remain unquestioned. Property could be seized, books banned, religious practices suppressed, individuals imprisoned without trial, and taxes arbitrarily raised with virtually no redress.

The expectation was that the state is always and forever a threat to individual freedom. The protection of individuals from abuse of power, it was maintained, can be guaranteed only through a 'higher law' which draws its legitimacy from nature or god and which, therefore, no state has the authority to violate. In the idiom of the time, this higher law was said to be 'the natural rights of man'.

Despite the value put on religious freedom in the Enlightenment, the supernatural was routinely invoked to justify the existence of these 'natural rights'. 'Sacred' was how rights were described in the Preamble to the French Declaration of Rights. The American Declaration of Independence famously declared that 'all men . . . are endowed by their Creator with certain unalienable Rights'.

The second factor explaining support for a bill of rights was the project of creating a new democratic state which did not mirror the worst excesses of the old one. The fear was not only of a new despot but of 'mob rule' or powerful majorities trampling on the interests of minorities. It became apparent that moving from autocracy to democracy would not of itself guarantee individual rights.

This was especially a motivating factor in America. On 31 August 1787, a disillusioned George Mason, who had written so expectantly about the eyes of America being upon the Constitutional Convention in Pennsylvania three months earlier, now declared that he 'would sooner chop off his right hand' than accept the Constitution as it then stood. As prime author of the Virginia Declaration of Rights, he was very disappointed that the delegates had not agreed to include a bill of rights.

The anti-Federalists, those most opposed to what they saw as the centralizing tendency of the new Constitution at the expense of individual states, were particularly concerned that a bill of rights upholding individual liberties had not been included.[14] They demanded that the rights of the people be written down. What they wanted was a bill of rights which would spell out the immunities of individual citizens. The concern was that a democratically elected government would reflect only the 'will of the majority' and would ignore the needs of minorities – defined in numerical terms – whether they be slave-owners or religious dissenters.

Even Thomas Jefferson, who was generally in favour of the new Constitution, wrote to James Madison, the young Virginian delegate, that a bill of rights was 'what the people are entitled to against every government on earth.'[15]

In the event the American Bill of Rights was adopted in 1789 and ratified two years later. It fused historic rights which descend directly from the Magna Carta and the English Bill of Rights (notably jury trial, non-excessive bail and freedom from 'cruel and unusual punishment') with claims that were closely tied to the specific circumstances of the day. These included prohibitions on where soldiers should be 'quartered' and, famously, 'the right of the people to keep and bear Arms.'[16]

Other classical Enlightenment liberties, like free expression and freedom of religion, were common to both the American Bill and French Declaration as were rights to liberty, property and fairness in criminal proceedings. But there was also a significant difference between the two charters.

France had its own famous Enlightenment theoreticians – Voltaire and Rousseau among them – who had considerable influence on the developing 'natural rights culture' as the eighteenth century wore on. There could not be a much more evocative distillation of the prevailing world-view than Rousseau's ringing declaration that 'Man is born free and everywhere he is in chains.'[17] Probably as a consequence of this heritage, the French Declaration is a more philosophically driven, less pragmatic document than its American counterpart, although Thomas Jefferson, one of the Founding Fathers of the American Constitution, assisted in both drafts.

Rights and duties

A rousing Preamble to the French Declaration demands that it be a 'perpetual reminder' of both 'rights and duties'. Tom Paine, the English radical who witnessed the French Revolution, tells us that the issue of rights and responsibilities was addressed by members of the French Assembly in terms not unfamiliar to today's debate:

While the Declaration of Rights was before the National Assembly, some of its members remarked, that if a Declaration of Rights was published, it should be accompanied by a Declaration of Duties. The observation dis-covered a mind that reflected, and it only erred by not reflecting enough. A Declaration of Rights is, by reciprocity, a Declaration of Duties also. Whatever is my right as a man, is also the right of another; and it becomes my duty to guarantee as well as possess.[18]

This sentiment is reflected in some of the clauses of the French Declaration. Liberty is defined as 'the power to do whatever is not injurious to others'. There are limits to the 'natural rights of man' but only those which 'assure other members of society the enjoyments of those same rights; such limits may be determined only by law'.[19]

So while the overwhelming value in first-wave rights is liberty, the French Declaration of the Rights of Man acknowledges that freedoms can, indeed must, be restricted to protect the rights of others. There are also limits to the manifestation of opinions on public order grounds and a reference to the responsibilities entailed by the exercise of free speech.[20]

Taken as a whole, this amounts to a recognition in the French Declaration of what Henry Shue calls 'negative duties – duties not to deprive people of what they have rights to'.[21] Interestingly, there was also a specific statement of duties in Section 16 of the Virginia Declaration of Rights, a forerunner to the American Bill, drafted by George Mason.

it is the mutual duty of all to practice Christian forbearance, love and charity toward each other

Perhaps unsurprisingly this did not make it into the rather more prosaic, freedom-orientated American Bill of Rights which, unlike its French counterpart, was influenced by the unwritten English common law. There was no specific mention of limitations on rights in the American Bill, even to protect the rights of others.

Enforcement

Also unspoken in both the rights charters was the role of the courts, although their general functions were described in other sections of the American Constitution. It was perhaps an inevitable consequence of the forces driving the first-wave human rights movement that over time judges would take it upon themselves to enforce fundamental rights. James Madison predicted that a bill of rights would 'naturally' lead courts to 'resist every encroachment upon rights'[22] by legislatures and executives.

In America this judicial activism developed over time as the courts came to be seen as the only independent bodies with enough authority to protect citizens from their governments and numerical minorities from majorities. In 1803, in the celebrated case of *Marbury* v. *Madison*, the American Supreme Court established its authority to overturn congressional legislation which the judges ruled had breached the Bill of Rights.[23] Although this power is not undisputed, the courts have continued to build on it, acting as the ultimate arbiter of legislation concerning civil and political rights in the US.[24]

From the very beginning, of course, the great rights revolutions failed to live up to their promises. Women were excluded from many of the reforms. Slaves were shockingly counted as three fifths of a person in the original American Constitution.[25] The American Bill of Rights was subsequently used to protect slave-owning[26] and the institution was not declared unconstitutional until 1865 in the US.[27] The French Declaration proved to be no more than a paper shield in the face of 'the terror' unleashed by the erstwhile proponents of fundamental rights. In the years that followed, it was the revolutionaries who hurled each other before the guillotine in open mockery of the 'rights of man'.

Yet the idea of fundamental and inalienable rights did not die with this betrayal. One hundred years after the American Bill of Rights was used to protect the property rights of slave-owners it became a potent weapon in the campaign to desegregate the South, with a little help from the liberal Chief Justice, Earl Warren.[28] If anything, the incongruence between powerful concepts like liberty and equality and the reality of continued inequality and oppression drove the quest for inalienable rights forward, encouraging it to evolve over time.

The British contribution

The contribution of Britain and the British to the first wave of rights is characteristically eccentric but not insignificant. Although we have not adopted a bill of rights until now, the English common law tradition, while generally presented as the polar opposite of the continental and American written rights approach, was both influential on and influenced by the first-wave rights movement.

The Magna Carta and the 1689 Bill of Rights

To this day the Magna Carta is often cited as the first human rights document. Erica-Irene Daes, writing as the UN Special Rapporteur on minorities, described her hope that the Universal Declaration of Human Rights may be accepted as 'the true Magna Carta of mankind'.[29]

The placing of the Magna Carta at the head of the human rights family tree gives a somewhat distorted picture. It is probably more accurate to describe it as a distant ancestor from a wayward branch of the family. On the one hand, it is nothing more than a series of concessions extracted by the barons from King John in 1215 which reflected the casual anti-Semitism and misogyny of the day. There were special provisions singling out the payment of debts to Jewish people:

And if anyone dies indebted to the Jews his wife shall have her dower and pay nothing of that debt.

And there was a commitment that:

no one shall be arrested or imprisoned upon the appeal of a woman, for the death of any other than her husband

On the other hand, the basic idea that the king as an embodiment of the state was bound by law, was the first step in the direction of recognizing the rule of law. The provision that 'to no one will we deny or delay justice or right' finds expression in the right to a fair trial in the French and American rights charters and all subsequent modern human rights instruments.[30] Most famously, the right to jury trial stems directly from the Magna Carta.

Similarly, the 1689 Bill of Rights which emanated from England's so-called 'Glorious Revolution' of the previous year is a very different creature from the descendants which bear its name. It must be the only Bill of Rights in history which had more to offer the rulers than the ruled. Reflecting the anti-Catholicism which partly fuelled the upheavals of the period (only Protestants were to 'have arms for their defence'), it was primarily aimed at establishing the rights of (pre-democratic) parliamentarians *vis-à-vis* the monarch. In many ways it forms the basis of our current, unwritten constitutional settlement and explains why we talk of 'parliamentary sovereignty' rather than 'the people's sovereignty'. But other rights to individual justice have survived to find their way into modern human rights instruments. The right to bail and not to be inflicted with 'cruel or unusual punishment' flow from that document.

The basic flaws in these early texts were well described by James Madison, one of the architects of the American Constitution. Writing with colleagues in the *Federalist Papers* to defend the absence of a bill of rights from the original constitution, which he was subsequently to go on to draft, Madison and his co-authors dismissed the Magna Carta and the English Bill of Rights as highly inferior documents. They were:

stipulations between kings and their subjects, abridgements of prerogative in favour of privilege, reservations of rights not surrendered to the prince. Such was Magna Carta, obtained by the barons, sword in hand, from King John. Such were the subsequent confirmations of that charter by subsequent princes. Such was the *Petition of Right* assented to by Charles the First in the beginning of his reign. Such, also, was the Declaration of Rights presented by the Lords and Commons to the Prince of Orange in 1688 and afterwards thrown into the form of an Act of Parliament called the Bill of Rights[31]

Probably the greatest legacy of the 1689 Bill of Rights to the modern human rights movement is the term 'bill of rights' itself. The Scottish Claim of Right of the same year likewise affirmed the idea of fundamental rights in Scotland. The precedent of enacting basic rights in a written charter had been set.

Locke and the Levellers

Whatever judgement is brought to bear on those early rights documents, there is little doubt that some of the first examples of the idea of basic or 'natural' rights fuelling popular movements stem from these shores. A loosely bound set of radicals active during the English Civil War in the 1640s, known as the 'Levellers', are most famous for their economic egalitarianism but they also demanded safeguards against arbitrary rule, religious intolerance and argued for the introduction of a guaranteed, fundamental law.[32]

In their *Agreements of the People*, the Levellers drafted what was effectively a basic constitution. They tried to promote it through subscription in a kind of imitation of a social contract. They argued that all political power in England had become morally bankrupt since the Normal Conquest as a result of arbitrary rule. Legitimate authority could be achieved only through the voluntary consent of the people, they maintained.

The adoption by the Levellers of the idea of 'natural rights' foreshadowed a line of thought most famously developed by John Locke, although expressed in a more moderate form. His 'natural rights' thesis was probably the single greatest influence on the subsequent development of the idea of fundamental rights. It was preyed in aid to legitimize the Glorious Revolution of 1688. His theory went on to inspire the French and American Revolutions although they took place nearly a hundred years after his death.

Writing in the late seventeenth century, Locke claimed to have 'proved' that 'man' was 'born . . . with a title to prefect freedom'.[33] Everyone is:

free equal and independent, no one can be put out of this estate and subjected to the political power of another without his own consent. The only way whereby any one divests himself of his natural liberty and puts on the bonds of civil society is by agreeing with other men to join and unite into a community for their comfortable, safe and peaceable living one among another, in a secure enjoyment of their properties and a greater security against any that are not of it[34]

In other words, Locke argued that people voluntarily exchanged their freedom and 'natural equality' as they entered society for their own self-protection. The exercise of power by rulers was acceptable provided 'natural rights' were respected. But if this unwritten contract were broken the people were entitled to remove their rulers and replace them with a government which did not violate the rights they were born with.

New ideas rarely emerge fully clothed from their author's pen. Locke's were no exception. He was extensively influenced by other philosophers and scholars[35] and drew heavily on the 'natural law' theories of Thomas Hobbes,[36] although he had many disagreements with him. What Locke was able to do was develop these ideas in a way which had resonance for the major political and constitutional debates of the era. Locke was probably the first influential writer to successfully establish the virtue of freedom in the popular consciousness and to succeed in equating rights and freedoms with each other. The English translation of his *Epistola de Tolerantia* included a Preface which said in capital letters:

ABSOLUTE LIBERTY, JUST AND TRUE LIBERTY, EQUAL AND IMPARTIAL LIBERTY, IS THE THING THAT WE STAND IN NEED OF.[37]

Admittedly this was not written by Locke, who was not a simple libertarian himself, but by his English translator, William Popple. Nevertheless it is indicative of the message which was now taking hold as a result of Locke's work.

The legacy of Tom Paine

It was Tom Paine, the eighteenth-century English radical, who set Locke's ideas alight to illuminate the upheavals of the late eighteenth-century; conflagrations at which Paine himself was present. His legacy spans three countries where at one time he had a major influence, America, Britain and France. Paine is probably the most famous exponent of the 'natural rights' theory from the Enlightenment period.

His classic work, *Rights of Man*, published in 1791, has been described by the historian E. P. Thompson as 'one of the two foundation texts of the English working-class movement'.[38]

Rights of Man had an extraordinary influence in its day and for decades to come. Dedicated to George Washington, the first President of the United States of America, the first part, published on 16 March 1791, was as much, if not more, about democracy than rights, as such. It was essentially a defence of the French Revolution, including the Declaration of the Rights of Man. Eleven months later the second part appeared.

This included a crucial 'social chapter', which came as close to proposing a welfare state funded through progressive taxation on landed property as could be imagined a hundred and fifty years before its introduction in the UK. Without challenging the Lockian idea that to own property is a fundamental right, Paine maintained that good government involved more than just changes to the constitution and republicanism; it also involved some pooling of resources.[39] His proposals were astonishingly detailed. Under Paine's vision every poor family would receive funds to raise and educate their children, there would be retirement pay from the age of sixty, and where necessary jobs would be provided for the unemployed.

It is difficult to imagine now the controversy and excitement Paine's book caused. Only a film or video would be likely to have such an effect today. It is estimated that the two parts sold a quarter of a million copies in a population of ten million.[40] Even more unusual, the book was read aloud to those who could not read on a previously unheard-of scale. The newly-founded London Corresponding Society, composed of tradesmen, mechanics and shopkeepers, set out to popularize the ideas of Tom Paine by networking with provincial societies through leaflets and handbills. They published a cheap edition of *Rights of Man* at only 6d a copy. Another organization, the Society for Constitutional Information, split over Paine. His supporters took control and encouraged its network of branches to follow suit.[41]

Paine's name became associated with agitation, especially among the poor, who were grossly exploited and disenfranchised. His work was distributed around the country from Cornish tin mines to the

Scottish Highlands. In Sheffield it was said that every cutler had a copy; in Newcastle it was in the hand of every journeyman potter. In the midst of all this interest in Paine's ideas one J. Massey complained in 1792 that:

More than Two Thirds of this populous Neighbourhood are ripe for a Revolt, especially the lower class of Inhabitants.[42]

On 21 May 1792 the government of William Pitt issued a proclamation against 'wicked and seditious writings'. When asked to explain why, the Prime Minister replied:

Principles have been laid down by Mr Paine which struck at hereditary nobility and which went to the destruction of monarchy and religion and the total subversion of the establishment of government.[43]

Paine and the societies which supported him were harassed and spied upon by government agents and became the object of massive, state-sponsored abuse. Bookshops selling *Rights of Man* were visited by government officials and the sellers were sometimes arrested and imprisoned. Paine was summonsed to appear in court on charges of seditious libel. He was by now a hounded dissident, persecuted for his beliefs. He fled by boat to Calais. The trial against him took place in his absence. He was found guilty. If he had returned to England he could well have been executed.

Paine died in 1809, an old man in exile in America. Only six mourners attended his funeral. But in his lifetime he had inspired millions of people in two continents to think in a new way about the world and their place within it. The direct lineage between Locke's writings, Paine's popularization of them and the Preamble to the American Declaration of Independence is as self-evident as the rights it proclaimed:

We hold these truths to be self-evident, that all men are created equal; that they are endowed by their Creator with certain inalienable Rights . . . to secure [these] rights, governments are instituted among men, deriving their just powers from the consent of the governed; that, whenever any form of government becomes destructive of these ends, it is the right of the people to alter or to abolish it, and to institute a new government, laying its foundations on such principles, and organizing its powers in such form, as to them shall seem most likely to affect their safety and happiness.

The rights of women

Tom Paine wrote very little about the half of the human race not mentioned in the title of his most famous work. This was left to Mary Wollstonecraft, often described as the first major feminist. Her book *A Vindication of the Rights of Woman* was written in 1791 and published the following year.[44] It was not, as may be supposed, so much a reply to Tom Paine as to the influential Whig political writer Edmund Burke and his castigation of the French Revolution.[45] In fact it was a sequel of sorts to Wollstonecraft's own *A Vindication of the Rights of Men*, published in 1790.

There had previously been books on improving women's manners and women's education. But this 'feminist manifesto' was the first 'single-minded criticism of the social and economic system which created a double standard of excellence for male and female and relegated women to an inferior status'.[46]

Could Wollstonecraft have written this in an earlier era? The circle in which she mixed included Dr Richard Price, a strong supporter of the French and American Revolutions, and Tom Paine himself. In this age of rights awareness it was now possible to suggest that even women should taste freedom. But not without being vilified and tormented for it. Horace Walpole famously dismissed Wollstonecraft as a 'hyena in petticoats'.[47]

The first rights backlash in the UK

Britain's contribution to the human rights story after Paine is less glorious. His work was trounced from all sides. The backlash against the idea of fundamental rights, which began almost as soon as Paine made it popular, makes today's attacks from communitarians and an array of other commentators seem mild in comparison.[48]

From the Right, the intellectual attack on the 'rights of man' took sustenance from the views of political thinker Edmund Burke, a

Conservative Party guru to this day. His unremitting condemnation of the upheavals in France, in *Reflections on the Revolution in France*, was a major incentive for Paine to write *Rights of Man*, just as Wollstonecraft had been similarly motivated.

The violence and tyranny unleashed in the years following the French Revolution, by many of the same people who had proclaimed their rights Declaration to the world, was reason enough for many to turn away from a cause they had once supported. Paine himself was a severe critic of the Terror that ensued.[49] But Burke's attacks were about the very idea that human beings are possessed of inalienable rights. Although they had once been friends, Burke's writings, and his determination to stem any contamination of revolutionary ideas from across the Channel to England, gave intellectual justification to the persecution of Paine and his work by the state authorities.

At another point on the political spectrum was the utilitarian philosopher and reformer Jeremy Bentham, who although an initial supporter of the French Revolution (he was made an honorary citizen of France in 1792) subsequently provided a scathing critique of the French Declaration of Rights. In *Anarchical Fallacies* he famously remarked that natural rights were 'simple nonsense' and 'natural and imprescriptible rights' were 'nonsense upon stilts'.[50] For Bentham and his fellow utilitarians, what is right is that which produces the best outcome for the most individuals; what is known as 'the greatest happiness of the greatest number' principle. This broad approach was to dominate British liberal political thought for generations.

Rights not created by specific laws are illusory according to Bentham. To say that men had an unbounded right to liberty was rubbish, he maintained, and to say they had a right to both property and equality was self-contradictory. In practice such rights would be limited by law, so rights which were apparently asserted against executive and legislative powers were in reality to be defined by them. Like the rights critics of today, Bentham concluded that declarations of rights burst the cords that bound 'selfish passions' when the cohesion of society depended on their restraint.[51]

Flying the flag for the *status quo* as the nineteenth century wore on was the constitutional law scholar A. V. Dicey. As we have seen, he argued powerfully that the uncodified English common law was a far better protector of individual liberties than bills of rights and written constitutions because the latter do not necessarily provide an effective remedy in law and because that which is written down can easily be rubbed out. Individual liberties cannot be destroyed by the government of Britain, Dicey argued, without abolishing an entire customary system of law upheld by judicial rulings.[52]

This argument – that the UK is freer without a written constitution or bill of rights than all those foreign countries that have them – has had an almost revered place in the British cultural imagination. In an almost identical form to that developed by Dicey it was used time and again by successive governments to defend their opposition to introducing a bill of rights into the UK right up until the present government bucked that trend. In the words of former Prime Minister Margaret Thatcher responding to the constitutional reform group Charter 88:

The Government considers that our present constitutional arrangements continue to serve us well and that the citizen in this country enjoys the greatest degree of liberty that is compatible with the rights of others and the vital interests of the state.[53]

The UK's Left rights backlash

Among the radicals and Socialists who were the natural successors to Tom Paine, his legacy waned over time. The abolitionists who fought to end slavery – outlawed in Britain in 1807 – were partly inspired by the Enlightenment ideals of equality and rights.[54] Paine's work could also be said to have influenced the Chartist movement for democratic and agrarian reform in the first part of the nineteenth century.[55]

But in the succeeding years the Left became massively influenced by Karl Marx's attack on the idea of rights as hopelessly individualistic and therefore inimical to the collectivist goals of Communism. Although Marx was not entirely hostile to the French Revolutionaries' identification of the rights of citizens,[56] he was so dismissive of the philosophy of fundamental rights as a progressive idea that this legacy was to last well into the twentieth century.

Marx, like Bentham, saw the very idea of rights as encouraging individualism and selfishness.

> None of the so-called rights of man ... go beyond egoistic man, beyond man as a member of civil society, that is, an individual withdrawn into himself, into the confines of his private interests and private caprice, and separated from the community. In the rights of man ... society appears as a framework external to the individual, as a restriction of their original independence. The sole bond holding them together is natural necessity, need and private interest, the preservation of their property and their egoistic selves.[57]

Even if Marx could have been convinced that declarations of rights can have an ethical content this would not have persuaded him of their value. The idea of a morality not based on class was itself a great deception, according to Friedrich Engels, Marx's closest collaborator:

> We therefore reject every attempt to impose on us any moral dogma whatsoever as an eternal, ultimate and forever immutable moral law ... as society has hitherto moved in class antagonisms, morality was always a class morality. A really human morality which transcends class antagonisms and their legacies in thought becomes possible only at a stage of society which has not only overcome class contradictions but has even forgotten them in practical life.[58]

Lenin sustained this attack, dismissing the French Revolution as 'bourgeois' in the wake of his own.[59] This was a description which influenced generations on the Left to see claims for civil and political rights in such terms. From a classical Marxist point of view, rights were a device for legitimizing the self-interested behaviour of the propertied classes, providing an obstacle to 'the organization of a polity for the welfare of the society as a whole'.[60]

Until the late twentieth century this discourse had a strong influence on a significant Left tradition, most of the supporters of which would probably not have described themselves as Marxists. It is easy to forget that, like communitarians today, many on the Left would routinely criticize the pursuit of individual rights as 'liberal', anti-collectivist and selfish. In addition there was the accusation of class-bias. Civil and political liberties would in many contexts be described as 'formal rights'; which could not be meaningfully exercised in an unequal society. Only social and economic rights were 'real'.[61] Compared to the fight against Capitalism, the struggle for human rights was depicted at best as a 'soft sideshow'.

Any appreciation of the differences between Enlightenment thinkers was all but lost in this broad critique. The radical message of Tom Paine and his supporters, for example, was rarely heard. A Tom Paine Society, patronized by a former Leader of the Labour Party, Michael Foot, exists to promote his ideas to this day, and there has been a campaign for a statue of Paine to fill the empty plinth in Trafalgar Square. But the story of the struggle for the 'Rights of Man', which had captured the hearts and minds of so many people in Britain two hundred years ago, was not generally absorbed into Left liturgy.

Yet Paine was far closer than Marx to being a natural prophet for many on the Left, if they had only known it. With his prototype welfare state, support for republicanism, opposition to slavery, abhorrence of capital punishment, antagonism towards tyranny in the name of revolution, and belief that rights and responsibilities flowed from the equal worth of every human being, his ideas could have continued to resonate far longer than they did. What prevented this was the faultline between Left and Right – or labour and capital – which dominated virtually every social and political issue in the last century, at least until the collapse of the Berlin Wall in 1989.

This did not mean, of course, that there was not a strong tradition of campaigning for civil liberties on the Left in the UK, usually in response to a particular abuse of state power. Quite the contrary. Ongoing violations of civil liberties in Northern Ireland, discrimination against minorities or women, high-profile miscarriages of justice cases and specific pieces of draconian legislation, such as the Prevention of Terrorism or Official Secrets Acts, would attract vociferous opposition, largely from the Left or from liberals.

But even these battles would quite often be fought within the Left/Right prism of national politics. In the 1980s, for example, the Left would fight for the right to demonstrate or to strike while the Right would campaign for the right of individuals to be allowed not to join a trade union or to be entitled to buy their own council homes. The battle lines between these positions would generally be thickly drawn with little attempt to veer a course between them.

The National Council for Civil Liberties (now Liberty) was born into a similar climate in the 1930s. It was set up in response to the oppressive treatment of hunger marchers and anti-fascist demonstrators by the police and from the outset attracted support from many of the Socialist luminaries of the day.[62] It continued to act as a focal point for Left (as well as other) opposition to civil liberties abuses by the state over the ensuing decades, although on occasions the tension between the Socialist and civil libertarian agendas of its members threatened to tear the organization apart.[63] In addition, of course, there have been single-issue groups associated with the Left which have used the idiom of rights to express their cause. These have ranged from some sections of the suffragette movement and more recent feminists to anti-racist, disability and homosexual equality groups.[64]

But until the last decade or so few of the members of these groups would have seen themselves as part of a broader human rights movement. Whatever formal links existed between organizations internationally, there was little understanding, except among the initiated few, that human rights thinking had evolved significantly since the Enlightenment era. Little appreciation that the old 'liberal' model of the individual pitted against an oppressive state had been superseded by a much more complex human rights vision. One which has developed principles that recognize that rights collide with each other, that states have a responsibility to mediate that collision, that governments protect liberties as well as violate them and that human rights abusers can be private companies, individuals or groups abusing other individuals or groups. A vision, in other words, which seeks to embrace the needs of the community as a whole as well as the liberties of its individual members.

It was the Second World War, and all the horrors associated with it, which led to a major revival of the idea of fundamental human rights as a political and moral force, and this time on a world-wide scale. And it was the cataclysmic nature of this event which shaped the evolution of rights from the first to the second wave.

CHAPTER 4

From Liberty to Community:
Second-Wave Rights

PART I: THE REVIVAL OF RIGHTS

At the beginning of the Second World War the celebrated British author H. G. Wells wrote a letter to *The Times* attached to a draft 'Declaration of Rights'. His letter was a cry for war aims to be articulated so that young and old know 'more precisely what we are fighting for'. He was, he admitted, looking for a set of principles to express what those who were prepared to go to war to fight Nazism stood for. Wells's point was that fundamental rights were not only a set of legal entitlements but also a set of values – perhaps the only set of values – powerful enough to inspire and bind people in the common undertaking of defeating fascism and defending their country from invasion.

Wells saw a common thread between what he was trying to achieve and what had gone before. He wrote:

At various crises in the history of our communities, beginning with Magna Carta and going through various Bills of Rights, Declarations of the Rights of Man and so forth, it has been our custom to produce a specific declaration of the broad principles on which our public and social life is based ... The present time seems peculiarly suitable for such a restatement of the spirit in which we face life.[1]

Wells and his supporters – largely on the Left of the political spectrum – were trying to revive an idea that had virtually died since the Enlightenment. They apparently felt that traditional modes of political discourse were unequal to the task of what was required.

Wells called for a great debate on the issue. The *Daily Herald* obliged and made available a page a day for a month for a discussion of the articles in the draft Declaration. The final version of the Declaration was published in the *Herald* in February 1940 with comments by distinguished personalities including J. B. Priestley, A. A. Milne, Kingsley Martin and Clement Atlee, the future Labour Prime Minister. Copies of the Wells debate were subsequently dropped on the European mainland during the War. Wells himself had the Declaration translated into many languages and distributed it widely.

In 1940 a Penguin Special, entitled *The Rights of Man or What We are Fighting For*, by H. G. Wells, appeared with a revised version of his 'Declaration of Rights'. In the Preamble Wells tried to explain why he was reasserting an idea which had weakened its grip on the popular consciousness in his home country over the previous hundred and fifty years:

It has been the practice of what are called the democratic or Parliamentary countries to meet every enhancement and concentration of power in the past, by a definite and vigorous reassertion of the individual rights of man. Never before has our occasion to revive that precedent been so urgent as it is now . . . To that expedient of a Declaration of Rights, the outcome of long ages of balance between government and freedom, we return therefore, but this time on a world scale . . .[2]

The Declaration enumerated a mixture of rights. It included classical Enlightenment liberties, newer rights like freedom of movement and access to personal information, plus, in the best tradition of Tom Paine, a range of what we would now call social and economic rights. These included rights to education, employment, 'nourishment, covering, and medical care and attention'. The concluding Article (10) sought to universalize these standards in the following terms:

. . . the provisions and principles embodied in this Declaration shall be more fully defined in a code of fundamental human rights which shall be made easily accessible to everyone. The Declaration shall not be qualified nor departed from upon any pretext whatever. It incorporates all previous Declarations of Human Rights. Henceforth for a new era it is the fundamental law for mankind throughout the world[3]

The book sold thousands of copies. It was translated into thirty languages and articles about it appeared around the world. Meanwhile Wells had sent a copy of his draft Declaration to his friend President Franklin Roosevelt, who wrote back to him with his reaction to it. When on 6 January 1941 Roosevelt made his 'State of the Union' speech he concluded it with his famous appeal for a world formed upon 'four essential freedoms' of speech and worship and from want and fear. He said:

Freedom means the supremacy of human rights everywhere. Our support goes to those who struggle to gain these rights or keep them.[4]

In the course of that year Roosevelt came back to the theme of the 'four freedoms' over and over again. On 1 January 1942, the Allied powers belatedly included the protection of human rights among their official war aims, stating, 'that complete victory over their enemies is essential . . . to preserve human rights and justice in their own lands as well as in other lands'.[5] The precise role of H. G. Wells and his supporters in inspiring that formulation must remain a matter of speculation.

The fallow years

Before the Second World War there were few international mechanisms to protect fundamental rights, or even vehicles through which concerns about them could be raised. The 1919 Covenant of the League of Nations, the forerunner to the United Nations formed in the wake of the carnage of the First World War, made no reference to human rights.[6]

Attempts to include some obligations concerning religious freedom were made, but these collapsed when the British and American delegates objected to a proposal to add prohibitions on discrimination against foreign nationals on the basis of race or nationality. The fact that one country ran a racially segregated Empire and the other legally discriminated against its own population on the grounds of race, may have had something to do with their wariness!

One important humanitarian organization created at this time was the International Labour Organization (ILO). It was established by the Treaty of Versailles, which concluded the First World War. The ILO was the first agency mandated to protect rights on a global scale. Its Preamble declared that the purpose of the League of Nations was to secure universal peace, which could not be achieved without 'social justice'. The ILO's constitution concentrated on employment conditions but it has also been active on the issues of forced and child labour. In its early days, though, it suffered from working largely in isolation until the birth of the international human rights movement after the Second World War.

The other significant development to come out of the Versailles Peace Conference in 1919 was the inclusion of 'minority clauses' in some of the peace treaties signed between the so-called Allies and former enemy states. This required countries like Hungary, Poland, Romania and Turkey to guarantee civil and political rights and religious and cultural tolerance to groups who, because of their race or language, differed from the majority populations. Similar clauses were included in two bilateral treaties involving Germany. Although these 'minority clauses' involved only a handful of countries, they did establish a historical precedent in the notional limits they set to national sovereignty or the right of a state to determine its internal policies.

The impotence of such mechanisms became obvious after Hitler came to power in January 1933. Anti-Jewish measures were introduced immediately. A few months later the issue of the Nazi persecution of Jewish people was placed before the League of Nations. A petition was submitted to the League's Council, citing a range of laws and decrees aimed at creating an apartheid-style existence for Jews, including in regions covered by the bilateral treaties. The measures effectively barred Jews from working in the civil service, law or medicine and severely limited their access to non-Jewish schools. At a subsequent session of the Assembly of the League of Nations in the autumn of 1933 the situation in Germany was discussed further. Criticism was made of the existing system for protecting minorities and there were calls for international guarantees for human rights everywhere.

On 3 October, the German representative, Mr von Keller, explained the new German philosophy. This was based on the concept of *Volkstum*: national identity defined in terms of race. He contended that the 'Jewish problem' was anyway outside the scope of the minority clauses. Three days after the session ended on 11 October Germany announced its permanent withdrawal from the League of Nations. The feeble attempt of the League to protect minorities of any description from the inferno that was to follow ended in abject failure.[7]

The UN Charter and human rights

The events that were witnessed and learnt about before and during the Second World War literally 'outraged the conscience of mankind'.[8] They led to questions about the very nature of humanity which inevitably drove thinkers and politicians back into the arms of theories about 'inalienable rights'. To rights activists it was unthinkable that the soon-to-be-established United Nations would not include the protection of human rights as one of its aims.

The United Nations Charter was signed on 26 June 1945, less than two months after the war in Europe ended and before peace had been concluded with Japan. A combination of Latin American states and non-governmental organizations (NGOs) – notably legal pressure groups, the American-Jewish Committee, the Federal Council of Churches and the National Association for the Advancement of Coloured People – lobbied the American delegation for human rights to be included in the Charter. Such pressure added to that already generated by the photos and reports that were travelling around the world as the Nazi death camps were liberated. This had its effect.

Earlier opposition by an unholy alliance of two of the Allied powers, the UK and the Soviet Union, to including references to respecting human rights among the purposes of the UN was overcome.

Thanks to the NGO lobby there were, in the end, several references to human rights in the Charter.

The first affirmed one of the defining features of second-wave rights – human dignity. This concept summed up what the Nazis sought to rob from their victims, dead or alive. The Preamble to the Charter reads:

We the people of the United Nations, determined ... to reaffirm faith in fundamental human rights, in the dignity and worth of the human person, in the equal rights of men and women and of nations large and small.

One of the founding purposes of the UN, under Article 1, is to achieve international co-operation 'in promoting and encouraging respect for human rights and for fundamental freedoms for all'. Article 13 requires the General Assembly of the UN to 'initiate studies' to assist in the realization of human rights, and under Articles 55 and 56 all members of the UN pledge themselves to achieve:

universal respect for, and observation of, human rights and fundamental freedoms for all without distinction as to race, sex, language or religion.

The Universal Declaration of Human Rights

Despite these references, the UN Charter disappointed many NGOs and smaller states by not including an international bill of rights within its terms. This proposal was opposed by all the major players. Most were colonial powers. America was racked by racial inequalities and legal discrimination. There was obvious nervousness about integrating a bill of rights into the very fabric of the UN Charter.

Closing the San Francisco Conference at which the Charter was agreed, the new US President, Harry Truman, felt constrained to address the disappointment many people felt at this intransigence. He promised that within the terms of the Charter:

we have good reason to expect the framing of an international bill of rights, acceptable to all the nations involved. That bill of rights will be as much a part of international life as our own Bill of Rights is part of our Constitution[9]

The Charter laid the responsibility for establishing a Commission to protect human rights at the door of the UN's Economic and Social Council (ECOSOC). This it duly did. ECOSOC charged the new Commission to produce recommendations and a report on an international bill of rights.

The first session of the Commission on Human Rights, chaired by Eleanor Roosevelt, wife of the former President, took place in January 1947.[10] Backed by the Soviet delegate, Roosevelt immediately proposed that the Commission concentrate on drafting a declaration, which would be of persuasive force only, while preparations would begin separately for one or more legally enforceable Covenants.

The Commission met for nearly two years and the end result was the Universal Declaration of Human Rights (UDHR). The first draft was written by John Humphrey, a Canadian law professor and social democrat who was appointed as the UN's Human Rights Director in 1946. René Cassin, the chief French delegate and an international jurist, had the largest influence on the draft after Humphrey, probably followed by Eleanor Roosevelt.

The Universal Declaration of Human Rights was adopted by the Third General Assembly of the United Nations on 10 December 1948, henceforth known as Human Rights Day. The vote was 48 to 0 with 8 abstentions. A further eighteen years were to pass before two International Covenants, one on civil and political rights and the other on economic, social and cultural rights, were adopted by the UN.[11] The three documents together provide the International Bill of Rights which President Truman promised would be drafted by the UN.

The UDHR represented the start of a new phase in human rights thinking by ushering in the idea that rights are universal. It marked the beginning of the end of the virtually unquestioned supremacy of the doctrine of national sovereignty which effectively denies that it is the business of any other government how the rulers of states treat their own subjects.[12] But the significance of the UDHR is far greater than that. It signified the beginning of a different conception of fundamental rights from that which dominated the Enlightenment era. As should become clear, the UDHR is truly the mother and father of all second-wave rights.

While it is not a legally binding treaty as such, the Universal Declaration has exerted a huge moral and legal influence around the world. The rights within it have formed the basis of all subsequent international and regional human rights treaties, including the European Convention on Human Rights. Virtually every one of these instruments refers to the UDHR as a source of inspiration in its Preamble. It has also served as the model for many domestic bills of rights around the world. Between 1958 and 1972 alone, twenty-five new national constitutions referred to it. Its provisions have been cited or used so often over the years that it is generally accepted that parts of it are now 'customary international law' and hence binding on states.[13]

The shadow of the Holocaust

The circumstances in which the Declaration was drafted were very different to those which galvanized the authors of the French or American rights charters a century and a half earlier. The idea that everyone was born with 'natural' or 'inalienable' rights was no longer new. There had been no revolution against a despotic government which had lost its legitimacy to rule in the eyes of its citizens. While state tyranny was clearly a feature common to both eras, the reality was that many people living under the Nazi regime had supported, or certainly not resisted, the ruthless oppression and annihilation of minorities or dissidents. Hitler was, of course, elected to power. He actually increased his share of the vote from 33 per cent at the end of 1932 to 44 per cent at the beginning of 1933.

What is more, all over supposedly democratic Europe, men and women, even if they opposed the Nazi occupation of their land, collaborated in the deportation and even murder of millions of innocent men, women and children who had been their neighbours, colleagues or friends. The rest of the world stood by and did very little to try to save the persecuted from their tormentors both before and during the war.

Even after President Roosevelt belatedly pronounced that the protection of human rights was a war aim little effort was made to rescue the doomed or bomb the death camps.[14] Although this is often denied, all the facts of what was happening inside the death camps were well-known to the Allied powers and even to those of the general public who cared to acquaint themselves with the facts.

An article titled 'The German Massacres of Jews in Poland' in the *Guardian* on 11 December 1942, for example, described how 'three to four million are in peril of ruthless extermination', and that 'of the weekly average of 25,000 Jews reaching Eastern Poland from the countries of occupied Europe the vast majority are going to a ghastly death'. The article called for a 'relaxation in the official methods which have hitherto so impeded the work of rescue as to make it almost impossible', such as providing assurances of help to 'countries still liable to an illegal influx of Jewish refugees'. The unmistakable message the journalist wished to convey, even as early as 1942, was that responsibility for what was happening in Nazi Europe could not be laid entirely at the door of a few hundred thousand fanatics.

The Nazi Holocaust of Jews, gypsies, homosexuals, disabled people and political opponents, and all its implications, was directly in the minds of the drafters of the UDHR. Johannes Morsink, an American professor of political philosophy, who has painstakingly recorded most of the debates on the various drafts of the UDHR, has gone so far as to say that 'without the delegates' shared moral revulsion against that event the Declaration would never have been written'.[15] Expression of this revulsion is found in the second paragraph of the Preamble which also reasserted Roosevelt's war aims:

Whereas disregard and contempt for human rights have resulted in barbarous acts which have outraged the conscience of mankind, and the advent of a world in which human beings shall enjoy freedom of speech and belief and freedom from fear and want has been proclaimed as the highest aspiration of the common people . . .

During the final General Assembly debate on the Declaration in December 1948 the drafters reiterated that it had been born out of the experiences of the war. Charles Malik, the Lebanese delegate, said that it 'was inspired by opposition to the barbarous doctrines of Nazism and fascism'. His Indian colleague made a similar point. Ernest Davies, a UK representative, said:

It should not be forgotten that the war by its total disregard of the most fundamental rights was responsible for the Declaration, for previous declarations had lived in history long after the wars and disputes which had given rise to them had been forgotten.[16]

A number of rights in the UDHR can be directly linked to the Nazi atrocities. In addition to the classical first-wave rights of life, liberty, property, free expression and free association there is, for example, a right to 'recognition everywhere as a person before the law' (Article 6). Along with the right not to be 'arbitrarily deprived of his nationality' (Article 15 (2)) this was a response to the stripping of all citizenship rights, and indeed all legal rights whatsoever, from those deemed to be *Untermenschen* by the Nazis. The right to marry and found a family 'without any limitation due to race, nationality or religion' was likewise a response to the 'Nuremberg laws' against intermarriage between Jewish and non-Jewish Germans.

But more significant than the effects of the Nazi era on individual rights was its influence on the overall vision of what the idea of fundamental rights is essentially about. There were three underlying values that came to the fore as a result of the horrors of the war, which helped to unpack the meaning of rights and drive them forward. These were dignity, equality and community, and they help to distinguish this second wave of rights from the first.

Dignity

There was no specific reference to the word 'dignity' in the first-wave rights charters. Respect for fellow human beings is, of course, an underlying theme of all fundamental rights instruments. But what the 'natural rights' advocates most wanted to bestow on individuals was freedom. Freedom to worship, to think, to move around, to own property, to pursue individual paths to happiness. The suffocating oppression of the regimes that the first wavers lived under pours out of every paragraph of those original documents. But this earlier preoccupation with the liberty of the individual should not be confused with the idea of dignity as it was developed by post-war human rights treaties. David Feldman, professor of jurisprudence, has commented:

We must not assume that the idea of dignity is inextricably linked to a liberal-individualist view of human beings as people whose life-choices deserve respect. If the state takes a particular view on what is required for people to live dignified lives, it may introduce regulations to restrict the freedom which people have to make choices which, in the state's view, interfere with the dignity of the individual, a social group or the human race as a whole.[17]

The drafters of the UDHR generally had a somewhat different vision in mind to the traditional libertarian one. First, of course, they were not themselves necessarily victims of repressive regimes. They were, instead, delegates of member states of the United Nations who had set themselves the task of creating a bill of rights for the whole world. In this sense it was an altogether more élitist enterprise than its predecessor a hundred and fifty years earlier. In essence, the international community, through the UN, surveyed the rubble and turned to human rights in their quest for a different future.

Second, the devastation that led the delegates to this task suggested that freedom may not be the only value that should be promoted, even for people living under a despotic regime. The inhumanity that individuals had shown to their fellow human beings, under orders or otherwise, conveyed to the drafters of the UDHR that a relatively neutral concept like freedom was an insufficient basis on which to build the peaceful and tolerant world they sought to achieve. Images of the systematic humiliation and degradation that the Nazis and their supporters inflicted on their enemies, disabled people and those they considered their racial inferiors were transmitted around the globe in the aftermath of the war. Almost as a statement of defiance, the drafters chose to underline their belief that human dignity is an essential value by including the concept in the very first line of the Preamble to the UDHR.

Whereas recognition of the inherent dignity and of the equal and inalienable rights of all members of the human family is the foundation of freedom, justice and peace in the world.[18]

The 'dignity and worth of the human person' is further affirmed in the fifth paragraph of the Preamble. Likewise, Article 1 begins with a resounding affirmation of the central place of human dignity in the UDHR:

All human beings are born free and equal in dignity and rights. They are endowed with reason and conscience and should act toward each other in a spirit of brotherhood.

The vision expressed by such sentiments goes to the heart of the matter. In summary, the transition from the first to the second wave of rights is represented by a shift from a preoccupation with the rights and liberties of individual citizens within particular nation states to a concentration on creating a better world for everyone. The first wave emanated from a struggle against despotic rule by the citizens whose rights were proclaimed; the second was a noble attempt to create a benign set of universal values promoted by the statesmen and women who set themselves this task. Both waves were aimed at protecting individuals from tyranny but the vision of how to achieve that goal had shifted. In the earlier era the main target was to set people free; in the later period it was to create a sense of moral purpose for all humankind.

Dignity as the foundation of rights

The term 'dignity' is never explicitly defined in the Universal Declaration but there is clearly a link between the concepts of dignity, respect and integrity. The prominent use of the term in the UDHR suggests a recognition that human beings have more complex needs than simply to be free from restraint. The message appears to be that human beings, endowed with 'reason' and 'conscience', have a 'personality' whose 'free and full development' are essential elements of human dignity (Article 29).

As David Feldman argues, it makes very little sense to talk of a right to dignity as such.

Dignity is thus not an end in itself or even a means to an end. It is rather an expression of an attitude to life which we as humans should value when we see it in others as an expression which gives particular point and poignancy to the human condition.[19]

In a sense the adoption of the term 'dignity' can be understood as the delegates' answer to the natural rights debate. The concept of dignity replaced the idea of god or nature as the foundation of 'inalienable rights'. This completed the transition from 'natural rights' to 'human rights'; a term which did not come into common usage until this time. Indeed, an attempt to tie human rights to nature in the Preamble of the UDHR and bring god into Articles 1 and 16 (on marriage) were specifically rejected. No longer was a higher being or pre-existing state of nature cited as the source of fundamental rights. Rights were to be accorded to all human beings without distinction because of the essential dignity of all humanity.

Religious and cultural influences on the UDHR

This emphasis on the concept of dignity had two, very different, consequences. First, it allowed delegates with different religious and philosophical convictions to find common ground. Although the idea that human dignity can provide the foundation of human rights was meant to replace the former quasi-spiritual explanations, the concept of dignity unquestionably has theological roots. Bishop Carlos Belo, the East Timorese 1996 Nobel Peace Prize winner, maintains that the idea that dignity is inherent in every person is of 'divine origin', although it also has a 'purely moral origin in lay philosophical thought'.[20]

While agreeing on the centrality of the value of dignity, the different convictions that the delegates brought to bear on the drafting process created a number of tensions that dogged the entire proceedings.

There was the natural law approach versus positivism; liberalism versus Marxism and communitarianism; West versus East; and the religious versus the secular world-view.[21] The drafters never agreed upon a formal definition of human rights. According to the Soviet delegate there was a tacit understanding that they would not do so:

To make the Declaration on Human Rights dependent on the application of a common conception of the nature of rights and freedoms would destroy its very purpose. The Commission's discussions had clearly shown the divergences which existed between the members in the fields of philosophy and ideology; that difference of ideas had not prevented fruitful co-operation, because even though there had been disagreement on the nature of the rights, the Commission has, nevertheless, come to a satisfactory agreement as to the nature of their application.[22]

Despite this, as Morsink points out, there was clearly some philosophical consensus that human dignity is an essential value, that 'human rights are inherent in people and therefore inalienable moral birthrights' and that it is through 'conscience and reason' that we know there are inherent rights.[23]

There were also obvious advantages as well as drawbacks to this creative tension. The drafters were able to draw from the ethical principles of all the major religions as well as from Socialist, liberal and other secular thinking.[24] This has meant, for example, that, while the claim that the UDHR represents universal values is hotly contested (and is one that will be returned to in the Conclusion of this book), it has proved possible for some religious leaders to square the broad approach to human rights in the UDHR with their own beliefs.[25] The South African Bishop Desmond Tutu and Hossein Mehrpour, a professor of law in Teheran and an Islamic scholar, are from this tradition. Mehrpour writes:

that apart from that aspect of religion which consists of the important duty to spiritually guide and instruct, there are no serious differences or contradictions in their social aspects and application between religious teachings and human rights[26]

Allied to its links with a quasi-religious perspective, the concept of dignity as a central value in second-wave rights has enhanced the understanding of the Declaration as being more than just a list of entitlements or legal standards but also a set of ethical values; a moral beacon to the world. Mary Robinson, the UN High Commissioner for Human Rights and former President of Ireland, has tried to get this point across:

My vision of the Universal Declaration, however, strays beyond its legal and political significance ... I would venture to suggest that it has become an elevating force on the events of our world because it can be seen to embody the legal, moral and philosophical beliefs held true by all peoples and because it applies to all.[27]

Addressing the General Assembly of the UN, René Cassin, the chief French delegate and one of the major authors of the Declaration, said:

something new ha[d] entered the world ... [this was] ... the first document about moral value adopted by an assembly of the human community[28]

This 'moral' approach is a world away from the British legal positivist tradition, expressed by Bentham, Dicey and others, within which a right is a legal concept only and meaningless unless a specific remedy is attached to it.[29] The Universal Declaration, by contrast, established the principle that the concept of right can combine the idea of 'the right thing to do' with legal entitlements, thus helping to shape the nature of those entitlements.[30] In other words, it built on the pioneering steps of the first-wave rights charters to establish the idea of a 'higher law' against which all 'positive laws' can be measured. This world-view is reflected in the third paragraph of the Preamble to the UDHR where it says:

it is essential, if man is not to be compelled to have recourse as a last resort, to rebellion against tyranny and oppression, that human rights should be protected by the rule of law

Social, economic and cultural rights

The other implication of the second-wave concept of dignity is the consequence for the role of the state. If the dignity of human beings is to be respected then it follows that the state has to do more than refrain from interfering or oppressing. It has to ensure that the basic requisites of human dignity are provided for. With this concept in mind, a shift starts to occur in the second wave from seeing the state as the prime body against which protection is needed to the idea that the state has a major role in protecting human rights.

Of course in practice this distinction has never totally held. Proactive state action, and the resources that are needed to sustain this, has always been required to ensure that fair trials are held, or that some kind of policing system is maintained which protects the right to life of all citizens, for example.[31] Tom Paine's visionary 'welfare state' would certainly have cast government in this more proactive role. But whereas the first-wave conception of rights was built around the notion of government as the enemy or potential enemy, the second wave implicitly takes a different stance. While the state can clearly be a source of oppression it is also the main guarantor of human rights. It is the body which all international human rights treaties address. It is the state which has legal obligations under international law, including the obligation to take 'positive action' to protect individuals' rights, whether through the criminal justice system, the police force or the benefits agency.

The equal emphasis in the UDHR on social, economic and cultural rights – to work, to just remuneration if in employment and to social security if not, to rest and leisure, to food, clothing, housing and medical care, to necessary social services, to education and to participate in the cultural life of the community – flows from the concept of human dignity.

The fifth paragraph of the Preamble ties the 'dignity and worth of the human person' with 'equal rights for men and women' and the determination of the UN 'to promote social progress and better standards of life'. Article 22 introduces the social and economic section of the Declaration with the statement that these rights are 'indispensable for his [sic] dignity and the free development of his personality'. The reference to a 'just and favourable remuneration' in Article 23 is also explicitly linked to 'an existence worthy of human dignity'.

The reasons for giving equal emphasis to social, economic and cultural rights in the UDHR, and hence bucking the trend of the Enlightenment documents, are of course broader than this. They are linked to the Socialist background of many of the delegates, especially from Latin America. Morsink states that much of the wording and virtually all the ideas in the social and economic section came from 'the tradition of Latin American Socialism' expressed in draft bills of rights submitted by Panama, Chile and Cuba.[32]

There was also some 'trading' of social and economic rights for civil and political rights between the West and the Communist bloc. Then there was the pressure from trade unions and an acceptance of the crucial role of workers in the war. But the concept of dignity undoubtedly helped to drive the idea of rights forward.[33] Many commentators consider that these social and economic rights – often referred to as second-generation rights – are what most distinguishes post-war rights from their Enlightenment ancestors.

Social and economic rights are expressed differently from the civil and political rights in the UDHR. They are rights dependent on 'national effort and international co-operation and in accordance with the organization and resources of each state' (Article 22). The inevitability of this formulation or otherwise will be briefly discussed in the Conclusion. But many commentators insist that the intention of the drafters of the UDHR was that the two types of rights should be indivisible. This is something Mary Robinson has been keen to emphasize frequently.[34] The human rights barrister Rabinder Singh describes the interconnectedness between the two sets of rights in this way:

Just as you cannot worship at the temple of liberty if you have nothing to eat, so if you want to protest about people going hungry in a land of plenty you need to have freedom of expression.[35]

It is clear that in practice civil and political rights were from the beginning given more weight by the UN (to the annoyance of many member states from the 'South') than social and economic rights. But the point is that the UDHR, through the concept of inherent dignity, forces the issue to stay alive. The concept illuminates the obvious point that the protection of the right to life, for example, involves providing the wherewithal to live as well as refraining from murder. It suggests that the freedom to choose your own path in life is a pretty hollow freedom if in reality you have few choices. The old Marxist complaint that fundamental rights are only 'formal rights', whereas 'real rights' involve access to a reasonable standard of living and so forth, was addressed by Socialists fusing with liberals and others to produce second-wave rights.

Equality

The second defining value of the post-war rights era is equality. When the drafters of the American and French charters spoke of everyone having equal rights, they did not mean it in the way we understand it now. As we have seen, women were initially largely excluded. The French Declaration of the Rights of Man and Citizen spoke partly to all men and partly only to its own citizens, as its title indicated. In the America of the Enlightenment slaves were not even counted as full human beings who were in possession of inalienable rights.[36] In a notorious case in 1857 the Supreme Court ruled that Constitutional rights did not apply to freed slaves either.[37] As the *Harper's Weekly* of the day put it:

[T]he court has decided that free negroes are not citizens of the United States.[38]

The Americans who most needed the Bill of Rights were therefore denied its protection in defiance of one of the Bill's founding principles: the protection of minorities against the will of the majority.

It is true that there was also a strong and ultimately successful tradition of opposition to slavery in the USA. The issue literally tore the country apart and was one of the factors in the Civil War. After the war was over the XIVth Amendment was passed to begin to address the issue of equal treatment within the states of America. But the fact that many of the revolutionaries, who in poetic language claimed 'that all men are created equal' and 'are endowed by their Creator with certain inalienable Rights',[39] could so systematically deny rights to a whole section of humanity, must partly be explained by their (implicit or explicit) denial that anyone of African origin was a truly human being at all.[40]

On this point, there are clearly parallels with Nazi Germany. This was not just a totalitarian state, but one for which racism, in particular against Jews, was the ruling ideology. The dehumanization of non-German 'races' was a defining feature of Nazism from the outset. In *Mein Kampf* Hitler defined the state as an:

organization of a community of physically and psychologically similar living beings for the better facilitation of the maintenance of their species[41]

His specific charge was that Jews were trying to dilute Aryan purity. Rudolf Hess, one of Hitler's right-hand men, was scarcely exaggerating when he declared in a meeting in 1934 that National Socialism was 'nothing but applied biology'.[42]

It was with this ideology in mind that the drafters of the UDHR approached the issue of equality. They chose not just to repeat the Enlightenment dictum that 'all human beings are born free and equal' but also to introduce the thoroughly modern formulation that everyone is entitled to the rights in the Declaration 'without distinction of any kind, such as race, colour, sex, language, religion, political or other opinion, national or social origin, property, birth, or other status' (Article 2). Article 7 goes further by emphasizing a positive right to 'equal protection of the law' as well as equality 'before the law' and protection from 'incitement' to discrimination. Unsurprisingly the South African delegation opposed this Article. They were, interestingly, one of only eight countries to abstain from voting in favour of the UDHR in its entirety. The others were the six nations from the Soviet bloc and Saudi Arabia.

The legacy of colonialism

There were some parallels between the drafting process of the UDHR and the American Constitution on this issue. Just as the need to bind the slave-owning South to the new Constitution helped to blind the

American Founding Fathers to the absurdity of their position on equality, so the impact of colonialism, which was still rife in 1948, left its mark. The Declaration was drafted just as the era of Empire was starting to end, with India, Pakistan and Burma all gaining independence in 1947 and the Lebanon and the Philippines the previous year.

The regions of the world were not fairly represented in the drafting committees. Because of colonialism, only four African nations took part. Conversely the West was disproportionately represented, severely denting the claim to 'universality' in authorship of the Declaration. Nevertheless, some of the most active participants in the drafting process were from Chile, the Soviet Union, pre-Communist China and the Lebanon as well as France and the US (in the person of Eleanor Roosevelt). The 'second tier' of drafters included delegates from Egypt, India, Pakistan, the Philippines, Turkey, Haiti, a range of Latin American countries and the Soviet bloc, as well as Australia, the UK and a number of other European states.[43]

The colonial powers were coy about introducing too many and too sweeping references to discrimination, with the Soviet delegation taking the opposite view.[44] Nevertheless the Preamble, and more emphatically Article 2, emphasized that the rights upheld by the UDHR apply to people in 'non-self-governing' territories, a euphemism for colonies, as well as everywhere else. The right to participate in the government of 'his country' in Article 21 was likewise not limited to citizens. However, the attempt to introduce an Article protecting minorities as a group failed, with opposition from both the US and the UK.

Undoubtedly, the idea of equality had come a long way since the late eighteenth century, again helping to define the evolution from first- to second-wave rights. By and large, in the first wave of rights, the term 'equality' applied only to white European men. It meant, in Dicey's terms, 'equality before the law', that is, that all laws should be applied equally. It did not mean that the law should actively protect individuals from discrimination, although the seeds of this idea were planted.[45]

The minorities that the Enlightenment charters sought to protect were generally numerical minorities, often property-owners or religious dissenters or even slave-traders. The widely held view was that their need for protection did not end with the demise of despotic rule. Indeed, as the nineteenth-century English utilitarian philosopher John Stuart Mill wrote in his classic work *On Liberty*, 'the will of the people ... practically means ... the majority' who can oppress minorities.[46] As we have seen, this was one of the reasons why democrats supported the idea of a bill of rights from the Enlightenment onwards.

But by the end of the Second World War the concept of minorities had become strongly associated with religious or racial minorities. The idea of equality was developing to include, as in Article 7 of the UDHR, not only 'equality before the law' but also measures to outlaw discrimination on any grounds. This evolution is not surprising. For, in addition to the effects of the horrors of Nazism, the very idea of equality contains within it the seeds of its own expansion, pushing out the boundaries of the term to ever-increasing inclusivity. We have seen this in the way that the 14th Amendment of the American Bill of Rights was latterly used to combat racial discrimination, both symbolically and legally, leading ultimately to the overturning of segregation, at least in law if not in practice, in the recalcitrant Southern states.[47]

Similarly, Kevin Boyle, professor of human rights law, has commented that:

The assertions of the entitlement of all human beings to freedom, equal rights and equal dignity in the UN Charter and the Universal Declaration, constituted revolutionary language at a time when large parts of the South of the world were ruled from Northern empires.[48]

By the time the two UN International Covenants were adopted in 1966 (see below), which together with the UDHR form the International Bill of Rights, they included in their first Article a right of 'all peoples' to 'self-determination'.

Nelson Mandela, former President of South Africa, has made the point that despite the fact that the UDHR was adopted only a few months after the Apartheid regime formally took power, its resounding endorsement of equality proved inspirational:

For all the opponents of this pernicious system, the simple and noble words of the Universal Declaration were a sudden ray of hope at one of our darkest moments. During the many years that followed, this document ... served as a shining beacon and an inspiration to many millions of South Africans. It was proof that they were not alone, but part of a global movement against racism and colonialism, for human rights and peace and justice.[49]

Equality as a driving force

The principle of equality continues to drive rights forward. Once it was accepted that human rights values require states to proactively take measures to root out discrimination between private individuals, then the characterization of rights was inevitably going to shift. It began to change from a shield against state tyranny to a vision that includes strongly implied injunctions on how private individuals should behave towards each other.

The significance attached to the idea of equality was also a further factor in the decision of the drafters of the UDHR to include social and economic rights. This resulted in the adoption in 1966 of the International Covenant on Economic, Social and Cultural Rights, a legally binding human rights treaty. The post-war concept of equality has also led to UN treaties on the elimination of racial discrimination and discrimination against women, adopted in 1965 and 1979 respectively. All three treaties have been ratified by the UK.[50]

The scope of equality has gradually been extended by international human rights supervisory bodies, like the European Court of Human Rights, to include people discriminated against on grounds of sexual orientation, gender reassignment and disability, although progress has been limited and uneven.[51] There was a 1960 UN Declaration on the right to self-determination,[52] Conventions on Apartheid, and a Declaration against religious discrimination.[53] The Preamble to the 1973 Apartheid Convention, for example, cites the commitment to equality in the UN Charter and the UDHR to justify declaring Apartheid a 'crime against humanity'.[54]

The International Covenant on Civil and Political Rights, part of the International Bill of Rights, which came into force in 1976, included not only a far-reaching right to equality (Article 26) but also a 'minorities clause'. In 1992 the UN agreed a Declaration on the rights of minorities.[55] And there is also now a Council of Europe Framework Convention for the Protection of National Minorities, ratified by the UK, which entered into force on 1 February 1998.

Community and responsibilities

Perhaps the most striking feature of second-wave rights is the incorporation of concepts like community and responsibilities. One obvious lesson drawn from the descent into barbarism that had contaminated virtually the whole of Europe in the Second World War was that the same individuals who require protection from tyranny can also contribute to it. Creating mechanisms to prevent states from abusing the rights of their citizens was plainly not enough. Individuals themselves needed to be inculcated with a sense of moral purpose if there was 'never again' to be a holocaust like the one unleashed by the Nazis.

Although it is generally states who are the bearers of responsibilities under international law, the 1946 Nuremberg Tribunal, established to try war criminals, developed a doctrine of individual responsibility. The Tribunal declared:

That international law imposes duties and liabilities upon individuals as well as upon states has long been recognized ... Crimes against international law are committed by men, not by abstract entities, and only by punishing individuals who commit such crimes can the provision of international law be enforced.[56]

The same principle was repeated in the Convention on the Prevention and Punishment of the Crime of Genocide, adopted on 9 December 1948, the day before the UDHR:

Persons committing genocide ... shall be punished, whether they are constitutionally responsible rulers, public officials or private individuals. (Article 4)

The view that the UDHR should include the responsibilities as well as the rights of the individual was widespread among delegates from the outset. The main dispute was whether there should be a list of separate duties corresponding to the Declaration of Rights or whether one general Article would suffice.

The drafters of the American Declaration of the Rights and Duties of Man, which was adopted by the Organization of American States a few months before the UDHR, had decided to include a catalogue of duties in ten separate Articles, including the duty to work, the duty to obey the law 'and other legitimate command of the authorities' (Article 33). The Latin American delegates to the UN wanted to emulate this approach in the UDHR. They were supported in this by the Chinese and Egyptian representatives. In explaining his agreement with this proposal, Dr Peng-chun Chang, the delegate from China, described the enterprise many of the delegates felt themselves to be engaged in:

the aim of the United Nations was not to ensure the selfish gains of the individual but to try to increase man's moral stature. It was [therefore] a necessity to proclaim the duties of the individual, for it was a consciousness of his duties which enabled man to reach a high moral standard[57]

The communitarian vision of the UDHR

The issue of whom individuals owed responsibilities to ranged in the discussions from the state (supported especially by the Soviet bloc) to society to the community. The proposal that individuals owed duties to the state raised strong objections. Charles Malik, the Lebanese delegate, helped focus the issue when he said:

The world was faced with a tendency to 'statism' ... The state insisted on the individual's obligations and duties to it. This [too] was a grave danger ... There were innumerable other intermediate loyalties which the individual must respect, such as those towards his family, his profession, his friends and also towards his philosophical laws ... Real freedom sprang from the loyalty of the individual not to the state but to those intermediate forms. These must find their place in the general social picture.[58]

In the end, although majority support was in favour of one separate Article on obligations, and most of the delegates rejected the idea that these should be to the state, its terms were not incompatible with Chang's description of the task the delegates had set themselves. The first clause of Article 29 simply states that:

Everyone has duties to the community in which alone the free and full development of his personality is possible.

The wording of this Article expresses two interconnected ideas. First, that individuals have responsibilities as well as rights. Second, that individuals do not exist in the world as isolated beings but live in societies, or more specifically communities, towards which they must act responsibly if they are to develop their true humanity. The insertion of the word 'alone' is significant here. A UK delegate explained that its use 'stressed the essential fact that the individual could attain the full development of his personality only within the framework of society'.[59]

According to Morsink, 'this word "alone" may well be the most important single word in the entire document, for it helps answer the charge that the rights set forth in the Declaration create egotistic individuals who are not closely tied to their respective communities'.[60]

Erica-Irene Daes, writing as the Greek UN Special Rapporteur on discrimination and minorities, maintains that, in choosing the word 'community', the drafters were not only emphasizing the social nature of human beings. They were also suggesting that they have duties, not to the state whose legitimacy depends on it upholding the rights in the UDHR, but to the group in which they live.[61] She says of Article 29:

this provision is of a moral nature in the sense that it lays down a general rule for individual behaviour in the community to which the individual belongs[62]

According to one interpretation, the wording of Article 29 also suggests that the existence of individuals' duties towards society or their community are contingent on them being given the conditions for 'the free and full development' of their personality.[63] Fernand Dehousse, the Belgian delegate, maintained that the Article establishes a contract between the individual and community in which society has the responsibility to ensure that the social and economic rights in the UDHR, in particular, are upheld.[64]

Either way, this portrayal of the rights of human beings had travelled a long distance since the Enlightenment era. This was a self-conscious endeavour by some of the delegates. The French representative, René Cassin, who drafted the original duties clauses along with much of the rest of the Declaration, was keen not to present the UDHR as 'a mere offshoot of the eighteenth-century tree of rights'.[65] For despite the old revolutionary call for solidarity, it was widely understood that first-wave rights were primarily driven by the impulse for liberty.

The post-war vision is also a far cry from the caricature of human rights as an entirely libertarian project portrayed at various times by the Left, the Right, utilitarians and communitarians of all shades. If Jeremy Bentham should ever pop out of the glass box where he remains in the foyer of University College London, he might be surprised to see that the 'selfish passions' he feared would be incited by rights documents are more likely to be tamed by the Universal Declaration of Human Rights.[66]

The second-wave rights vision does not begin and end with isolated individuals pitted against mighty states; individuals who, in the words of the French Declaration of Rights, should have the power 'to do whatever is not injurious to others' (Article 4). Instead it is a vision in which the 'personality' of individuals can effectively develop only in community with others. This is an idea also developed in Article 1 of the UDHR, which links 'dignity' and 'conscience' with what reads almost like a Commandment:

All human beings ... should act towards one another in a spirit of brotherhood.

These communitarian themes – there is no better word for them – partly reflected the philosophical and religious backgrounds of a number of the delegates, which, as we have seen, included Islam, Socialism and Confucianism.[67] But they stem mainly from the same precipitating factor which influenced so much of the contents of the

UDHR. In other words, the emphasis on the social nature of human beings and their responsibilities to others and the wider community flowed from the task the delegates set themselves. This task was not just to set the people free but also to find common values in which the liberties of individuals would be respected without weakening the bonds so necessary for human development. It was a different understanding of the concept of freedom.

Duties flow from rights

On the other hand, the conclusion reached, after much discussion, was that it was not appropriate to elevate duties above rights either. This contradicts the approach of many modern communitarians including, as we have seen, some in the present government.[68] An earlier proposal to have the duties clause placed at the beginning of the Declaration was also defeated because it was felt not to be logical to describe limitations before mentioning rights.[69] Interestingly, US representatives were particularly opposed to giving too high a priority to the duties of the individual in a Declaration concentrating on rights. Whether this concern partly reflected the culture of their own Bill of Rights can only be a matter for speculation.

The decision not to enumerate specific duties in the UDHR meant that, by strong implication, responsibilities were presented as flowing from the rights upheld. This approach is reflected in three places in the UDHR. First, there is the statement in Article 30 that nothing in the Declaration 'may be interpreted as implying' that the state, any group, or 'person' can engage in any activity aimed at 'the destruction' of others' rights or freedoms in the UDHR. This formulation put individuals and groups on an equal footing with states in this Article. It was explicitly aimed at checking the growth of fascism or other totalitarian ideologies. The intended message to all people was that in exercising rights you are not entitled to use them to destroy those of others.

Second, and related to this, is the second part of Article 29, where the concept of legitimate restrictions on rights, and the grounds on which these can be made, is expressed:

In the exercise of his rights and freedoms everyone shall be subject only to such limitations as are determined by law solely for the purpose of securing due recognition and respect for the rights and freedoms of others and of meeting the just requirements of morality, public order and the general welfare of a democratic society.

This clause simultaneously sets limits on how far governments can go in restricting rights while establishing the acceptable limits of individuals' rights. The limits on rights thus set the boundaries within which a right can be exercised.[70] This in turn provides a guide as to where the exercise of rights might hurt others, for example, by inciting racial hatred through freedom of speech. In this sense the obligations of individuals to others and to the broader society in which they live flow from the exercise of rights and are established through such limitations. The placing of this limitation clause in the same Article as the statement of responsibilities stresses the link between limitations on rights and the duties of individuals.

The principle that rights must be limited to protect others was almost unanimously approved by the delegates on the UN Commission of Human Rights. The adoption of specific grounds for limiting rights – 'morality, public order and general welfare in a democratic society' – was to ring-fence the scope of the state to determine what limitations are required.[71]

There are echoes here of the French Declaration, which, as we saw, differed from the American Bill of Rights in explicitly recognizing that there could be limitations on certain rights provided they were 'determined by law' and aimed at protecting 'others', 'society' and 'public order'.[72] This followed logically from the statement in Article 4 of the French Declaration that 'Liberty consists of the power to do whatever is not injurious to others.' In one sense this exercise of 'negative duties' in the fulfilment of rights is axiomatic, as Tom Paine pointed out in *Rights of Man* and John Stuart Mill elaborated on in *On Liberty*.[73] It is simply not possible for privacy rights to be upheld, for example, if neighbours continually pry on each other.

But in its third major reference to responsibilities, the UDHR goes much further than this. In the last paragraph of the Preamble it is clear that the Declaration is actually addressed to the people of the world and that they have an obligation to take positive steps to both promote and protect human rights:

The General Assembly proclaims the Universal Declaration of Human Rights as a common standard of achievement for all peoples and all nations, to the end that every individual and every organ of society, keeping this Declaration constantly in mind, shall strive by teaching and education to promote respect for these rights and freedoms and by progressive measures, national and international, to secure their universal and effective recognition and observance . . .

This is not, of course, a legally binding obligation on individuals but it is a strongly worded moral exhortation on everyone to carry out their positive duty to 'secure universal and effective recognition' of fundamental human rights.[74] This message is all at one with an enterprise which at its heart is about creating a better world for all. With this exhortation the evolution from first- to second-wave rights is complete.[75]

PART II: RIGHTS ENFORCEMENT AND THE MORAL MAZE

The UDHR remains the foundation document of second-wave rights. About twelve million people worldwide signed a petition on the fiftieth anniversary of its adoption, in 1998, calling for its values to be upheld. The many legally binding international human rights treaties which have followed it are all essentially drafted in its image.[76] Most of them cite the UDHR in their Preambles and the rights and freedoms enshrined in these instruments generally follow closely in the Declaration's footsteps.

In legal terms, though, there is a significant difference between them. Treaties are essentially legal documents. They are not primarily a statement of ethical values like the UDHR. If an instrument is legally binding between nations then it is the state which is the prime bearer of any obligations it confers and it is to the state that such instruments are addressed in formal terms (although, as we have seen, individuals can be directly liable under some treaties).[77] This is a matter of international law. It is also a matter of policy. Like the rights charters of the Enlightenment, international human rights treaties are substantially aimed at safeguarding the rights and freedoms of individuals. It is the state's responsibility to refrain from oppressive acts and to restrain private forces from rights violations, although increasingly there is a recognition that states also have to be proactive in promoting and protecting rights.[78]

That said, all post-war treaties are recognizably affected by the evolution from first- to second-wave rights – from a liberty-driven to a more community-orientated world-view. There is still a powerful moral ethos running through such treaties whose broad message speaks to society as a whole. In each and every one of them there are clear limits set to the liberty of the individual in order to protect not just the rights of others but also the common good. The three concepts – dignity, equality and community – which drove forward the vision of rights in the UDHR are to a greater or lesser degree visible in each post-war treaty. Combined with the first-wave principles of liberty and justice, they compose the underlying values of such instruments.

The communitarian vision of the International Covenants

The twin International Covenants on civil and political and social and economic rights, which were adopted in 1966 to give legal force to the principles in the UDHR, affirm the communitarian vision which informs second-wave rights.[79] Individuals do not just have duties to other individuals but to the wider community. The Preambles to both Covenants draw on the precise wording of the Universal Declaration to declare:

the individual, having duties to other individuals and to the community to which he belongs, is under a responsibility to strive for the promotion and observance of . . . rights

Erica-Irene Daes, a UN Special Rapporteur, maintains that this Preamble, although without direct legal force, has to be understood as an aid to interpretation of the legally binding Articles which follow it. Her reading of it is that, while it is 'an indisputable fact' that the Covenants are concerned with 'the obligations of states to individuals', the fact is that 'states are the sum of individuals' and so 'the individual must co-operate' if the rights in the Covenants are to be upheld.[80]

This underlines the crucial role for individuals in upholding the vision of post-war human rights instruments, including those that are legally binding. It is particularly relevant, of course, in democratic societies where governments are to some degree constrained by the wider electorate in the choices they make, at least if they want to be re-elected. One of the original purposes of rights charters from the Enlightenment onwards, as John Stuart Mill and others recognized, was to prevent governments from simply following the latest populist demand. But if the public are constantly braying for more draconian policies, for less protection for suspects and longer prison sentences, for example, then this is likely to leave its mark.

While under the classic Enlightenment model judges are supposed to act as a bulwark in such circumstances, as we have seen it is not realistic to assume that they will not also be affected by the prevailing climate.[81] What the Preambles to the Covenants are saying, in other words, is that laws on their own will not safeguard rights if there is little or no popular human rights culture.

The obligations individuals have under the Covenants, therefore, go beyond the 'negative duties' that are the corollary of rights under the first-wave model.[82] They are obliged not only to refrain from abusing others' rights but also to promote the ideal of human rights or what has been called the 'human rights ethic'.[83] It is not just a question of behaving responsibly to others. It is also about encouraging others to do so. It is about speaking out when there are cries to lock people up and throw away the key or restore capital punishment or hound out paedophiles on their release from prison until they are forced to return to captivity for their own protection. It is about making the case for human rights as a set of moral values.

The highs and lows of the ECHR

There is no equivalent exhortation to individuals to promote human rights in the European Convention on Human Rights (ECHR), which has been incorporated into UK law through the 1998 Human Rights Act. In fact, the only specific reference to the concept of duty is in Article 10 on free expression and opinions where 'the exercise of these freedoms, since it carries with it duties and responsibilities, may be subject to' a list of restrictions.

There is also a powerfully worded prohibition on destroying the rights and freedoms of others (Article 17). As in the UDHR and the twin Covenants, this Article is explicitly addressed to individuals and groups as well as governments.

Generally speaking, the more philosophical aspects of the Declaration and Covenants are missing from the ECHR. There is no explicit reference to dignity or equality. There is a broad anti-discrimination Article (14), which potentially has an overriding effect in that it applies to all the other rights in the Convention. But, unlike its equivalent in the International Covenant on Civil and Political Rights (ICCPR Article 26), it does not outlaw discrimination in general terms; only in relation to the civil and political rights enumerated in the ECHR.

This narrowing of the scope of some of the more loosely expressed ideals in the UDHR may have something to do with the fact that, while the basic rights and freedoms were drawn from the Universal Declaration and the emerging draft of what became the ICCPR, British Foreign and Home Office officials played a significant role in the drafting process of the ECHR.[84] Cabinet minutes and unpublished papers reflect the difficulties they had in moving beyond the British positivist tradition to an understanding of the broader ethical message of human rights. A Mr L. A. Scopes in the UN Department of the Foreign Office, for example, commented in a memo to the Foreign Secretary, Ernest Bevin:

We can freely admit that the Convention lacks the precision of a document drawn up in the framework of an established body of national law but, as the Lord Chancellor admits, it represents the results of a series of compromises and ... it is probably the best compromise we shall be able to achieve.[85]

The Cold War, which at this point was more strongly felt within Europe than anywhere else, also had its effect on the nature of the draft. For the delegates at the Council of Europe, concern about the spread of Communism from the East was almost as strong a motivating factor for adopting the ECHR as the aftermath of fascist rule.[86] This may have had some effect on the decision not to include any of the social and economic rights in the UDHR in the European Convention (although rights to education and 'to the peaceful enjoyment of possessions' were added to the First Protocol).[87] The Council of Europe's Committee of Ministers' report on this issue justified the decision in terms which suggested that the delegates were well aware of the Socialist or social democratic influences on the UDHR:

It is necessary to begin at the beginning and to guarantee political democracy ... and then to co-ordinate our economies, before undertaking the generalization of social democracy.[88]

The growth of totalitarianism in Eastern Europe also partly explains the emphasis on the value of democracy in the Convention which in the Preamble is described as one of the means by which fundamental freedoms are maintained. This is an area where the Convention speaks in much more direct language than the Universal Declaration. The terms 'democracy' or 'democratic' barely got a mention in the UDHR because of the difficulty the delegates had in achieving agreement among the nations of the world on what the terms meant. A number of the UN member states could not be described as democratic under any definition, and many of those that could ran decidedly undemocratic empires (the UK included, of course).

The UK government's ambivalence over ratifying the ECHR
The implications of legally enforceable human rights treaties for the running of the British Empire surfaced in Cabinet discussions by the Atlee Labour government about whether or not to ratify the ECHR.

The Colonial Secretary, James Griffiths, opposed ratification because it was:

likely to cause considerable misunderstanding and political unsettlement in many colonial territories ... where ... the bulk of the people were still politically immature ... This confusion would undoubtedly be exploited by extremist politicians in order to undermine the authority of the Colonial Government concerned[89]

As former Labour Home Secretary Roy Jenkins once pointed out, George III could not have expressed it better at the time of the American War of Independence.[90]

In a letter of 29 September 1950, the Colonial Secretary admitted what was nearer the truth: that the adoption of the Convention by Colonial governments could be extremely damaging politically:

The Convention, if applied to the Colonies, cannot be other than an embarrassment to Colonial governments and if it were possible for the United Kingdom to decline to accept it, so that the question of its application to the Colonies would not arise, the Colonial Office would be very glad.[91]

In the end, the fact that several of the member states of the Council of Europe ran undemocratic and racially segregated empires did not prevent the final paragraph of the Preamble referring in a self-congratulatory way to the common 'ideals' they shared, including a heritage of 'freedom and the rule of law'.[92]

Second-wave influences on the ECHR

Despite the more limited scope of the ECHR, it would be entirely wrong to see it as devoid of the values which define the UDHR. The Preamble to the Convention pays homage to the Universal Declaration twice and clearly shares a common ethos of trying to create a better world. As early as 1979 the judges at the European Court of Human Rights sought to place the ECHR in a broader human rights context. They continue to develop their case law or jurisprudence in that spirit and there are increasing references to other post-war human rights treaties to strengthen their interpretation of Convention rights, including the ILO Conventions and the 1961

European Social Charter.[93] In this way some of the weaknesses and gaps in the ECHR are beginning to be addressed; for example, by reference to the UN's Conventions on race and on children.[94]

Notwithstanding the absence of specific references to the values of dignity or equality, the ECHR jurisprudence has evolved to give some recognition to these principles, even if this is often unstated. The right to privacy, for example, has been interpreted to mean more than the right to be left alone. In true second-wave rights fashion, the judges at the European Court of Human Rights have ruled that it also covers 'the right to develop one's own personality and to create and foster relationships with others'.[95] Although still slow to develop, this perspective has allowed the right to privacy to encompass issues concerning sex, sexuality and child abuse (through the concept of 'physical integrity'), partly from the point of view of safeguarding the dignity of the individuals involved.

Similarly the right not to be subject to degrading treatment has been interpreted to cover both dignity and equality. The European Court of Human Rights, for example, has recently ruled that lack of medical care when someone is suffering from a serious illness can amount to degrading treatment.[96] In an earlier landmark case concerning the withdrawal of the automatic right of entry to the UK of British East African Asians, the European Commission on Human Rights[97] ruled that:

publicly to single out a group of persons for differential treatment on the basis of race might, in certain circumstances, constitute a special form of affront to human dignity[98]

New protocols to the ECHR have been passed from time to time; for example, concerning deportations, equality between spouses and the death penalty, only some of which have been ratified by the UK.[99] These have also been aimed at bringing the ECHR up to speed with developing human rights norms. A new draft protocol has been drawn up to broaden the anti-discrimination provision of the ECHR. If adopted as drafted, it will cover any right 'set forth by law', not just the civil and political rights in the Convention. The commitment to equality in the UDHR is cited as a reason for this extension. At the time of writing it is not yet certain whether the UK government will sign the new protocol.[100]

Positive obligations under the ECHR

It would also be incorrect to view the Convention as being more in the mould of the Enlightenment charters than the second-wave treaties so far as the role of the state is concerned. The strong tone, and positive expression, of the first Article of the ECHR, which requires states to 'secure to everyone within their jurisdiction' the fundamental rights and freedoms in the Convention, has encouraged the European Court of Human Rights to emphasize the 'positive obligations' on governments to protect and promote rights.

As we have seen, this means that the state is viewed not only as a potential abuser of rights from which individuals need eternal protection, as was largely the case under the first-wave model. It is also the prime body responsible for securing rights. The European Court of Human Rights has declared time and again that the state is obliged to take proactive steps to protect people's rights, even when it is not directly involved. In other words, governments are increasingly being required to 'hold the ring' between private parties in a way which ensures that fundamental rights are protected. This has brought the ambit of human rights law into smacking,[101] domestic violence[102] and the rights of fathers concerning abortion,[103] for example.

Through such cases individuals are effectively being given guidance as to what is appropriate behaviour in human rights terms. For example, through the smacking case a stepfather was indirectly told that he had subjected his nine-year-old son to 'inhuman and degrading treatment', in breach of Article 3 of the ECHR, by regularly beating him with a cane. In the UK Court the man had been successfully able to plead 'lawful punishment'.[104] Before the Human Rights Act came into force there was no obligation on the domestic courts to reinterpret the law to embrace Convention rights in such circumstances; even rights which, in the case of torture and degrading treatment, are absolute.[105]

In the abortion case the father of an unborn child was effectively told that while he was entitled to raise his concerns, he had no fundamental right to be consulted on, or to stop, his partner's abortion. This was because it was the mother's private life, and not any right to life that the foetus may or may not have, which was at stake.[106]

The time has long passed since the ECHR spoke only to states. Although the procedures of international law require that it continues to speak through states, for only states can be taken to the European Court of Human Rights, the vision it upholds is addressed to society at large.

Limitations on rights and the obligations of individuals

As was intended by the drafters of the UDHR, limitations on rights – which are extensive under the ECHR – also give guidance as to where the exercise of an individual's rights might harm others or the common good. The drafters of both the ECHR and ICCPR decided against an all-encompassing limitations clause like Article 29 of the UDHR.[107] Instead restrictions are joined to specific Articles.

There is, in fact, a hierarchy of rights under the ECHR. Some rights – like the prohibitions on torture, inhuman or degrading treatment, or slavery – are virtually absolute. Other rights, like the right to liberty and a fair trial, are qualified in explicit and finite circumstances. The right to liberty, for example, can be curtailed to bring someone to court on 'reasonable suspicion' that they have committed a crime.[108] Other rights can be limited on more general grounds, like the rights to privacy or freedom of assembly and association, which, in the ECHR, can be curtailed to protect, among other things, public order, national security, health, morals and the rights and freedoms of others.[109]

The lists of qualifications and restrictions on rights in the Convention are sometimes bafflingly long, and some of them appear to reflect the concerns and interests of the European governments which drafted them rather than internationally recognized human rights principles. Dubious examples include the curtailment of liberty to detain 'alcoholics or drug addicts or vagrants',[110] limiting free expression to maintain 'the authority and impartiality of the judiciary',[111] and restricting privacy to protect 'the economic well-being of the country'.[112] None of these are replicated in the ICCPR.

In a throw-back to the French Declaration of the Rights of Man the ECHR even goes so far as effectively to discriminate against non-citizens. Article 16 allows states to impose 'restrictions on the political activity of aliens'.

It would be incorrect, however, to see most restrictions on rights as merely a sop to state interests or as operating outside human rights philosophy. As we have seen, limitations on rights frequently express individuals' obligations to each other or the wider community which in turn flow from the exercise of their rights. In relation to some Articles they have also conferred new rights on individuals. This is a process in evolution but it is gaining in frequency. The European Court of Human Rights, for example, has to some degree sought to balance the right to a fair trial with the rights of victims and witnesses. The judges have recently declared that:

principles of fair trial also require that in appropriate cases the interests of the defence are balanced against those of witnesses or victims called upon to testify[113]

A rape trial could be one of those circumstances. In one case the Strasbourg organs acknowledged that rape trials 'are often conceived of as an ordeal by the victim, in particular when the latter is unwillingly confronted with the defendant'. It was accepted that in sexual abuse cases 'certain measures may be taken for the purpose of protecting the victim' provided they could be reconciled with 'an adequate and effective exercise of the rights of the defence'.[114]

On the other hand, all attempts by the victims of crime or their relatives to argue for the right to actively participate in the sentencing process of a convicted criminal, as happens in some states in America, have so far failed.[115]

Maybe this will yet come. But one thing is certain, the case law will not develop in a way that denies the very purpose of the Convention. From the outset the European Court of Human Rights has emphasized its teleological approach to interpretation. This means that rather than getting bogged down in the meaning of words, as the UK courts are wont to do, it seeks to realize the objects and purposes of the ECHR in its judgments. The Court will sometimes consult the preparatory documents that went into drafting the treaty but that is relatively rare. Part of fulfilling the purposes of the treaty is to treat it as a 'living instrument'.[116]

To sum up, the evolving ECHR philosophy, as would be expected from a second-wave rights document, continually balances the rights of the individual against the rights of other individuals and the needs of the community. But not to the extent of extinguishing 'the very essence of a right' laid down in the Convention.[117]

Contrasts with the American Bill of Rights

The affirmation that individuals have inalienable rights simply because they are human and that these are of a higher order than any particular law, remains the enduring principle that binds all fundamental rights charters from the Enlightenment to the present day. This philosophical orientation suffers from caricature and misrepresentation by those who either oppose the very idea of fundamental rights or who misunderstand the world-view it represents. From Marxists on the Left to Conservatives on the Right and utilitarians and communitarians somewhere in the middle, the rights enterprise has been dismissed as selfish and dangerously individualistic.[118]

Professor Mary Ann Glendon, an American communitarian, spoke for many others of a similar view, for example, when she described 'American rights talk' as prodigious 'in bestowing the rights label', 'legalistic', and characterized by:

its exaggerated absoluteness, its hyperindividualism, its insularity and its silence with respect to personal, civic and collective responsibilities[119]

While it is fair to say that over the last three decades an increasing number of claims have been expressed as fundamental rights, from smoking to hunting to partying without restrictions, it is highly misleading to portray the rights movement, in the US or elsewhere, as nothing more than legalized license. As was recognized by the

French revolutionaries from the outset, any attempt to draw up the fundamental rights of the people in one document as a declaration or bill of rights inevitably involves establishing the responsibilities of individuals in the process of balancing rights against each other. By their very nature, such declarations require that fundamental rights and freedoms be distinguished from other claims masquerading as rights and that the former be given special protected status.

In addition, it has been pointed out that 'some of the core liberal rights – such as freedom of speech and association – are designed to encourage forms of deliberation and communal interaction, practices that the critics of "rights talk" otherwise seem to favour'.[120] Examples include joining a trade union, putting a newspaper together, communicating with others in groups or through the media, demonstrating and protesting.

Nevertheless there are different characteristics which distinguish the first and second waves of rights from each other. These need to be understood, particularly in modern Britain, where we have just incorporated a second-wave rights treaty into our law. While liberty – as distinct from license – was the predominant value in first-wave rights charters, the picture was more complex post-war. Protecting individuals from tyranny and abuse of power remained fundamental. But other values emerged in the endeavour to create a better world through the language of fundamental rights. As we have seen, dignity, equality and community stand alongside liberty and justice as the hallmarks of second-wave rights. Even Glendon has recognized this difference in her critique of 'rights talk':

Try, for example, to find in the familiar language of our Declaration of Independence or Bill of Rights anything comparable to the statements in the Universal Declaration of Human Rights that 'everyone has duties to the community' and that everyone's rights and freedoms are subject to limitations.[121]

It is, admittedly, harder to obtain a vision of what a 'good society' would look like from the plain words of the American Bill of Rights than it is from the UDHR. But it is not necessary to go as far as the distinguished American philosopher John Rawls in maintaining that the state should largely remain neutral between different conceptions of how to live, simply safeguarding the freedoms which allow individuals to make their own choices.[122] Even the American Bill of Rights can be subject to a 'moral reading', as Professor Ronald Dworkin suggests:

I believe that the principles set out in the Bill of Rights, taken together, commit the United States to the following political and legal ideas: government must treat all those subject to its dominion as having equal moral and political status; it must attempt, in good faith, to treat them all with concern, and it must respect whatever individual freedoms are indispensable to those ends, including but not limited to, the freedoms more specifically designated in the document, such as the freedoms of speech and religion.[123]

One of the difficulties with the American Bill, however, is the absolute terms in which some of the Articles are framed. It is hard to imagine a clearer illustration of the difference between the first- and second-wave approaches to rights than the contrast between the absolutist Ist Amendment of the American Constitution – which declares that 'Congress shall make no laws prohibiting free speech' – and the responsibilities-driven right to free expression under Article 10 of the ECHR. Actions taken by the authorities in Holland and Germany to protect minorities from race hatred, for example, have been upheld by the European Court of Human Rights.[124] The ICCPR goes further. Incitement to 'national, racial or religious hatred' is explicitly prohibited as part of a vision of what a society based on human rights should look like.[125] In contrast, as Professor David Feldman has commented, the American Supreme Court:

has tended to adopt an individualist approach, protecting freedom of individual expression rather than the sensitivities of groups or communities at whom expression is directed. There is a brand of pluralism which demands that members of ethnic or cultural groups should be treated with respect[126]

On a similar theme, the influential communitarian writer Amitai Etzioni has criticized the US Bill of Rights – fairly or otherwise – for being too absolutist. In a book on privacy rights in the US, Etzioni pleads for a conception of privacy which 'systematically provides for a balance between rights and the common good', by which he means public health and public safety. Apparently unaware of the doctrine of proportionality developed by the European Court of Human Rights to balance rights and any limitations on them,[127] he goes on to advocate that the US courts apply a not dissimilar approach. He expresses the fear that he will be condemned for assaulting 'a sacred American value' in the process.[128]

To a significant extent what these communitarians are criticizing is not so much the jurisprudence which has flowed from the American Bill of Rights as the framing of its original contents and the cultural norms it has encouraged. In this idiom, fellow communitarian Chris Brown, professor of international relations at the LSE, has complained that:

The absolutism of rights claims can be a menace to a civilized society as the inability of the American public authorities to control the ownership of firearms in the United States illustrates quite vividly. Even in a less extreme case, it is not clear that the free-speech absolutists who defend all forms of expression in Ist Amendment terms are not acting against the public interest.[129]

A further factor which sets the first and second wave of rights apart is the role allotted to the state under various rights charters. In America the original conception of the state as a body which violates, rather than also protects, rights still largely holds (although, as we have seen, in reality even this involves governments making provisions for fair trials and a criminal justice system, for example). There has to be state action before the constitutional protections in the Bill of Rights apply.[130] In 1989 the Supreme Court refused to hold the relevant state authorities responsible for the severe physical abuse suffered by a child from his father – even though they knew the boy was at risk – which left him permanently retarded after falling into a coma. In rejecting an application from the son and his mother, Chief Justice Rehnquist, a conservative Supreme Court judge, articulated an entirely contrary view of the responsibilities of the state to that which has been developed through the European Convention on Human Rights:

[The clause's] purpose was to protect the people from the state, not to ensure that the state protected them from each other. The Framers were content to leave the extent of government obligation in the latter area to the democratic political process.[131]

Judges at the European Court of Human Rights, by contrast, have ruled that states *do* have 'positive obligations' to protect rights even, in some circumstances, where private individuals are the only protagonists. As we have seen, they have provided protection to a boy who was beaten by his stepfather in similar circumstances to the ones just described.[132]

In reality, of course, American jurisprudence is not always as far from its European counterpart as these illustrations would suggest. The Supreme Court has developed doctrines to limit rights to meet 'compelling interests', even in relation to those rights which are expressed in absolutist terms.[133] Given that rights inevitably collide in many circumstances this is hardly surprising. However, in a culture like America's, where the premium on liberty and free speech is extremely high and the Bill of Rights is still discussed in much the same terms as when it was drafted,[134] it is individual freedom which comes across as its overwhelming value.

There is a difficulty in this for a country like the UK where there has been no real fundamental rights tradition (as opposed to a common law liberties one). It is because American cultural hegemony is so strong that it can affect the reading of second-wave human rights treaties. The automatic association between human rights and traditional liberal individualism can be made by even the most erudite of judges. The Court of Appeal Judge Sir John Laws, in an otherwise brilliant piece on morals and rights, declared, without any apparent awareness of the controversial nature of his argument:

the autonomy of every individual . . . is the ideal which drives all the post-war international human rights texts

Expanding on this point, Laws continued:

the individual's autonomy is a function of man's moral nature, which cannot be defined in terms of rights, though it gives rise to them. An attempt to define it in terms of rights is a serious mistake. It would be to deny man's shared morality. If it becomes a systematic feature of a prevailing social philosophy, it would give rise to a community of selfish individuals and therefore no community. A society whose values are defined by reference to individual rights is by that very fact already impoverished. Its culture says nothing of individual duty[135]

Etzioni could not have put it better! As far as most British people are concerned, anecdotal evidence suggests that when they are informed that they are getting a bill of rights, if they have any notion of what this means at all, they assume the American model with its Supreme Court and ban on gun control. Practically the only popular link most people in this country have with such ideas comes from American movies.

An interesting exchange between Mary Robinson and journalist and broadcaster Michael Ignatiev illustrates the hegemonic influence of the American approach. Following her lecture at the Royal Festival Hall in September 1999, Ignatiev insisted that 'However you cut it, human rights language is individualistic and claims of individuals must prevail in any conflict with the community.' The UN High Commissioner for Human Rights begged to disagree: 'There are the rights of the individual but they are not unlimited in the sense that they live in a community.' Earlier in the exchange she had referred to Article 29 on the duties of the individual to the community and the need to listen to the Islamic perspective on this: 'they have a very developed sense of what Article 29 of the Universal Declaration on Human Rights means'.[136]

First- and second-wave rights compared

The interpretation of all bills of rights everywhere has, of course, evolved over the decades. The Founding Fathers of the American Constitution would never have dreamt that the right to abortion could be deduced from their Bill of Rights one day.[137] In the same way, the framers of the ECHR would not have imagined that before the century was out it would have been affording protection to gays and lesbians[138] or, as now seems likely, transsexuals.[139] But what is involved in tracing waves of rights is more than just a question of the evolution of case law or jurisprudence reflecting changing philosophical and social mores over time.

In understanding this evolution from first- to second-wave rights it is important to be clear that the idea of first-wave rights is not a static notion which applies only to a particular period, the Enlightenment. Although that was its origins it lives on as an ideal today. This applies not only to the US, where the American Civil Liberties Union routinely defends the Ku Klux Klan's right to march in minority areas on free speech grounds, but also to other countries where liberty from tyranny remains the main impulse in calling for the recognition of inalienable rights. When a new generation in Iran protested under the banner 'Freedom or Death' in July 1999, they too were invoking the idiom of first-wave rights.[140]

The use of the term 'waves' rather than 'generations' is intended to counter any suggestion of a rigid distinction between the two sets of rights. The metaphor is deliberately chosen to imply a sense of overlap and exchange which continues unabated. The South African Bill of Rights, for example, is clearly influenced by both first- and second-wave impulses as well as other, indigenous factors. Even the American Bill of Rights, the original first-wave model, has, through evolving jurisprudence, come under the influence of second-wave values; for example, in the growing weight given to the principle of equality over the years, on which it has both led and followed. The extent of this influence, however, has been somewhat truncated by the refusal of successive US governments to ratify international human rights treaties until this was partially rectified by President Clinton in 1994 with regard to the ICCPR and some other UN treaties. The US has always maintained that its standards of human rights protection are higher than international norms though a fairer description might be 'different' rather than 'higher'.[141]

The major factor explaining the different waves is the social context in which the drafters of the various charters operated. After the Second World War the UN's project to protect fundamental rights sought to establish a set of common values to guide public and private life in a democracy. Related to this was the view that responsibility for upholding human rights values must, to be effective, engage everyone, not just governments. The sense was that freedom was most enduringly protected through such an approach.

Perhaps the best exposition of how the value of liberty has evolved in the second-wave rights era is given by Daes, the Greek UN Special Rapporteur, who deserves to be quoted in full:

Personal freedom means the freedom of every law-abiding individual to think what he will, say what he will and go where he will ... This freedom must be matched with the peace and law of the community in which the individual lives. The freedom of the just individual is worth little to him if he can be preyed upon by murderer or thief [sic]. Every individual should respect the rights and freedoms of other individuals and carry out his lawful obligations to the community ...

So long as the individual, on the one hand, respects the rights and freedoms of other individuals and fulfils his responsibility to strive for the promotion and observance of the rights recognized in the Universal Declaration on Human Rights ... and other international and national instruments on human rights, and the state, on the other hand, properly and lawfully exercises its powers, a balance is achieved which constitutes a safeguard of freedom.[142]

It is this pursuit of a vision for the whole community that marked the birth of second-wave rights. As we have seen, every international instrument which has been drafted since the Second World War to a greater or lesser extent reflects this goal. This includes the ECHR, the treaty that forms the basis of the 1998 Human Rights Act, the UK's first modern Bill of Rights. But before returning to look at the implications of this Act it is necessary to consider whether we are now witnessing the emergence of a third wave of human rights, one characterized by the concept of mutuality. If so, could the Human Rights Act be regarded as a third-wave – as opposed to a third-way – bill of rights?

CHAPTER 5

Globalization and Third-Wave Rights[1]

While rights critics and opponents still tend to conflate first- and second-wave rights charters and characterize the post-war rights movement in the image of its Enlightenment ancestor, a third wave of rights is gradually emerging. Trends like this are often not discernible until well after they are established. But there are signs of a new development in human rights thinking which is worthy of comment.

The end of the Cold War

Three major factors have contributed to an emerging third wave of rights. The first was the collapse of the Berlin Wall in 1989. Without wishing to exaggerate the effects of the Cold War on human rights thinking, there is little doubt that it did get caught up in the rhetoric of the period, particularly in the 1980s. Increasingly, human rights became a vehicle for the West to abuse the East.

There was, of course, a powerful, authentic human rights movement within Eastern Europe which was enormously influential in breaking down the 'Iron Curtain', and doing so in a way which respected the ethos of human rights. Hence the label 'Velvet Revolutions', so different to their predecessors in France and Russia.[2] But there was an uncomfortable sense in which the idea of human rights was being used as a pawn in a superpower game.

The Helsinki Accords of 1975,[3] aimed at bolstering East/West *détente*, combined human rights declarations with a guarantee of the territorial *status quo*. There was no effective enforcement mechanism. Although the Accords were symbolically important in that they gave confidence to the then fledgling human rights movements in Eastern Europe, they were also used in the UK and elsewhere to portray the West as a beacon of freedom which the rest of the world should follow.

The role of the state in these Accords was closer to a first-wave than a second-wave vision. Governments were assigned the task of guaranteeing the classical liberties of free expression, movement, association and religion. Individuals' responsibilities faded from view. Although reference was made to the UDHR, social and economic rights – the contribution of Socialists to the second-wave enterprise – were nowhere to be seen in the Accords.[4]

More importantly than anything that was written down, the rhetoric that tended to surround calls for improvements in human rights from the leading Western political figures of the day – notably British Prime Minister Margaret Thatcher and US President Ronald Reagan – tended to mention human rights and free enterprise in the same breath. Human rights abuses were simultaneously ignored or underplayed when carried out by friendly nations. This had two major consequences which retarded the evolution in human rights thinking. First, the association between the idea of human rights and the Enlightenment conception of liberty (or an extreme version of it) was powerfully reaffirmed. Second, among some progressive circles in the West, the idea of human rights was nearly discredited altogether as a superpower tool.[5]

When the wall came tumbling down so did the plaster cast which had kept the idea of human rights paralysed in a developmental limbo. It was now set free again to evolve in response to the changing conditions of the late twentieth century.

Globalization

One of the most significant of these changes is what has come to be called 'globalization', the collapsing of national boundaries in economic, political and cultural life.[6] From the expanding role of the world's financial markets and the spread of transnational corporations to the revolution in communications and information technology, more and more areas of people's lives are affected by regional, international or transnational developments whether they are aware of this or not. This is the second major factor contributing to an emerging third wave of human rights.

Of course, in one sense, the post-war human rights enterprise embraced globalization before its modern form emerged. The quest for universal human rights standards was an early attempt to communicate across national boundaries. As we have seen, it was a rather faltering endeavour, with claims to universality challenged both in terms of authorship and content (a theme which shall be returned to in the conclusion).

One of the consequences of globalization has been a loosening of the reigns of the human rights dialogue. It has broadened out from the rather phoney internationalism of representatives of nation states meeting under the auspices of the United Nations to a conversation involving a growing cast of people.

As we have seen, an increasing range of pressure groups now frame their aspirations in human rights terms.[7] Before Amnesty International was established in 1961 there were very few human rights non-governmental organizations (NGOs). Now there are thousands operating all over the world. Modern campaigns for the protection of the environment, for third-world debt relief and for development aid all engage in the debate about what fundamental human rights are and the appropriate way to enforce them. It is no longer just a soft sideshow.

The fact that, through satellite television and other technological innovations, we can all see live, or close to, what is happening to others around the world from our armchairs has also had an enormous impact on the way the struggle for human rights is viewed. That strangers from different countries can communicate with each other through the worldwide web is having a similar effect. For example, during a recent major human rights trial in Malaysia over sixty websites sprang up to cover the proceedings while sales of the government-controlled newspaper plummeted.[8]

It would not be remotely believable to argue nowadays that 'we didn't know'; the excuse given for the lack of serious international intervention against the Nazi regime in Germany until the necessity for self-defence made inaction impossible. Now people have no excuse to wait for the end of wars or massacres, when the dead are already buried, to declare in UN statements that 'disregard and contempt for human rights have outraged the conscience of mankind'.[9] This was why the lack of UN action to prevent the widely predicted massacres in Bosnia and Rwanda in the mid-1990s caused such international outcry.

The quest for common values

Both the spread of globalization and the end of the Cold War are closely related to the third factor that accounts for a new wave of human rights. It concerns the quest for a set of common values.

The latest developments in the globalization of communications which have enhanced human rights awareness have coincided with the demise of the ideological paralysis that had kept the world frozen in Left/Right camps for most of this century. With the end of the Cold War came the collapse of old political certainties.

This has been a particular problem for the Left as the values of Socialism, or even social democracy, have survived less well than those of Capitalism into the twenty-first century. While the wounding of Socialism has to some extent been engineered by the very centre-Left forces who are actively seeking new heritages to draw inspiration from, the attempt to galvanize a dispirited Left under the heading of the 'third way' in a number of Western countries has so far proved lame, particularly in the UK.[10]

This political vacuum has happened to coincide with what a number of commentators view as a decline in a shared set of ethics which defines what society stands for. Not all of these are religious leaders. John Dunford, for example, the General Secretary of the Secondary Heads Association, has talked of 'a society which is increasingly unsure about its values'.[11]

The decline in organized religion in modern Britain is nevertheless presented as a major factor in this perceived 'moral crisis' by some commentators. A recent poll revealed that belief in God continues to shrink. Less than four million people attend church on Sundays and anecdotal evidence suggests that synagogue and even mosque attendances are down.[12] While this may not necessarily mean a reduction in spirituality, for some commentators it points to the 'privatization' of beliefs along with much else in society. Dr Carey, the Archbishop of Canterbury, spoke for many of this view when he warned against:

moral relativism and privatized morality. There is a widespread tendency to view what is good and right as a matter of private taste and individual opinion only. Under this tendency, God is banished to the realm of the private hobby and religion becomes a particular activity for those who happen to have a taste for it[13]

In the UK context, many of the rights critics discussed earlier are motivated by what they see as a spiralling relativism in which there is little common agreement about what is right and wrong.[14] A number of them accept that there is no turning back the clock to recreate the certainties of a previous era when the Church of England and widespread deference to authority provided the social cohesion they believe to be currently lacking. They are searching for a new set of ethics as relevant to those of any religion as to those of none; what could be described as 'values for a godless age'.

In the light of this perceived moral and political vacuum, the characterization of human rights as a set of values – as an evolving ethic establishing rights and responsibilities for all, rather than as a set of legal rules – has its attractions, particularly in the West.[15] While this presentation of rights can be traced back to the renaissance of the human rights ideal after the Second World War, it is now appealing to a more fertile ground than existed earlier.

The widening net of who is responsible for upholding human rights

These three factors – the end of the Cold War, globalization and the quest for common values – each have their counterpart in the developing third wave of human rights. First, there is the changing conception of the state and the widening of the net of human rights liabilities.

Building on the new role for the state which emerged post-war, human rights thinking has evolved to broaden the scope of its responsibilities. As we have seen, not only must states not infringe rights, not only must they enforce those rights which fall within their direct sphere (like providing a criminal justice or education system or holding fair elections), but they also have 'positive obligations' to uphold rights enshrined in human rights treaties, even when it is private parties which have violated them.[16]

This approach, which was largely pioneered by the European Court of Human Rights, did not really kick off until the late 1970s, gaining momentum in the last ten years.[17] The end of the Cold War has almost certainly indirectly contributed to this acceleration by hastening the process of detaching the idea of human rights from an eighteenth-century conception of the state.

The Inter-American Court of Human Rights, the regional human rights court which is responsible for enforcing the American Convention on Human Rights, has likewise developed a 'positive obligations' doctrine. It ruled, in the context of 'disappearances', presumably at the hands of a paramilitary force, that private individuals can violate fundamental rights and the state has a responsibility to prevent them.[18]

A great deal of international human rights law and standards, therefore, have evolved to hold the ring in a fair and just way between different sectors of civil society rather than between the individual and the state *per se*. This not only squashes the idea that human rights equals small or no government. It also means that private companies – and even individuals – who wield the kind of power that can breach human rights are increasingly liable in law.

The effect has been to continually broaden the net of who is legally liable, directly or indirectly, under international human rights law. In part, as we have seen, this is an acknowledgement that even private individuals need to be held responsible for flagrant breaches of others' rights, whether these are preventing protesters from peacefully demonstrating[19] or abusing the rights of children.[20]

In part it is also a recognition of the ever-widening scope of private power both within states and on a global scale. The European Court of Human Rights has made it clear that states cannot absolve themselves of the responsibility to uphold European Convention rights by delegating tasks like education to the private sphere.[21] The 1987 European Convention for the Prevention of Torture likewise does not distinguish between people detained in private or public prisons.[22]

On a global scale, increasingly, it is not strong states that are the problem but weak ones. States that fail to protect their citizens from private power, whether it is paramilitaries committing murder and torture or transnational corporations (TNCs) spreading contamination and pollution. It has been noted that 'paradoxically, in such circumstances, it may be in the interests of human rights organizations to seek to reinforce the legitimacy and authority of the state, within a regulated global framework'.[23]

The problem is that the growth of globalization makes this a pointless goal in certain circumstances. In a world where individual states – the traditional bodies to which international human rights treaties are addressed – are no longer the major player in many contexts, bolstering their authority is an insufficient strategy. TNCs with multiple subsidiaries operating in a number of countries simultaneously wield significant economic and political power. In these circumstances it is extremely difficult for the state – both home and host governments – to exercise effective legal control over them.

Part of the new trend in human rights thinking is to search for a strengthening of international law to include powerful private bodies within its remit, not just states. The International Commission of Jurists (ICJ) has explored ways in which international human rights standards could be directly applied to TNCs. The results of this review were published in 1999 in a unique pamphlet on *Globalization*,

Human Rights and the Rule of Law. The issue to be faced is whether to treat TNCs and other corporations 'as large para-state entities to be held accountable under the same sort of regime as states', or whether to look for different approaches to accountability 'that are promulgated by consumer groups and the corporations themselves'.[24]

Globalization and mainstreaming

The difficulties in relying on international law to enforce human rights standards in the scenarios created by globalization have resulted in a search for new structures of international accountability, much of this led by a thriving NGO sector (often from the aid and environment lobbies).

This growing emphasis on alternative methods of rights enforcement is a second third-wave tendency. It is not that the more traditional route of rights observance – courts and official monitoring committees – have fallen out of favour. Quite the contrary. Recent years have seen the establishment of *ad hoc* international tribunals to try war criminals from Rwanda and the former Yugoslavia. In 1998 a treaty to establish a permanent International Criminal Court to bring to justice anyone indicted of 'crimes against humanity' was finally signed.[25]

Related to this is the relatively recent proliferation of Human Rights Commissions around the world to encourage promotion of, and compliance with, human rights standards. Some of these are toothless, of course; others, like the Australian, New Zealand and South African Commissions, have adjudication or conciliation powers.[26] The UN's 'Paris Principles', adopted in December 1993, aim to establish common standards concerning the status of these institutions.[27] Mary Robinson, the UN High Commissioner for Human Rights, has reported that in the last few years her office has responded to requests from forty countries wishing to establish national human rights commissions; the most recent being from Dublin and Belfast.[28]

But a largely unstated distinction is developing over two types of rights. First, absolute rights, like protection from arbitrary killing, torture or slavery, then qualified rights, like liberty and fair trial, which can be curtailed only in specifically defined circumstances. It is generally recognized that, although supplementary means of enforcement of such rights are welcome, the international community has hopelessly failed to protect individuals across the globe from widespread violations of such rights, largely because of inadequate judicial enforcement mechanisms.[29]

Second, there are those rights which attract much broader limitations and are inevitably balanced against each other, like free expression, privacy and association. Although these are, of course, also judicially enforceable through domestic courts and bodies like the European Court of Human Rights, it is rights like these which are ever more amenable to alternative methods of enforcement.

'Mainstreaming' is the current jargon for the new approach to human rights enforcement. Kofi Anan, the Secretary-General of the UN, has pioneered this new trend. Human rights have been placed on the agenda of all the most important management structures of the UN, moving them out of the ghettoized rights units.[30] The emphasis is on prevention; on ensuring that human rights enforcement is part of the day-to-day diplomatic endeavours of the UN.

But this new approach is about much more than just the bureaucratic structures of the UN. It is a direct response to the challenges of globalization, which means, according to Robinson, that 'the debate at this stage is business driven'.[31] Anan has challenged transnational companies to what a UN report describes as 'a "Global Compact" of shared values and principles, to give a human face to the global market'.[32] The immediate goals are to incorporate universal human rights values into the mission statements of both individual (usually transnational) businesses and global governance structures like the IMF or World Bank, to change management practices and to share learning experiences. Interestingly, the more such bodies are pressurized into addressing their policies and practices from a human rights perspective the more social and economic rights, which have always taken a back seat in the judicial context, are receiving attention.

Initiatives taken by companies in response to pressure from unions, investors, NGOs or international monitoring bodies like the ILO include investment policies tied to the human rights standards of the host country, codes of conduct governing the behaviour of the companies themselves, and social labelling, allowing consumers to monitor the human rights standards of TNCs and other bodies. According to the ILO, nearly half of all codes of conduct include reference to child labour, about a quarter cover forced labour, and only about 15 per cent refer to freedom of association. Very few codes deal with other civil and political rights although some mention freedom of conscience and speech.[33]

The American State Department has intervened to encourage such initiatives. The business motive for becoming involved seems to be a mixture of preventing a 'potent backlash' against globalization[34] and concern over 'international condemnation and the damage to reputation which would ensue' by ignoring human rights.[35] In 1996, for example, Shell, the Anglo-Dutch oil company, embarked on the process of developing business principles which drew upon the UDHR following international condemnation of its stance in Nigeria. No doubt, in some instances, this creeping corporate awareness, such as it is, stems from the genuine commitment of company directors as the idea of human rights grows in strength.[36]

The problem, of course, is verification, and the abuse of mainstreaming initiatives for self-promotion purposes. Accountability procedures for corporate violations of human rights are being explored but Robinson has acknowledged the difficulties: 'we want to make sure it's not public relations . . . having a code of conduct . . . we want to make sure it's implemented on the ground'.[37] Legal academic Andrew Clapham laments the fact that there has been no equivalent initiative in the field of human rights to the World Bank's Inspection Panel, which rules on actions affecting environmental rights.[38]

The most significant aspect of these extra-legal developments from the point of view of this book is that they are a further sign of a new wave of human rights thinking. The spotlight on TNCs is itself a reflection of the acknowledgement that the private sector has a growing responsibility for human rights violations, which in turn is a by-product of globalization.[39] As the German sociologist Ulrich

Beck, whose theories on risk have been influential in New Labour circles, has commented:

Who will uphold human rights in a world that has left behind the nation state?[40]

Understanding human rights as a set of ethical values

The third indicator of a new wave of human rights thinking comes from the recent attention to the communitarian drift of the UDHR and the twin International Conventions discussed in the last chapter. This is sometimes presented as evidence of the increasingly universality of the human rights message; the communitarian orientation being said to reflect an 'Asian approach'.[41] This may be so but, as we have seen, this theme was self-consciously there from the beginning of the second wave, although somewhat neglected until recently.

Much of this new emphasis on responsibilities and duties is connected with the mandate in the Preambles to the UDHR and the International Covenants that individuals should strive to promote human rights; the statement in Article 29 of the Universal Declaration that 'individuals owe duties to the community'; and the requirement that the right to education should involve strengthening respect for human rights.[42]

The African Charter on Human and People's Rights, the most recent general regional human rights treaty to be drafted,[43] which has been in force since 1986, went further than this. It has a separate chapter on the duties of individuals, aimed at reflecting African, rather than Western, norms. This includes the duty to work and to 'preserve the harmonious development of the family'.[44]

The African Charter is, in fact, the only human rights treaty (as opposed to declaration) with a separate duties section where obligations do not flow directly from the rights enumerated. This may be connected to the fact that when it was established the African Commission on Human and People's Rights had no associated court or any other legal powers to enforce the Charter.[45] A new Protocol establishing an African Court on Human and People's Rights has just been adopted and it will be instructive to see whether the individual duties in the African Charter will be declared legally enforceable or not. Interestingly, the 1989 UN Convention on the Rights of the Child, while integrating responsibilities with rights, also refers explicitly to the 'rights and duties' of 'parents, legal guardians, or other individuals legally responsible' for children.[46]

The UN initiatives related to this new emphasis on individual responsibilities and human rights promotion are too numerous to list here. They include: the Vienna Declaration, adopted at the second World Conference on Human Rights in 1993, which proclaimed that the individual 'should participate actively in the realization of [these] rights and freedoms'; the creation of a UN Decade for Human Rights Education in 1995; and the adoption in 1998 by the UN General Assembly of a Declaration on 'the Rights and Responsibilities of Individuals' to promote human rights.[47]

Declarations on human responsibilities

Recently there have been attempts to draw on the values in the UDHR and produce them as new 'duties declarations'. In 1998 a high-level group chaired by Justice Richard Goldstone, former Chief Prosecutor at the UN war crimes tribunal for the former Yugoslavia,[48] drafted a Declaration on Human Duties and Responsibilities to mark the fiftieth anniversary of the UDHR. Produced under the auspices of UNESCO, the Valencia Declaration, as it is known, sets out the duties implied by each Article of the UDHR and establishes which actors are responsible for upholding them. That the major responsibility for rights enforcement lies with the state is clear from the text but, referring to Article 29 of the UDHR, the new Declaration emphasizes:

that the assumption of the duties and responsibilities implicit in human rights and fundamental freedoms rests upon all members of the global community[49]

The previous year the InterAction Council launched a Universal Declaration of Human Responsibilities. Chaired by Helmut Schmidt, the former German Chancellor, the document received the endorsement of a number of heads of state. However, unlike Justice Goldstone's Declaration, the Schmidt document contains some strange departures from the philosophy of the UDHR. These include the injunctions that 'Sensible family planning is the responsibility of every couple' and 'All people have a responsibility to develop their talents through diligent endeavour.'[50]

Justice Goldstone has commented that people who involve themselves in such initiatives include those who see the exercise of elaborating responsibilities and duties as complementing the values in the UDHR, those who believe duties should take precedence over rights, and those who consider that as a consequence of globalization and technological advancement a fresh approach to human rights is required.[51]

Whether the proposition that duties precede rights threatens the human rights project is discussed further in the next chapter. The interesting point to note here is that the post-Cold War search for new ideals and common bonds in an era of failed ideologies appears to have contributed to a growing appreciation of human rights as a set of values.

This has significantly affected political discourse at certain crucial moments. Where once wars were fought in the name of saving the world from Communism, or spreading Christian civilization, or plain self-interest, it is now human rights which are presented by Western leaders as the justification for intervention (most recently in Kosovo and East Timor). True or false, it suggests that the idea of fundamental rights is growing more powerful than even our Enlightenment forefathers predicted.

The democratization of rights discourse

It is not just political leaders who have turned to human rights in the search for new meaning in this millennial era. The language of human rights increasingly enters ordinary discourse as a way of setting down a basic framework within which wider issues can be discussed, from global inequalities to domestic crime policies to medical ethics. Its attraction is probably greatest for those who are stumbling for a new way to make sense of the world in the wake of the collapse of the pre-Cold War certainties. In particular those on the Left or centre Left who have come out the worst in this stand-off.

But human rights values can never be more than a set of broad principles. Although they challenge many assumptions, they are not a substitute for a fully fledged ideology or belief system which speaks to every facet of human life. As such they generally have the capacity to form the basis of a shared ethos without necessarily disturbing all other points of reference in people's lives, whether these be political or religious or neither of these.[52]

The third wave of rights will have properly arrived when this understanding of human rights is more widely shared. Too often they are still portrayed by commentators, the media, lawyers, etc., as narrow, technical rules rather than as a challenge to Britain's positivist legal tradition.[53] Of course, when human rights are incorporated in law and enforced by courts they become legal standards as well. An essential quality of human rights values is that they have claims attached to them; that is what distinguishes them from other values and makes them rights. But they are a very special kind of legal standard. Once you bring broad concepts like 'a fair hearing' or 'a private life' into the law, extra-legal moral theory is required to interpret them.

Modern times show us that when human rights are breached, they do not simply vanish. History reveals that Bentham was wrong about this.[54] As a set of values human rights have the power to go on living long after their much-predicted death and to bring about significant changes to both political and legal culture which go beyond the strict enforcement of particular laws.

The former General Secretary of Amnesty International, Thomas Hammarberg, has described the broadening horizon of the human rights ideal:

we note that human rights issues today are high on the political agenda in a number of countries. This is not surprising, the rights issues relate to central and sometimes controversial political issues: restraints on power and the essentials for everyone's daily life. The language of human rights has infiltrated political debate[55]

At the end of the last century Kofi Anan said he wanted 'to make the next century the century of human rights'.[56] Although it is too early to predict this with any certainty, the implications of Anan's goal begin to establish the shape of things to come in this third wave of rights.

The human rights vision has evolved over two hundred years from protecting individuals from state brutality, to establishing a set of ethical standards essential to creating a decent society, to providing people with the contours of a value system by which to lead their lives. If this is to be the trend, then the big issues that the idea of human rights makes us confront can no longer remain the preserve of official standard-setters and enforcement bodies.

The corollary to this must be a much more robust acceptance than is likely to be found in any current legal textbook that there are few once-and-for-all human rights answers. Besides the fundamentals, like, for example, protection from inhuman punishment and slavery – given special protected status by the ECHR[57] – all international human rights treaties, as we have seen, recognize that most rights exist in conflict with each other and have to be qualified or limited to protect the rights of others or the common good.

Decisions have to be made as to where to draw the line between, for example, protecting the rights of even the most despised groups like rapists or paedophiles and adequately defending their victims or potential victims.[58] Outside clearly defined boundaries, such as no death penalty and no torture, this line cannot be permanently fixed. It is inevitably going to have to be porous enough to absorb some prevailing norms without compromising on fundamental human rights principles.

This leaves space for some 'democratic' involvement in where boundaries between rights should lie. If human rights are to play the crucial role now allotted to them, then wider participation in such debates is both inevitable and to be welcomed. Even though the final decisions in actual cases must lie with the law courts, the same does not apply to the issues that underlie them. Without this 'democratization', there is little hope that the preservation of human rights can become the mainstream activity that the UN seeks. Nor is it likely that the idea of human rights can help to fill the values void in Western societies.

Mutuality and participation

With these developments in mind, the major new feature of the emerging third wave of rights can be described as 'mutuality'. It builds on the values of community and liberty that are the defining features of first- and second-wave rights. It reinforces rather than dilutes them. But the essential factor behind this new emphasis on mutuality is participation; involvement in the human rights enterprise by a growing number of people and a wider range of peoples around the world. As such this emerging third wave does not so much involve a new conception of rights – as to some degree occurred in the shift from the first to second wave – as a change in the place of rights in society. In this one sense they are closer to their Enlightenment roots as the focus shifts from the essential, but somewhat élitist, standard-setting phase in the post-war era, to a project whose development everyone can participate in.

Based on current trends, it is possible to sketch out how the third wave of rights could develop. There is an increasing appreciation through human rights education, discussions on the web, debates in the media, etc., that human rights are not just something governments secure or take away but that we are all implicated in their observance. My right to privacy entails your obligation to respect it, as well as the state's duty to pass laws to uphold it, and so on and so forth. The more that people understand that mutuality is an essential feature of human rights compliance, the more they are likely to participate in a growing world-wide debate about the nature of human rights. And the more they participate the greater will be the awareness that human rights values involve us all.

Within established human rights norms that set the boundaries of debate, we might find ourselves caught up in a dialogue about how compliance can best be achieved, where the boundaries between conflicting rights should lie, what limitations on rights are necessary in a democratic society, how far the interpretation of rights should reflect diverse cultural values and so forth. Increasingly, many of these 'human rights conversations' are likely to take place on a regional basis in the first instance, to take account of the different histories and cultures people bring to these debates. But with the aid of modern technology, cross-cultural dialogues are, if anything, likely to increase.[59] In this way the concept of community developed in the second wave should evolve from a rather rigid conception of mutual obligations laid down from on high to a shared set of ethical values in whose development everyone is encouraged to participate.

Although his conception of mutuality is slightly narrower in scope than this, the eminent American professor of philosophy Alan Gerwith describes how it can create what he calls a 'community of rights'. In opposing the standard communitarian critique of rights he says:

The concept of human rights thus entails a mutualist and egalitarian universality; each human must respect the rights of all the others while having his rights respected by all others, so that there must be a mutual sharing of the benefits of rights and the burdens of duties . . . By the effective recognition of the mutuality entailed by human rights the society becomes a community. So the antithesis between rights and community is bridged.[60]

Supposing that this is right, and that mutuality and participation represent the human rights terrain of the near future, then some difficult questions are posed. How reconcilable are the goals of the third wave with the original idea of inalienable rights? Is it possible to engage the wider society in the question of where the boundary between conflicting rights should lie, for example, and still provide the courts with sufficient authority to protect individuals against abuse of state power, which was the initial motivation for first-wave rights?

How can equality be guaranteed for minorities if the voice of the majority is to be reflected in the interpretation of rights? And if human rights are to provide a set of common values, from where do they derive their legitimacy and authority? These were all questions faced to some degree by the framers of the UK's new Bill of Rights. Its significance as arguably the first 'third-wave bill of rights' shall be explored in the next chapter.

CHAPTER 6

The Human Rights Act:
A Third-Wave or Third-Way Bill of Rights?

For the first hundred and fifty years after Tom Paine and his followers agitated for the 'rights of man', things went pretty quiet on that score in the UK. Paine's legacy was effectively wiped from the national conscience. His ideas have probably received more attention in modern America than in this country. Even now, he does not warrant a mention in the Department for Education and Employment's (DFEE) new list of recommended non-fiction authors for schools, nor in its recommended history syllabus for Key Stages 2 and 3.[1]

Establishing the fundamental rights of the people in a written document has always been considered to be something other countries were preoccupied with. The UK government was involved in drafting the constitution for the new Germany after the Second World War, including its 'Basic Law' of rights. Bills of rights and written constitutions were bequeathed to former colonies on obtaining independence from the 'Mother Country'. But with the exception of H. G. Wells's wartime initiative there was no significant lobby for a bill of rights during the last two centuries in the UK until the late 1960s.

The campaign for a UK Bill of Rights

What kick-started this issue back to life was the 1968 Commonwealth Immigrants Act. Passed in only three days by a panicky Labour government, the sole purpose of the Act was to deny entry to the UK to British Asians who were expelled from East Africa, precisely at the time that they needed their UK citizenship.[2] A slumbering consciousness began to stir. Old debates from across the Atlantic about whether parliamentary democracies without constitutional rights can adequately protect minorities began to filter among some lawyers and informed observers. Pamphlets in support of a bill of rights were published by two prominent lawyers from the Labour and Liberal Parties, Anthony Lester and John Macdonald respectively.[3]

The 1970s

This gradual reawakening of the old idea of inalienable rights took a further jolt in 1974 when the esteemed judge and subsequent Law Lord Leslie Scarman chose to deliver the first of his Hamlyn Lectures on a bill of rights. In a famous passage harking back to episodes like the 1968 Immigration Act, he said:

When times are normal and fear is not stalking the land, English law sturdily protects the freedom of the individual and respects human personality. But when times are abnormally alive with fear and prejudice, the common law is at a disadvantage: it cannot resist the will, however frightened and prejudiced it may be, of Parliament.[4]

Scarman argued for a bill enforced by judges who would in certain circumstances be able to override Parliament when legislation breached its terms. The *Guardian* newspaper led on the story and it was discussed in the media over the next few days.

The proposal found little support on the right or among those in favour of the *status quo* because of the dent it would make to the principle of 'parliamentary sovereignty'. Under this doctrine the legislature must always remain supreme. Dating back to the constitutional settlement of 1688 which led to the first bill of rights, 'parliamentary sovereignty' means that no Act of Parliament has higher legal status than any other. Every statute can unmake or amend any law that precedes it. No former Parliament can bind its successor under this doctrine. The idea that certain laws have a higher moral claim on the basis of which the courts can overturn other legislation which breaches them was, until the latter part of the twentieth century, entirely alien to the legal tradition in the UK.[5] A. V. Dicey, a nineteenth-century constitutional law theorist, famously proclaimed that:

The sovereignty of Parliament is (from a legal point of view) the dominant characteristic of our political institutions.[6]

The concern on the Left was presented in different terms but partly amounted to the same thing in practice. There was still opposition to what was seen as an individualistic philosophy of little obvious benefit to the collective needs of the poor or working class. There was, at this time, massive ignorance about the drift away from libertarianism in post-war human rights thinking. Even by the 1980s, all that most people on the Left knew about the ECHR was that it had apparently led to the outlawing of the trade union closed shop.[7] The fact that the Convention explicitly enshrined a right to trade union membership, for example, was mainly unknown.

But the debate largely focused on the issue of enforcement. The worry was that bills of rights inevitably undermine the capacity of Left-wing governments to carry through the programme they were elected on. At best a fuzzy liberal consensus would be foisted on the political process by the judges. At worst a democratically elected Labour government would be prevented from carrying out its programme and a conservative agenda would dominate regardless of who was formally in power. These fears were genuinely held, and not without foundation given the track record of the judiciary in the UK over the years.[8]

The argument on the Left of the political spectrum that ran throughout this period went something like this: In so far as bills of rights involve ringing declarations of fundamental principles, their translation into laws which govern practice requires a considerable degree of interpretation of the original text on the part of the enforcer. If, in a nutshell, the primary enforcers of a bill of rights are to be judges then this gives them considerably more scope for what is, effectively, law-making – as opposed to law-interpreting – than under the current system.[9]

If, the argument continued, judges are given the power to overturn Acts of Parliament which they believe breach fundamental rights, then their legislative power is even more extensive. Given that judges are almost exclusively white, middle- or upper-class males educated at public school and Oxbridge, this effectively transfers powers from democratically elected representatives to an astonishingly small and unrepresentative oligarchy. The chances, from this perspective, of the courts protecting minorities over a sustained period when, in Scarman's words, 'fear is ... stalking the land', are not high. The fate of pro-union and pro-working-class legislation is likely to be even more ominous.[10]

The problem, in terms of moving the debate forward, was that from this time onwards the idea of fundamental rights expressed in a bill of rights became hopelessly intertwined with the constitutional question of the respective powers of the executive, legislature and judiciary. Mention bills of rights and people thought judges (if they thought anything at all). For this reason, if for no other, the debate in the UK largely remained trapped in the ether. It never really came down to earth to become a truly popular issue.

The power of the courts under a bill of rights had been a concern in many other countries before they went on to adopt one, including in Canada and India.[11] But the dialogue there centred also around the idea of fundamental rights, not just the detailed constitutional implications.

Support for a bill of rights in the UK was largely the preserve of liberals (with a capital and small L). The campaign, such as it was, came to be largely conducted by lawyers and Liberal MPs in favour of incorporating the European Convention on Human Rights (ECHR) into UK law.

On the Tory side there were a few prominent supporters over the years from all wings of the Party, particularly when they were out of power. These included former Education Secretary Sir Keith Joseph, former Attorney-General Sir Michael Havers, ex-Cabinet ministers Lord St-John Stevas, Jonathan Aitken and Leon Brittain, and a former Lord Chancellor, Lord Hailsham.

There was also a small group within the Labour Party who became interested in the idea. Anthony Lester, QC, played a leading role in keeping the issue alive.[12] After he resigned as Home Secretary, Roy Jenkins also acknowledged his support for incorporation of the ECHR.[13] But most of the Left, in and outside the Labour Party, were either uninterested or opposed.

A discussion document called *A Charter of Human Rights*, published in 1976, was the first formal Labour Party document to propose incorporation of the ECHR into UK law. Until the early 1990s this was the only paper to seriously address the issue of how to reconcile support for a bill of rights with the legitimate anxiety that it would be used to stop Labour from carrying out its programme. The document emanated from the Human Rights sub-committee of the National Executive Committee (NEC), which was chaired by Shirley Williams, MP, and included others of a like mind.[14] The NEC would not allow the paper to be presented as official policy but only as an issue for debate.

The Home Office, meanwhile, published its own discussion document on incorporation in 1976[15] following the interest in the policy aroused by Scarman's Hamlyn Lecture. It examined the issues involved in some detail without coming to a conclusion either way. The following year the Northern Ireland human rights quango, the Standing Advisory Committee on Human Rights (SACHR), proposed a charter of rights based on the ECHR for Northern Ireland which would preferably extend to the whole of the UK.[16]

The swan-song of this period was the 1978 House of Lords Select Committee on whether the UK should adopt a bill of rights and, if so, what kind. Six members were in favour and five against (of which three were from the ruling Labour Party). The report recommended that any bill of rights be based on the ECHR.[17] It was debated in the House of Lords. The Liberal Peer Lord Wade, who doggedly introduced draft bill after draft bill to incorporate the ECHR in this period, moved a motion in support of the Select Committee Report. After a five-hour debate this was carried by 56 votes to 30.[18]

The Tories were elected on a manifesto in 1979 which was committed to holding all-party discussions on a bill of rights. Once in power, the downside of a policy that would curb the freedom of the executive was soon apparent to the new Prime Minister, Margaret Thatcher, and her government. Her line tended to be that, while her government supported the principles in the ECHR, this was the freest country in the world and we believe that it is for Parliament rather than the judiciary to determine how these principles are best secured[19]

The 1980s

The case for a bill of rights at this time was mostly presented in terms of protecting individuals and minorities from the abuse of state power. The rights under consideration were usually civil and political, drawn mainly from the ECHR. Social and economic rights, given equal status to other rights in the Universal Declaration of Human Rights, were generally deemed to be not appropriate for judicial enforcement and hence were not on the agenda of most projects of incorporation of the ECHR.

Opposition or indifference to a bill of rights by all but a small group continued right up until the late 1980s or early 1990s.[20] It was not until the late 1980s that the National Council for Civil Liberties (NCCL) began to take a consistent interest in this issue, for example.[21] Although rarely articulated in these terms, until that time the struggle for civil liberties in the UK tended to take place within the tradition of the common law liberties which defined the British system. An exception to this was Northern Ireland, where links with human rights campaigns around the world had some influence on the direction of the civil rights movement.

But in Britain the civil liberties lobby operated mostly in splendid isolation rather than embracing the international human rights movement.[22] Like everything else in British politics until the late 1980s, this lobby also had a Right- and Left-wing incarnation, although the latter was far stronger.[23] The aim of both wings was to be free not to do things, on the whole, rather than obtaining the written right to something. The drift was clearly libertarian. However, NCCL, as befitted an organization with strong trade union links, also championed some rights which were defined as collective, like the right to strike. Its support for anti-discrimination and equal opportunities legislation was also strong. But there was little attempt to turn these somewhat conflicting currents into a coherent movement or philosophy.

The turning-point was the 1987 general election. The failure of the political system to brook virtually any challenge to a Conservative government which, on the basis of three elections on a minority vote, could bring in almost any measures it wished, was hitting home. The reputation of Parliament as a bulwark against the executive was pretty much in tatters. It became obvious that the government of the day could control Parliament through the party whip and the tantalizing carrot of promotion to ministerial office.[24] By now the judges were beginning to get a reputation as the only source of effective opposition to the government.[25] Even some of the Left started to look at them in a different light.

The formation in 1988 of Charter 88 was a milestone. A pressure group for constitutional reform, which collected thousands of signatures in its first year, Charter 88 called for a bill of rights as part of its ten basic demands. Law Lords, other judges, lawyers, academics and celebrities started to come on board.

The 1990s

By the beginning of the next decade the NCCL – which was relaunched as Liberty in 1989 – was starting to situate itself squarely within the broader human rights movement. Directed by Andrew Puddephatt and chaired by Alf Dubbs and Fiona Mactaggart respectively,[26] Liberty formally overturned any previous opposition to bills of rights and began to describe itself as a human rights organization.[27]

In 1991 Liberty published *A People's Charter*, its own draft bill of rights. This was based on a wider range of instruments than the ECHR and included the broader equality right contained in the International Covenant on Civil and Political Rights (ICCPR),[28] children's rights drawn from the UN Convention on the Rights of the Child, and trade union rights taken from ILO Conventions.[29]

The Institute of Public Policy Research (IPPR), the influential think-tank close to the Labour Party, published its bill of rights, drawn from both the European Convention and International Covenant, in the same year.[30] The Scottish Council for Civil Liberties and the equivalent body in Northern Ireland, the Committee for the Administration of Justice, published bills of rights for their jurisdictions in 1990 and 1992 respectively, both of which included some social and economic rights.[31]

The heat was on. But there was still broad resistance from a significant section of the Left, in so far as they cared about the issue at all or thought it relevant to most people's lives. This included Neil Kinnock's Labour Party. The Deputy Leader of the Opposition and Shadow Home Secretary, Roy Hattersley, was particularly opposed.[32]

This Left opposition did not generally centre on the nature of the rights themselves any more. While civil and political rights were still regarded as merely 'formal' rights in many quarters, the perceived threats to civil and political liberties posed by Thatcherism, along with a dim awareness that some international human rights treaties (though not the ECHR) did in fact seek to protect social and economic rights, combined to make the nature of the rights less of a concern than previously. The news that the Tory government's poll tax, one of the most divisive policies of the period, would probably have been overturned in the US as unconstitutional did the rounds, helping to give bills of rights some much-needed cachet on the Left.

The main sticking-point continued to be the role of judges. Although their reputation was improving on the Left, there remained the significant point of principle that democratically elected politicians might be prevented from carrying through their programme as a result of a bill of rights.

The Conservatives, too, continued to be worried about the role of judges under a bill of rights in that it would disturb the balance of the much-vaunted British Constitution. When Home Office minister Charles Wardle, for example, spoke in one of a growing number of parliamentary debates on the issue, it was as if Dicey had been reincarnated:

this country's approach to rights and freedoms is more permissive than found elsewhere. The possession of rights and freedoms is assumed. It is not dependent on their enshrinement in statute or through some other constitutional device. That means that only through specific action by Parliament . . . can those rights be curtailed[33]

Maintaining parliamentary sovereignty remained the meeting-point between the Labour and Conservative Parties. Giving Parliament, not the courts, the last word on legislation was the issue which bound opponents of a bill of rights. There was little attempt by the major players on any side of this debate to present it publicly in any other than these constitutional terms.

Behind the scenes, however, the Labour Party was working with Liberty and others sympathetic to finding a way through this paralysis. Liberty's *A People's Charter* was distinctive in that it recommended what it called a model of 'democratic entrenchment' for enforcing bills of rights. This involved distinguishing between absolute rights (like protection from death, torture and slavery), where judges would have the final say, and other rights, where elected MPs, working through a special Select Committee, would have the last word on whether Acts of Parliament conformed with the ECHR.[34]

Liberty's proposals were too complicated to be adopted in full but their broad approach now began to be taken seriously in Labour circles. Derry Irvine, QC (now the Lord Chancellor), took a particular interest in them as did some key players in the Society of Labour Lawyers. The result of all this was that the 1992 Labour Party Manifesto pledged that a

Charter of Rights backed up by a complementary and democratically enforced bill of rights will establish in law the specific rights of every citizen

Labour was not, of course, in a position to honour this commitment, as the Party suffered its fourth election defeat in a row. Then John Smith became the new Leader of the Labour Party. For Smith, a Scottish lawyer, democratic reform was 'unfinished business' from the last time he had held government office in the late 1970s. The new Shadow Home Secretary, one Tony Blair, dropped his former opposition to bills of rights and proceeded to work on the policy.

By February 1993 the Labour Party's internal Policy Commission on Constitutional Reform was debating papers by Tony Blair and Derry Irvine in favour of incorporating the European Convention on Human Rights into UK law as a first step to establishing a British Bill of Rights.[35] The author of Liberty's draft bill of rights was invited to discuss her proposals for democratic entrenchment with the Party's internal policy commission.

The following month Smith made a keynote lecture to Charter 88 embracing most of its constitutional reform programme, including 'a Human Rights Act that incorporates the rules of the Convention directly into British law'.[36] This was the first time that Labour had made such a public commitment to a bill of rights.

Liberty held a series of seminars with backbench MPs to galvanize interest in the policy. Concern remained about the role of judges but the message that incorporation did not necessarily have to mean the end of parliamentary democracy as they knew it was getting through to MPs. Graham Allen, MP, then a member of the Shadow Home Affairs team, was active in trying to secure the support of the wider party, even issuing a series of newsletters on 'Labour and the Constitution'. The general line was that Labour would commit itself to incorporation of the European Convention at the next election followed by consultation on a home-grown bill of rights that could fill in the well-known gaps in the ECHR.[37]

At the initiation of former *New Statesman* editor Stuart Weir, a campaign was formed by Liberty and Charter 88 called the Labour Rights Campaign, directed at the grass roots of the Labour Party. It was far more effective at attracting interest in the issue than the numbers involved would suggest. Resolutions in favour of a bill of rights were successfully tabled at Party conferences, fringe meetings were held and local wards addressed.

To try to create a broader political constituency in favour of a bill of rights, Liberty organized a human rights convention in June 1995 in the centre of London. Over 3,000 people participated in a three-day 'super-conference' involving lectures, debate and cultural events. Although there was vigorous dispute about the idea of fundamental rights and its relevance to people's lives there was also discernible excitement that it could help to shape a much-needed new political vision.

To help keep up the momentum a consortium of human rights NGOs started to meet regularly to plan a co-ordinated strategy in favour of a bill of rights. This was led largely by Liberty, now directed by John Wadham, and JUSTICE, which, under Anne Owers's new leadership, was turning from being a criminal justice group to an avowedly human rights one.[38] The Constitution Unit, a research institute attached to University College London, published a major review of human rights legislation, helping to maintain debate about alternative models for incorporating the ECHR into UK law.[39]

When Tony Blair stood as Leader of the Labour Party following the death of John Smith in May 1994, he included support for a bill of rights in a candidate statement not overburdened with specific policies. But by 1996 this policy had been trimmed to one of support for the incorporation of the European Convention on Human Rights (ECHR) only, with just the merest hint that it might be followed up by the introduction of a specifically British Bill of Rights. What's more, there was a clear shift of emphasis. Whereas policy documents in 1993 sought to tie support for a bill of rights with the Party's historic championing of 'the oppressed and underprivileged against the power of the strong and powerful',[40] three years later the new Leader of the Opposition was keen to present his honed-down policy as one dictated by good sense rather than high ideals.

When the mantle of leadership passed to Tony Blair after John Smith's death the constitutional reform package was maintained. Some would say that this was to provide a veneer of radicalism for a party fast shedding its old Socialist clothes. For Peter Mandelson, MP, the opposite appeared to be the motive. The point of supporting a bill of rights, he wrote, was that 'no one will ever be able to accuse Labour of being prepared to sacrifice individual rights on the altar of collectivist ideology'.[41] Others would argue that New Labour have never had a vision to drive constitutional reform but felt themselves saddled with a series of unconnected policies by their dead leader.[42]

Whatever the truth of this speculation, it is hard to see that it adds up to an adequate explanation of why New Labour stuck to its guns and incorporated the ECHR into UK law. Although most of the judges and legal profession had come round, and opposition on the Left had largely faded away, there was no groundswell of enthusiasm for incorporation. It did not even attract the level of grass-roots support which existed in Scotland (and to a lesser degree Wales) for devolution or in London for a new assembly. Given its implications for fettering the executive, the policy could not have survived into government without the personal support of one or two key players.

There is little doubt that at specific times genuine interest in, and commitment to, incorporation of the ECHR was shown by the new Shadow Home Secretary, Jack Straw, his predecessor, Tony Blair, and the future Lord Chancellor, Lord Irvine. At various points they spent a significant amount of time thinking through the difficult constitutional and philosophical issues the policy posed and defending it from attack by other senior party figures as an irrelevance at best and damaging at worst.

Jack Straw, together with the Shadow Minister in the Lord Chancellor's Department Paul Boateng, published a consultation paper on incorporation of the ECHR in December 1996 called *Bringing Rights Home*.[43] Different models were canvassed. But there was no real possibility that one would be adopted which would completely overturn parliamentary sovereignty and give judges the power to strike down primary legislation and effectively replace it with their own, in imitation of the American Supreme Court.

After the Labour Party won the general election in May 1997 Jack Straw, the new Home Secretary, pushed hard at an early Cabinet meeting for a bill to incorporate the ECHR into UK law. In this he was successful. The consortium of human rights NGOs became involved in working with the Home Office on the details of the policy, which resulted in a model that was far more ambitious than the technical incorporation of a human rights treaty.

A White Paper, *Rights Brought Home*,[44] was published along with the Bill in October 1997. The latter was introduced first in the House of Lords by Lord Irvine, working with Home Office minister Gareth Williams (now Attorney-General), and subsequently by Jack Straw in the House of Commons. By 9 November 1998 the Human Rights Act (HRA) had become law. It came fully into force with much razzmatazz on 2 October 2000. Jack Straw declared the Act to be 'the most significant statement of human rights in domestic law since the 1689 Bill of Rights'.[45]

The unique features of the Human Rights Act

The New Labour Government adopted a model for incorporating the ECHR into UK law which is not (yet) replicated by any other state. Our domestic courts are empowered, for the first time, to review Acts of Parliament for compliance with human rights standards and are required to read these standards into legislation wherever possible. But, as we saw in Chapter 1, the judges are still prohibited from overturning Acts.

On the presumably rare occasions where judges in the higher courts cannot, through this method, reconcile an Act with Convention rights they can formally make a 'declaration of incompatibility' to that effect.[46] The government can then swiftly introduce legislation to comply with a court's declaration using special 'remedial orders' which bypass the usual legislative process where there are 'compelling reasons to do so'.[47]

Taken as a whole, the Human Rights Act is the first UK statute that can fairly be described as a 'higher law'.[48] It will influence all legislation already on the statute book and all laws yet to be passed. For this reason, and because judges are not restricted to ECHR jurisprudence when they interpret the Act, it can fairly be described as the UK's first modern Bill of Rights. Although parliamentary sovereignty has not been overturned, it no longer has a free rein.[49]

In some ways, though, the Human Rights Bill, when it was published, was a disappointment to a number of those who had campaigned so long for a bill of rights. It was clear that any earlier intention to follow up incorporation with consultation on a home-grown bill of rights, which would be broader in scope than the ECHR, was dead and buried. What is more, a commitment Labour had made to the Liberal Democrats in their Joint Consultative Committee on Constitutional Reform – which met prior to the election – to entertain the establishment of a Human Rights Commission or Commissioner was clearly not likely to materialize this side of a general election. Sarah Spencer, Director of the Human Rights Programme at IPPR, had researched the impact of different commissions around the world in the hopes of influencing the government to create one here.[50]

The ECHR, on which the Bill was based, is widely recognized as being out of date.[51] This accusation, as we have seen, could have been levelled at it from the time it was drafted in 1950. It was never as far-thinking as the UDHR, a number of whose principles it sought to enforce. It did not include social and economic rights (other than education and property rights). Nor did it include even the same range of civil and political rights as the ICCPR.[52] The gap between the anti-discrimination provisions of the two treaties is particularly acute.[53] What is more, the Human Rights Bill and subsequent Act omitted two Convention rights from its terms, Articles 1 and 13.[54] While the government insisted they were procedural rights covered by the process of incorporating the Convention into domestic law, others disagreed.[55]

There was also some disappointment about the Act among those for whom ending parliamentary sovereignty was one of the main points in favour of incorporation.[56] There was concern that the 'declaration of incompatibility' provision did not adequately protect victims of rights abuses. If the government of the day refused to act to comply with a Declaration he or she could be left 'hanging in the air' and might still need to go to Strasbourg to claim relief; whether compensation or release from jail![57]

Although it was realized that relatively few cases would involve judicial review of Acts of Parliament (rather than the discretionary actions of officials or ministers) there was also concern that the judges would be encouraged to be cautious by the knowledge that Parliament still retained the last word on statutes. MPs could legislate to overturn the effects of any court ruling safe in the knowledge that, once ensconced in an Act of Parliament, the policy at issue would be protected from judicial repeal (unless the European Court of Human Rights subsequently ruled otherwise).

There had been some false hopes that the Canadian approach to enforcement would be adopted whereby courts can overturn Acts of Parliament as a general rule, but are stopped from doing so if legislation is passed in acknowledged defiance of their Charter of Rights.

The problem with this model is that governments are rarely, if ever, prepared to own up to violating fundamental rights. For that reason this special provision, or 'notwithstanding clause', has never been used by the Federal Parliament, giving the Canadian Supreme Court effectively the same powers as its American equivalent.[58]

But despite some criticisms of the Human Rights Act, mainly from those who prefer the 'American way', generally speaking there was support from all sides. On the Right there was consolation that parliamentary sovereignty had not, in the event, been overturned (only dented), undoubtedly a factor in the Tories deciding not to vote against the Human Rights Bill passing into law. On the Left, there was relief that the Act stayed true to the tradition they had always feared losing through a bill of rights. The decision to keep the last word on Acts affecting civil and political rights with Parliament – which effectively means the government of the day – meant that most of the opposition on the Left to incorporation largely fell away. The law professor Keith Ewing, known as a staunch opponent of bills of rights in the past, put it this way:

incorporation of the Convention has been secured in a manner which subordinates Convention rights to constitutional principle and democratic tradition. We should not diminish the importance of the fact that the Human Rights Act does not give the courts the power to strike down legislation ... By ensuring that legal sovereignty continues to rest with Parliament, the government has retrieved the first constitutional principle of democratic socialism, and overcome one of the principle concerns about incorporation of the Convention[59]

Perhaps the most striking feature of the Human Rights Act is that it has a reasonable claim to being the first ever third-wave bill of rights. This is not only because of its late entry into the world, coming into force at the beginning of the third millennium after nearly all the democracies in the world have written constitutions or bills of rights. It is also because of the combined effect of its provisions, and the way it is being promoted by government and human rights NGOs.

There are three distinctive qualities to the Act which bring to mind the three major characteristics of third-wave rights. First, its conception of the role of the state. Second, the means of enforcement, in the widest sense of the word, envisioned by the Act. Third, its promotion as a set of values encouraging the broad development of a human rights culture.

The role of the state under the Human Rights Act

Ministers consciously chose not to imitate the classic Enlightenment model, where the traditional arms of the state are the only bodies against which individuals need protection, in their approach to incorporation of the ECHR. On the other hand, they also decided not to allow individuals to sue each other directly for breaches of human rights. The formula that was adopted keeps the government in the frame but brings in private bodies, and even individuals in certain circumstances, as potential players in the cast of characters who have responsibility for upholding rights under the Act. This contrasts with a number of other jurisdictions, notably the US and Canada, which take a more classical liberal stance on this issue.[60]

There are three ways in which non-state actors can be drawn in. Number one, some private sector bodies are included through the prohibition on public authorities acting incompatibly with Convention rights.[61] While 'public authorities' are not listed, the orbit of responsibility under the Act is far wider than just the obvious arms of the state.

Any body that carries out 'functions of a public nature' is legally liable.[62] This is deliberately framed to bring the private, voluntary and charitable sectors within the scope of the Act to the extent that they provide a public role like running private prisons, or elderly people's homes. It also includes bodies which regulate the activities of the public or which act under statutory powers. Those likely to be affected include, for example, private companies like Railtrack, or the privatized utilities to the extent that they carry out functions on the state's behalf; charities like the NSPCC in respect of functions which are governed by law; or regulatory bodies like the Press Complaints Commission (PCC) or the British Medical Association (BMA).[63]

Number two, the courts are explicitly named as a public authority.[64] This is the same as in the New Zealand and South African Bills of Rights but again different from America and Canada. The Lord Chancellor, Lord Irvine, explicitly stated that this was intended to make sure that the common law complies with Convention rights, including when it applies to individuals:

We also believe that it is right as a matter of principle for the courts to have the duty of acting compatibly with the Convention, not only in cases involving other public authorities, but also in developing the common law in deciding cases between individuals.[65]

Most commentators agree that this will lead, in time, to the common law plugging gaps it can't presently fill. There is currently no general right to privacy in UK law, for example.[66] Gordon Kaye, a star of the television series 'Allo 'Allo, discovered this to his cost after a serious car crash in 1990. He was recovering in bed when a journalist and photographer from the *Sunday Sport* entered his hospital room and took pictures of him. When Kaye tried to claim damages from the paper for violating his privacy, he failed. In finding against him Lord Justice Bingham lamented:

the failure of both the common law of England and statute to protect in an effective way the personal privacy of individual citizens[67]

The Human Rights Act will not immediately remedy this void as the press is not a public body although it is widely accepted that the Press Complaints Commission and broadcasting regulatory bodies are. However, as a result of the Act, a right to privacy is likely to emerge eventually through the development of the common law, even if Parliament fails to legislate in this direction. As the courts are required to interpret the common law compatibly with the Convention so current civil claims against newspapers, like nuisance or breach of confidence, will probably develop into a recognizable right to privacy over time.[68]

Number three, and related to this, is the requirement on courts to interpret *all* legislation compatibly with Convention rights (so far as possible), which includes private law.[69] This means that disputes between individuals, should they come before the courts, must be settled according to human rights norms where they involve the interpretation of legislation. Divorce, domestic violence, discrimination cases; all these and more involving private individuals will be influenced by human rights values in this way.

All this is in addition to the 'positive obligations' doctrine of the European human rights court, which UK judges are bound to take into account. This, as we have seen, indirectly brings private parties into the net of responsibilities under the ECHR in a range of circumstances.[70] This approach is given a boost by the Human Rights Act, which includes 'failure to act' on the part of a public authority as a potential violation of Convention rights. A train company that fails to invest in the most effective safety technology required to protect lives, for example, could be found to have breached the Act.[71]

The picture, therefore, that will gradually emerge once the case law gets going, is of a society widely affected by enforceable human rights standards. As expected, the obvious arms of the state – central and local government, the NHS, the immigration service, the police, the armed forces, the criminal justice system, and so forth – will have the main liability for human rights breaches. Individuals can cite the rights in the Human Rights Act in their defence if they are prosecuted as well as take such bodies to court for breaching their fundamental rights. But responsibility for human rights compliance will also extend to a network of private bodies to the extent that they carry out public functions, private bodies that breach human rights norms under the common law and even, in some circumstances, private individuals who take disputes against other individuals to court or whom the state requires to respect the rights of others.

Mainstreaming compliance under the Human Rights Act

The second reason why the Human Rights Act has a reasonable claim to third-wave status is the vision it contains of how rights should be enforced. The enhanced role of the courts in protecting rights has already been explained.[72] The extent to which, prior to this Act, judges were blocked from using human rights values to check the abuse of power of officials or ministers will probably amaze most people. When you are told all your life that you are living in the freest country in the world it comes as a bit of a surprise to find that human rights considerations could not be used by the courts to determine whether a woman could use her dead husband's sperm to conceive a child,[73] or whether the former Conservative government was entitled to ban the nation from hearing the real voice of the Sinn Fein leader, Gerry Adams, on the news.[74] This is to name but two random examples from thousands of cases over the years.

For as long as the Human Rights Act (HRA) remains on the statute book the miserly place that international human rights values were allowed in the courtrooms of the UK will be a thing of the past. Repealing such a high-sounding Act is almost inconceivable in the foreseeable future. It is fair to say that enforcement of human rights standards through the courts is here to stay.

But this is far from the whole story. While the term 'mainstreaming' is nowhere to be found in the Act or White Paper which accompanied it, it is a term as beloved by New Labour as it is by Kofi Anan, Secretary-General of the United Nations, who, as we saw, is trying to change the culture of the UN.[75] The goal of 'mainstreaming' is reflected in the whole scheme of the HRA.

Before any new government Act is introduced, the minister responsible must make a statement as to whether or not it is compatible with ECHR rights.[76] While it is refreshing to see human rights considerations mentioned on the face of statutes alongside financial ones, this provision has a farcical element. A ministerial declaration of compatibility is as certain to accompany every piece of legislation as a cry of 'order, order' from the Speaker, making its value appear somewhat dubious.

However, this provision has the potential to get the slumbering beast of Whitehall moving in terms of human rights scrutiny of policies and legislation in the way nothing else ever has. Civil servants maintain that all legislation and policy have long been monitored for compliance with the ECHR, at least since two Cabinet circulars required this in 1987. But this was mainly an exercise in risk management in recognition of a 'consistently high level of applications and decisions' in Strasbourg concerning the UK.[77]

If backbench MPs from all parties start using government statements of compliance as a reason to interrogate ministers about the human rights implications of their legislation at an early stage in a bill's life, then this should alert Whitehall. Although this has got off to a slow start, it is hard to believe that even the more robotic tendency among backbenchers will not use this opportunity in time. The government maintained that an increase in parliamentary scrutiny was one of the purposes of this provision. Rejecting a Liberal Democratic amendment that would have required ministers to give reasons for their 'statement of compatibility', Lord Irvine said:

Of course Parliament will wish to know the reasons why the Government have taken whatever view they have taken ... the reasoning behind a statement of compatibility or the inability to make such a statement will inevitably be discussed by Parliament during the passage of the Bill.[78]

The new Joint Parliamentary Committee on Human Rights, which is empowered to scrutinize draft bills for their compliance with the Human Rights Act, as well as conduct general investigations, could have an even more significant watchdog role.

The knock-on effect on civil servants is likely to be an increase in scrutiny levels at the earliest stage of policy formulation. This should take the responsibility for human rights compliance outside the offices of the lawyers, who have monopolized this process in the past, and into the domain of a wider group. The tendency of lawyers to mystify how they arrive at a decision of compliance is likely to decrease if only because they would not be able to cope with the sheer volume of work if they do not share their expertise with a wider range of colleagues. Of course the legal officers of the various departments will need to remain closely involved with the scrutiny process, but any person with a reasonable education can understand human rights values and the way they are broadly applied if they familiarize themselves with the basic principles.

This 'mainstreaming' of human rights values has already begun.[79]

In addition to the range of high-quality material for the public sector produced by the Human Rights Unit in the Home Office, together with the government-appointed Human Rights Task Force,[80] there is also a well-informed Human Rights Unit website and a regular newsletter. Material aimed at the private and charitable sectors has also been produced.[81] This is particularly important for so-called hybrid bodies which, although privately owned, can be taken to court if they are accused of breaching the Human Rights Act in the exercise of their public functions.

The tone of the various pieces of material is much more about good practice than simply risk management. In this there is a precedent from the Policy Appraisal and Fair Treatment (PAFT) Guidelines issued for Northern Ireland by the last government. On paper, at least, these aim to achieve a cultural shift in policy-making by requiring a 'positive approach' to be taken to 'equality of opportunity and fair treatment'.[82]

Each department in Whitehall has specially designated Human Rights Act officers with responsibility for reaching out to the relevant bodies that come under their area, such as the NHS, Inland Revenue and Immigration Service. The Local Government Association (LGA), the Association of Chief Police Officers (ACPO) and the Crown Prosecution Service (CPS) are all represented on the Task Force, increasing liaison with those sectors.

The absence – to date – of a Human Rights Commission, for anywhere but Northern Ireland, to fulfil at least a promotional and public education function will obviously limit the extent to which this momentum can credibly be maintained. There are also additional proposals for entrenching human rights scrutiny within Whitehall, many of which have not yet been adopted.[83]

Most essential of all for the long-term effectiveness of 'mainstreaming human rights' will, of course, be the attitude the government takes to its own Bill of Rights. If, as is likely, it starts having to amend some of its most treasured legislation, or to accept new interpretations to it, as a result of court rulings or civil service advice, then defensiveness could well set in, drowning out any other cultural message. Just maintaining the current practice of defending almost every case taken against it under the Act will put the government in the role of protector of unacceptable legislation rather than promoter of human rights. The message to start putting on the brakes, or even go into reverse, will percolate to all those public officials who had just started to drive in a new direction. This would not have to be a written message, or even a stated one. The point about 'main-streaming' is that communication takes place without issuing instructions. And this one will be heard loud and clear if it comes.

The values of the Human Rights Act

The third, and most important, factor which suggests that the UK's new Bill of Rights could be part of an emerging third wave of rights is the potential it has for communicating human rights values to society as a whole. As we have seen the government is increasingly keen to promote it in these terms. Jack Straw devoted virtually his entire speech to this theme at a major civil service college seminar on the Human Rights Act in December 1999. He began by posing the sixty-four thousand dollar question:

What do we mean when we talk of building a culture of rights and responsibilities in the UK? These aren't empty words or mere jargon. A rights and responsibilities culture *really is* our goal.

His answer could not have been more in line with the emerging third wave of rights:

In the human rights context we are basically talking about unconscious understandings and assumptions concerning politics, social life and justice ... Please don't make the mistake of seeing these changes as just about the legal system. We didn't incorporate the Convention principles and norms as playthings for the lawyers ... In time, the language of the Convention will be the language in which many of the key debates are settled. The language you need to speak to win an argument. And that's a real culture change.

He continued:

Consider the nature of modern British society. It's a society enriched by different cultures and different faiths. It needs a formal shared understanding of what is fundamentally right and fundamentally wrong if it is to work together in unity and confidence ... The Human Rights Act provides that formal shared understanding. It's an ethical language we can all recognize and sign up to. An ethical language which doesn't belong to any particular group or creed, but to all of us.[84]

This is as clear an exposition of the post-war human rights message as you will find anywhere. It could have been drafted by Mary Robinson, the UN Human Rights Commissioner, or even Eleanor Roosevelt. It is unusual to hear such sentiments come out of the mouth of a government minister, even one who introduced the Bill of Rights, but how realistic is it that these values will permeate the public imagination? Could they strike a chord or do they sound like the preachings of a pious politician?

In formal terms the government's Human Rights Task Force is preparing material aimed at the general public which draws on this message of human rights as a set of ethical values of relevance to people of all religions and none. This will be promoted through newspapers and other widely used outlets. NGOs are also producing their own material and staging public events.[85] Many of these are London-based but there is also considerable promotional activity being organized through the Scottish Human Rights Centre and the Northern Ireland Human Rights Commission.

A new statutory national curriculum entitlement on citizenship at Key Stages 3 and 4 is being introduced in 2002. Education Secretary David Blunkett, who shortly after taking office set up an advisory group on citizenship education chaired by Professor Bernard Crick, described the new subject as 'one of the most important steps in developing and understanding our democracy and encouraging active citizenship that has been introduced for a very long time'.[86]

The link between citizenship education and the values in the new Bill of Rights was, astonishingly, slow to be appreciated by the Crick advisory group although the connection was appreciated in the final report.[87] The citizenship curriculum will include a requirement that students know and understand 'the legal and human rights and responsibilities underpinning society'.[88] Although, at the time of writing, there is no explicit mention of the Human Rights Act in the guidelines published so far, the DFEE have told the Human Rights Task Force that relevant materials on the values underpinning the Act will be produced.

But whether the Home Secretary's prediction that human rights values will come to inform most of the great debates of the age is realistic or not depends on more than these formal preparations. The race relations and sex discrimination legislation of the 1970s are a case in point. Whatever their weaknesses, they have arguably achieved a new common language of equal opportunities and encouraged a greater avoidance of stereotyping. Who could deny that racism and sexism would be far more entrenched were it not for those Acts? But their effectiveness has depended almost as much on their declaratory and symbolic roles as on their technical provisions. Lord Williams, now Attorney-General, explicitly made this link between anti-discrimination laws and the HRA when as a Home Office minister he piloted the Human Rights Bill through the House of Lords. He expressed his hope that the new Act would have a similar effect on cultural change as these older ones have had.[89]

Identifying obstacles to cultural change through a bill of rights

There are many obstacles to realizing this vision of the UK's new Bill of Rights, but two stand out in particular. The first concerns the government and the second the legal culture of the UK.

Legislation in trouble

In addition to a government-inspired backlash like the one described earlier, the other damage this, or any future government, can do is consistently pass legislation which blatantly breaches human rights values and then deny it.[90] This is a difficult issue because unless there is clear jurisprudence from the European Court of Human Rights on an identical, or very similar, case it is not always possible to know exactly which way the courts will jump on any specific issue that may arise under the legislation.

Even if the European Court has ruled a particular way the domestic courts are not bound to follow. And in a surprising number of cases the Court has left it to the domestic authorities to decide whether a breach of the Convention has occurred, arguing that it is not appropriate for a regional court to impose its values on national ones provided certain procedural safeguards are followed.[91]

The press coverage of the responses of some civil rights lawyers to every piece of legislation which addresses crime or victims' rights could lead people to believe that they are all in breach of the ECHR. As we have seen, this is highly unlikely to be the case.[92] Indeed, there is increasing recognition by the European Court of Human Rights that there is a fundamental right to be protected from life-threatening crime and that the state has a duty to uphold this right.[93] Yet there is still a tendency to portray the Convention as a first-wave instrument – in which the state is an abuser and not also a protector of rights – and use this to attack the government at every opportunity. David Feldman, a professor of jurisprudence, has argued strongly against the presentation of the ECHR as a classical liberal document:

Convention rights are unlikely to operate in a purely liberal and individualistic way. Portraying them in that light would deprive the 1998 Act, and the whole idea of fundamental rights, of the support of all but an extreme group of liberals.[94]

That said, there is some legislation at the heart of the Home Office's own programme that appears to defy fundamental human rights values. Notable examples include aspects of the Prevention of Terrorism and Immigration and Asylum legislation, both introduced in 1999.

There is no bar in post-war human rights philosophy to special anti-terrorist laws. Indeed, if there was evidence that special laws were needed to prevent violent, ideologically driven acts, there could even be an obligation on a state to introduce them to uphold the right to life. But it is highly likely that, unqualified, the reverse onus of proof enshrined in the new anti-terrorism bill is in breach of the right to be presumed innocent under the ECHR.[95] This provision, condemned by Labour when it was first brought in by the Conservative government in 1994, could mean that if you were found in possession of some Cabinet ministers' addresses, for example, you might have to prove your innocence rather than the prosecution prove your guilt. A few readers of this book could be feeling a bit uneasy at this moment.

More worrying still is a new provision in the Bill which makes it an offence to incite terrorism abroad. Although obviously aimed at countering criticisms by some regimes that the UK harbours dangerous terrorists, its effects could be much broader. On the face of it, this provision will make it a criminal offence to support by words alone an armed struggle in another country, including one that flagrantly abuses human rights. It could theoretically have led to charges of terrorism against members of the African National Congress (ANC) in exile in the UK during the Apartheid years, and is potentially a breach of the right to free expression under Article 10 of the ECHR.[96]

Aspects of the 1999 Immigration and Asylum Act also appear to offend against human rights values. There is, again, nothing to stop governments controlling immigration under international human rights law. There is not even a direct right to seek asylum under the ECHR, although there is under the Universal Declaration of Human Rights and the ICCPR. But, significantly, the European human rights court has found that deportation to a country where you are likely to be tortured is a breach of Article 3 of the Convention.[97] This sets clear standards for government behaviour towards asylum seekers.

The human rights NGO JUSTICE has found thirteen potential breaches of ECHR rights in the new Immigration and Asylum Act. These include religious discrimination in the 'sham marriages' provision, the absence of a clear legal basis for detention and a lack of proper judicial control over its length. The most publicized aspect of the new law is the introduction of a cash-voucher scheme for asylum seekers. JUSTICE argues that the low level of support involved, and the fact that the new law allows all support and accommodation to be withdrawn from individuals seeking refugee status in some (admittedly quite rare) circumstances, raise the issue of whether the provisions could effectively starve someone out of the country. If an asylum seeker were forced back into a dangerous situation in their home state this would breach the right to be free from torture under the European Convention. Likewise, the extension of liability for transporting asylum seekers to lorry drivers without clear exemptions for those who bring in people in imminent danger 'of torture or inhuman treatment' is potentially in breach of the same provision.[98]

An unyielding legal culture

Even more threatening to the capacity of the new Bill of Rights to spread an understanding of human rights values is the traditional legal culture in the UK. Andrew Puddephatt, now Director of the international freedom of expression group Article 19, has warned that:

As with any bill of rights, there is a danger that lawyers, to the exclusion of a wider audience, dominate the debate.[99]

However well-meaning and committed individual lawyers may be, there is a tendency to redefine all laws within the 'positivist' or literal culture of British law.[100] This is a culture which has a historic respect for the principles of liberty and justice but which in many ways finds human rights philosophy alien to its mode of operation. It is a culture which tends to look for the 'true' meaning of words rather than the 'possible' meaning of statutes. A culture which looks to precedent rather than purpose. It is a culture so myopic that it was viewed as a revolutionary step when the courts accepted in 1993 that lawyers can refer in court to ministerial statements which explain the purpose of legislation, rather than relying on interpreting words which are obscure or ambiguous.[101]

In many ways the human rights legal culture could not be more different to this. Rather than looking back it looks forward. There is no formal doctrine of precedent. The European Court of Human Rights will usually follow previous decisions but is not bound to do so. The approach is dynamic rather than static in its orientation. This means that the principles in the Convention are considered in the light of subsequent developments, allowing them to evolve with changing norms.[102]

To put it bluntly, there is a real danger that the legal profession in the UK, which has a huge role in presenting the new Act to the rest of society, will miss the whole point. It is not just that radical and not-so-radical lawyers may try to argue hopeless cases by seeking an interpretation of a word in the Convention which was never meant to be applied out of the context of the treaty's overall aims and purposes. It is also that they could squeeze the life blood out of this new Bill of Rights by appearing to turn it into a statute as opaque and obscure to the woman on the Clapham omnibus as any other law.

Murray Hunt, a practising human rights barrister, has argued a similar point. He warned that:

the most cursory consideration of our current legal culture yields a number of examples of habits of mind and patterns of thought on the part of judges and practitioners which ... may impede the development of the type of human rights culture envisaged by the Act

In evidence Hunt cites the 'highly formalistic' legal culture which 'prefers to take refuge in the familiarity of well-known rules and interpretative approaches' rather than engage in modern debates. Although there has been some movement away from this, the 'positivistic' approach, which assumes that every text has 'an actual meaning', rather than one that can be constructed, still prevails.[103]

Dialogue and debate through the Human Rights Act

There is one sure protection against the legal profession inadvertently squeezing the soul out of the Human Rights Act. That is for a wider and wider group of people to participate in a national conversation about the nature of human rights, who should enforce them and how they should be applied in real-life situations.

That is precisely what happened on 16 December 1999. This was when the European Court of Human Rights in Strasbourg delivered its decision on the trial of Robert Thompson and Jon Venables, who had been found guilty six years earlier of the tragic murder of a toddler, James Bulger. When the abduction and violent assault on the two-year-old took place in February 1993 it is fair to say that most of the country was traumatized. This was not just because the two culprits were only ten years old; children themselves. It was also because of widespread revulsion at the appalling torture the little boy suffered and empathy with the despair of his parents. This capacity to identify with the common humanity of every individual is, of course, the base route to the survival of a human rights culture.

It is obviously most difficult for people to sustain this sense of solidarity or mutuality with all human beings when they are confronted with murderers, however young. When the European Court's ruling was announced, there were of course the predictable headlines like 'So What About James's Rights?'[104] There was also the usual confusion between the EU and the Council of Europe with a member of the audience on BBC Radio Four's *Any Questions* asking the panel, 'Should the decision on the Bulger sentencing have gone to Brussels?' And a number of commentators, including Tory MPs, ranted about foreign judges interfering with British justice.

But the debate that ensued over the following days in the letters pages of national newspapers, in radio phone-ins and on the television, was largely measured, despite strong feelings on all sides. What came across was that the European Court of Human Rights found that the adult trial process that the boys endured breached their right to a fair trial. Also that the setting of a tariff, or minimum detention period, in excess of that set by the trial judge, by the then Home Secretary, Michael Howard, was in breach of the requirement that the entire trial process, including the fixing of sentences, be independent from the executive or government. How much more considered still would the debate have been if human rights values had been more familiar?

While strong views on either side were expressed as to the wisdom of the Court's judgment, an overwhelming assumption was that victims were irrelevant to a court of human rights. No publicity was given to the judges' statement that:

States have a duty under the Convention to take measures for the protection of the public from violent crime.

Nor that the Court went on to say that:

It does not consider that the punitive element inherent in the tariff approach itself gives rise to a breach of Article 3 [degrading treatment] or that the Convention prohibits States from subjecting a child or young person convicted of a serious crime to an indeterminate sentence, allowing for the offender's continued detention or recall to detention following release where necessary for the protection of the public.[105]

Interestingly, there are ways in which the unique aspects of the Human Rights Act could, in the long run, facilitate a wider understanding that such views are not at all out of kilter with modern human rights values. Murray Hunt explains why:

It is clear from the Act's own provisions ... that it is designed to introduce a culture of rights that is more communitarian than libertarian in its basic orientation. In such a human rights culture the individual citizen is more than the mere bearer of negative rights against the state, but is a participate individual, taking an active part in the political realm and accepting the responsibility to respect the rights of others in the community with whom he or she is interdependent.[106]

It is worth quoting at length how Hunt describes the features in the Act which contribute to this culture. There is, he says,

a creative tension between the judiciary on the one hand and Parliament and the executive on the other. It binds the principal constitutional actors into a dialogue with each other in which all agree on the objective of securing Convention rights, and disagreements about their interpretation or the resolution of conflicts between them are mediated by a new relationship between courts and Parliament, both of which have an explicit role in pronouncing on human rights issues[107]

The 'participative model'

The only factor missing from this description is 'the people'. They – we – still have the opportunity, under the British Bill of Rights model, to engage in this 'dialogue' through participating in the political process directly or through various modern means of communication. This is especially important in relation to the big social issues of the day: tobacco-advertising bans; the outlawing of hunting; the ethical considerations raised by voluntary euthanasia or abortion; the debate over whether or not smacking is a legitimate punishment for a child; controls on the expenditure of political parties. These are all issues which could be, or have been, decided by the courts in America or Canada but will remain the ultimate preserve of Parliament under the 'British model'. In this way no one need be barred from the national debate over where the appropriate balance between rights lies. While ministers can be lobbied, judges can not.

What could be described as the participative model in the HRA – which was the consequence of all those years of debate on the respective roles of the courts and Parliament – implicitly recognizes that human rights are messy things, not clear-cut, neatly parcelled laws. They are ultimately a set of values with claims attached to them on a constant journey of evolution. As one commentator has observed:

Rights nudge each other. They do not fit together neatly in logic or in practice. They guarantee abrasions as well as peace between citizens. They call for debates between interests, claims and centres of power. For their exercise they require social pluralism, diverse power centres and possible appeals to diverging ultimate authorities.[108]

If human rights are to provide the set of values for a democracy that is the driving force behind the second and third wave of rights, then the debate about where to draw the line when rights collide has to embrace a wider group than the legal élite. In the end the line will just not hold if it has no legitimacy. And the legitimacy of the courts to overturn the decisions of elected MPs on major social or political issues – even in a system like ours where politicians are under the cudgels of the party whip and the government is often elected on a minority vote – is far from clear.

This is not to say that the emerging third wave of rights implies that future bills of rights worldwide should inevitably follow the UK model. Such a claim would be absurd. It merely means that the approach adopted by the HRA can claim a legitimate place within the human rights universe. Once it would have been dismissed as a half-baked piece of legislation, inherently inferior to 'real', judicially entrenched bills of rights whose defining characteristic is that they allow courts to overturn all legislation which judges consider breach human rights.

Where there has been no recent history of democracy, on the other hand, like in the new South Africa, or most former colonies undergoing independence – or for that matter in America and France two hundred years ago – it makes no sense to entrust a bill of rights to a democratic system which does not yet have the confidence of the people.

Interestingly, the courts in Northern Ireland and Scotland will be able to strike down the legislation of their respective Assemblies in much the same way as the American Supreme Court can. This is justified in the government's White Paper on the HRA in terms of devolution principles. Only Westminster Acts are deemed 'sovereign' and therefore not liable to be declared null and void by the judiciary.[109] Intended or otherwise, this will provide a useful means of comparing the effects of these two models operating simultaneously in the UK on inculculating human rights values within popular culture.

Of course, at the boundaries – the hard edges where the most fundamental of rights are at stake – there are, or should be, clear human rights answers, and it cannot be right that a government which threatens these liberties is also charged with determining how they should be protected. This is the *locus* of books like Geoffrey Robertson, QC's, recent *tour de force*, *Crimes Against Humanity*.[110]

There is an argument, therefore, for saying that the Human Rights Act should have allowed the courts to have the final say when, for example, life, torture and slavery are at stake (and perhaps also for qualified rights like fair trial or the right to liberty).[111] As we have seen, there is a parallel here with the European Convention of Human Rights, which distinguishes between absolute rights that cannot be derogated from even in an emergency and those that can be qualified or limited.[112]

Protecting minorities from 'the will of the majority'

The other obvious major critique of the participative model in the HRA is that it is all very well when it comes to the broad social issues which affect society as a whole, but what about minorities? How can a bill of rights which facilitates the broadest possible dialogue about where the boundaries between rights should lie protect minorities whose interests are not shared by the majority? Particularly if the term 'minority' is used in its widest sense to include *any* small group of people like prisoners, 'neighbours from hell' or even paedophiles.

Of course in one sense it cannot offer sufficient guarantees. The public campaign in Scotland and England in the first months of the new millennium against repeal of Section 28 of the 1988 Local Government Act, which some teachers complained stymied their capacity to respond to homophobic bullying in schools, brought home the timeless need for institutional safeguards for minorities.[113] Reports at the time that Kent County Council's education authority intended to issue its own guidelines on the 'intentional promotion of homosexuality' once Section 28 was repealed illustrate both the possibilities and limitations of the new Bill of Rights as far as protecting minorities is concerned.[114]

Should they be issued, such guidelines would be open to challenge in the courts as a breach of the Human Rights Act. Such broad protection against discrimination or unfair treatment was not available before the new Bill of Rights was in force. Whether such guidelines breached the law would have depended only on the terms of narrowly defined, specific legislation.

At the same time, because the courts do not have the final say on rights, as they do in the US, the debate could continue even if a court overturned guidelines of this nature. Parliament can still legislate to change the effects on policy of court rulings, although this would be to risk the charge that the government of the day was breaching fundamental human rights and ultimately to risk humiliation at the European Court of Human Rights. The Human Rights Act, then, combines a system of checks and balances with an approach which does not close off democratic involvement in an issue once the courts have ruled on it.

Can any system, anyway, honestly claim to guarantee complete protection of the few against the many, regardless of how 'unpopular' a given minority is? Although only occasionally acknowledged, most judges are to some extent influenced by the prevailing political and social culture and do not simply stand above it as supporters of judicially entrenched bills of rights would have us believe. There has been a degree of back-pedalling by the courts in Canada, for example, since the Charter of Rights gained a reputation in certain quarters as 'a criminals' charter'. Similarly, would the American Supreme Court have ever 'discovered' a right to abortion from the American Bill of Rights, which does not even mention the term 'privacy', if the year had not been 1973 and the second-wave women's movement had not been in full stride?[115] That is not to say that one caused the other, but to deny the latter's influence would be naïve in the extreme.

If judges are to be influenced by a human rights culture, which in the British context is essential if they are to interpret the Human Rights Act in the spirit that Parliament intended, then that culture has to take root in a wider field than the law. But if 'the people' are kept out of rights debates which are presented as too complex for the ordinary person, then it is hard to see how such a culture can emerge.

That said, it is essential that any bill of rights worth its name provides a counterbalance to the power of governments or parliaments to act at will. The Human Rights Act undoubtedly provides greater safeguards against arbitrary state power than has ever been known in the UK, and gives the courts a much greater authority to check such power than in the past. The Act, therefore, has the potential to act as a significant bulwark against executive decisions or panic-induced laws when 'fear is . . . stalking the land'.[116] This is one of its major strengths.

In the final analysis, the Human Rights Act can be said to reflect the emerging third wave of rights because it encourages popular participation in the enforcement of rights when bills of rights were once viewed as essentially anti-populist. Its special features reflect a growing appreciation that rights are evolving with social, political and economic changes and that the debate about where the line should be drawn between conflicting rights is a debate without end.

But it need not be just isolated individuals who can join this dialogue. Organized groups can also participate in debates about rights for they too have a legitimate stake in influencing their boundaries. The simple point is that it is not senior judges alone who are empowered to determine from on high what rights mean and how they should evolve through this new Bill of Rights. Their word is enormously influential but it is not God's. The courts are there to stop any derailment from the human rights message in the resolution of this dialogue. But they are not there to pre-empt it. If someone had not already coined the phrase, the Human Rights Act could be labelled the 'People's Bill'.

Third wave or third way?

The People's Bill of Rights nearly did not materialize at all, at least not in the year 2000. There was a last-minute 'wobbly' when it seemed as if Downing Street might delay implementation of the Act until after the next general election. Fear of some high-profile cases leading to tabloid headlines like 'Labour Introduces Criminals' Charter' or 'Paedophiles Released Early through New Labour's Villains' Rights Bill' seemed to create a last-minute panic in the higher echelons of government.[117]

It is doubtful whether the Home Secretary or Lord Chancellor could have overcome these objections had it not been possible to present the Act as a manifestation of the culture of rights and responsibilities which is a trademark of the third way. Jack Straw made a valiant attempt to do this in his speech to the Civil Service College on 9 December 1999. 'Rights,' he said, 'are the heading you find if you glance through the ECHR. But rights *and responsibilities* are what it is really about.'[118]

Of course, in many ways, he is absolutely right. As we have seen, the ECHR is very different from the classic libertarian mould of rights charters. To some degree there is a convergence between the communitarian values of New Labour and the Bill of Rights they have bestowed.

However, the story does not quite end there. There are some highly significant ways in which the Human Rights Act challenges some of the shibboleths of the new politics. This is in addition to any legal challenges to Labour's programme which, as we have seen, will undoubtedly arise and will sometimes be successful.[119]

First, the claim that rights emanate from duties and not the other way round, which the Home Secretary and the Prime Minister, along with a number of commentators, are prone to insist upon from time to time.[120] This begs the obvious question – outside the basics like is it wrong to murder or steal? – who, in a dvierse and pluralist society, has sufficient legitimacy to decide what these duties are which rights should flow from? Is it to be God, Tony Blair, the Queen, religious leaders, judges, or Parliament (for which, read the government of the day) whose set of 'fundamental duties' might change with each election if not each opinion poll?[121]

None of these have a remote chance of achieving sufficient legitimacy to successfully define a whole set of common responsibilities adhered to across classes, cultures and generations in a way that might conceivably be possible in a mono-cultural or mono-religious society. This is perhaps why all attempts to draft a separate charter of responsibilities by international figures have yet to make the impact some would say they deserved.[122] And as this 'duties-led approach' sometimes favoured by New Labour fails to lead to any significant cultural change in the UK there are calls for ever stronger punitive sanctions to control the behaviour of us all. This creates the danger of imitating the conditions which led to the demand for fundamental rights in the first place.

The reason why it is persuasive to argue that rights entail responsibilities and not the other way round is because their legitimacy lies not in some higher force but in a recognition of our common humanity; the dignity inherent in every human life.[123] The motive for accepting this approach is part self-interest, part concern for others, and part an appreciation of the mutuality that is required to live in a 'decent society', where all have a potential to flourish. This was the formula, as we saw, that the framers of the UDHR struck upon, after much debate. If any set of shared values is going to resonate in modern Britain then this is probably it.

The second major challenge to the 'third way' from the 'human rights way' flows from the implication, not necessarily stated, that you lose rights because you act irresponsibly. This is an impression that can be drawn, perhaps unfairly, from the government's insistence on coupling rights with responsibilities at every mention of the word and more particularly from the assertion that rights flow from duties and not vice versa.[124]

In human rights terms, you lose only those rights that are necessary to protect the rights of others and the broader community. And, if rights are limited for those reasons, this must happen in a proportionate way to meet a legitimate aim in a democratic society. So prisoners still retain the right to privacy and free speech within prison, ex-cons the right to be presumed innocent of any further crimes until proven guilty, and even heinous murderers the right not to be subjected to torture, to a fair trial and to retain their life. The concept of dignity – the most prevailing human rights value of all – requires this. For if any human being, or group of human beings, is deemed to fall so low as not to be deserving of any significant rights at all, this challenges our claim to a common humanity.

Finally, there is a requirement in human rights terms for individuals to act responsibly in quite a different sense than New Labour tends to voice. The Preamble to the ICCPR, a treaty which the government is legally bound to uphold, proclaims that part of an individual's duty to the community entails promoting fundamental human rights.[125] This, in turn, must mean challenging popular culture where it denies human rights values, from whichever source it comes. So it means encouraging others to see that even paedophiles need to live somewhere when they are released from jail. It means confronting the view that asylum seekers who make claims which fall outside the narrow grounds for refugee status are necessarily 'bogus' rather than just unsuccessful. And it means having the courage to challenge officialdom when power is abused at others' expense, not just your own.

If the Human Rights Act does achieve a wider understanding of these values then Jack Straw will surely be right. Historians will judge this Act to be 'one of the most important pieces of constitutional legislation the UK has seen'.[126]

Human Rights in an Era of Failed Utopias

The writing of this book has taken me on an unexpected journey. My initial motivation was to explain the significance of the new Human Rights Act – the UK's first modern Bill of Rights – to a largely uninitiated audience.[1] There had been staggeringly little popular engagement in this development. Had the ghosts of radicals past come back to haunt us, they would have been amazed at how little the passions have run over an idea which gripped the popular imagination two hundred years earlier.[2] The 'rights of man' – and woman – were finally being written down and enshrined in law and hardly anyone seemed to notice!

The Human Rights Act explained

The first most people will have learnt about their Bill of Rights will probably have been through reading press reports with titles such as: 'Rights Act Will Put British Way of Life on Trial' or 'The Judges – Our New Oppressors'.[3] Like other similar articles, these pieces predictably catalogued a list of measures that may be overturned by the courts under the new Act, with varying degrees of accuracy.

Despite attempts by the Home Office to promote it, at the time of writing there had been little opportunity to appreciate that the new Bill of Rights will have as much, if not more, significance for our democracy as devolution, freedom of information or the election of a London mayor. Few individuals will know that public (and some private) authorities have been rendered accountable for their actions where once they were immune from questioning.

189

Even fewer people will be aware that they can now directly challenge authorities for breaching their fundamental rights in circumstances where once they were powerless to do so.[4] They will scarcely realize that many people's lives could at some time be directly touched by the Act, not only the defendants or prisoners or oppressed minorities who most obviously need its protection.

People like those who live under the flight path of Heathrow Airport, whose right to enjoy their private lives in their own homes is potentially infringed by aeroplanes taking off and landing at night. Or like the children who were abused or maltreated in the North Wales' children's homes scandal that came to light in February 2000: young people who would have had a significantly greater chance of legal redress for the harm done to their physical and emotional well-being[5] if the Human Rights Act had been in force than they had under the old system.[6] My goal in writing this book was to explain all this.[7]

The Human Rights Act defended

I wanted, too, to defend the Act from three main, overlapping, criticisms. First, that it removes control in certain key areas from elected MPs to unelected judges, overturning the much-vaunted doctrine of 'parliamentary sovereignty'.[8] Second, that its greatest achievement will be to introduce an American-style litigious approach to public life, and third, that it will lead to the waning of political action in key areas.[9]

A leader in the *Daily Mail*, for example, flagged up the first two points six months before the Act was due to fully come into force under the heading 'A New Tyranny of Human Rights?'

No longer will Parliament decide on crucial matters of moral and social policy. In future the ECHR will be virtually a Supreme Court. Its every edict – however bizarre – binding on us. And who will be the beneficiaries? The answer is simple – the lawyers.[10]

The *Observer* columnist Nick Cohen expressed the third criticism in a withering attack on expectations raised by the Human Rights Act:

> In the leftish press, and in the small circles where civil rights activists meet, a giddy mood of liberal hubris is building after two decades of defeat ... The resurgent liberals believe, then, that the government has handed its critics an instrument that will shatter the very authoritarianism it propagates in every available tabloid. Citizens will defeat an overbearing state; not by electing MPs or organizing protests, but by turning to that vanguard of revolution – her Majesty's learned judges ... Only the credulous will be left believing that the law is an adequate substitute for politics.[11]

The Human Rights Act, I set out to demonstrate, does not need to lead to the shutting down of politics. Nor does it inevitably mean the substitution of parliamentary democracy for rule by judges. On the contrary, the unique model chosen – which still leaves the last word with Parliament on how Acts should be framed[12] – is aimed at creating a dialogue between the courts, government and Parliament in which we can all participate. If we do not like the results we can still use all the traditional methods of protest to make our point in the knowledge that in the UK – unlike in the US – judges will not have the final say on policies affecting fundamental rights.[13]

There is, on the other hand, no denying that the courts have more opportunities to hold the government and public officials to account under the Human Rights Act than they had previously. This is one of the reasons why it is remarkable that the government should voluntarily cede so much power by introducing a bill of rights. It is not as if the people were baying for one at the gates of 10 Downing Street.

After years in which the democratic process failed to check the excesses of central government, whichever party was in power, an increased role for the courts is one of the Act's purposes. This can be a boost for democracy in its own way in that it allows individuals a direct role in the interrogation of public policy to a degree which was denied to them before.[14]

But fears of litigiousness, although they will probably be borne out in the early days of the Act, may yet prove to be exaggerated. The new Bill of Rights creates a framework based on human rights values that should affect not only the courts. If the values it promotes take root, the Act should in time lead to a change in the culture of public (and to some degree private) life, rendering it more sensitive to individual needs. Eventually this could reduce the impetus for legal challenges.

Ethical and political debates

In writing this book in the run-up to the full enforcement of the Human Rights Act, I actually wanted to go further than suggesting what its legal and constitutional significance might be. I planned to examine what effect it could have on society's values generally. I wanted to demonstrate that the Human Rights Act is a 'higher law'[15], not only because it influences all other laws, but also because it has the potential to infuse a distinct ethical vision into life in the UK.

To make this case convincingly it was necessary to restore the reputation of the idea of rights from the mauling it has received from two debates that have rumbled on in the UK over a number of years. The first revolved around the claim that in our modern society there is no longer a set of shared, ethical values which, in crude terms, can help to determine right from wrong. In an era where the idea of god, if not dead, has become diffuse, and where hordes of young people are reared without a strong faith or any particular ideology, a recurring refrain is that morality has been privatized along with much else in modern Britain.[16] Ed Straw, Chair of the counselling service Relate,[17] put it this way:

We may be at a most unusual point in history; a time when people define for themselves the moral codes by which they live their family lives. For generations family and wider morality has come from elsewhere: transcendental, inherited, handed down, imposed . . . Suddenly, the roads are free of signs, markings and maps . . . No fixed points, no certainties, just miles and miles of choice[18]

For a number of commentators this freedom is the source of a modern malaise reflected in crime, truancy and an unspecified, but generalized, ethos of selfishness. For some, the only remedy is to try to regain the 'paradise lost' and restore the social order which characterized this country before the 'permissive' 1960s took its toll.[19]

For others, it is clear that there can be no turning the clock back. The race has been on to find an alternative source of a common morality for the UK. The challenge, as many see it, is to find a new set of ethics which goes beyond the idea of free choice and individual autonomy and which is neither anti-religious nor tied to an exclusive faith. In the words of Lady Mary Warnock, former Mistress of Girton College, Cambridge, and an adviser on medical ethics to the Archbishop of Canterbury:

I am convinced that it is possible to believe in a new source of morality, our common humanity, without rejecting religion in some form . . . the clergy . . . often make it impossible for their views on matters of morality to be taken seriously, simply because they have no language in which to discuss morality without reference to God.[20]

Parallel to this debate has been the search for a new political framework, in particular on the Left, to replace what are perceived as the failed ideologies of the last century. It may be that the label 'third way', and the communitarianism of Amitai Etzioni and others, which have attracted some support in the US, have not found resonance in this country beyond a small élite.[21] But many of the certainties of the old Left vision have faded. A number of commentators and activists are grappling with the contours of a new progressive politics. Charlie Leadbeater, a theorist of influence with 10 Downing Street, for example, has proposed that the future lies with 'a new synthesis of liberalism and communitarianism which should take us beyond the old language of Left and Right'.[22]

Both the quest for a common set of ethical values and the search for a 'third way' in politics have rights in their sight. With a number of key players in common, both pursuits view the idea of rights as a potential threat to their mission. For the former, rights encourage selfishness and relativism, the very forces that a new set of ethics is supposed to counter. For the latter, rights have similarly promoted individualism and license, which threaten the fabric of strong communities.[23] From both perspectives – which often overlap in practice

– rights are perceived as part of the problem rather than the solution. The target is not the Human Rights Act in particular but what is perceived to be an exaggerated emphasis on rights at the expense of duties in recent decades, or in Mary Warnock's words, 'the overuse of the concept of human rights'.[24] The danger is that much of the potential value of the new Act will get lost in this cross-fire.

One of the key purposes in writing this book was to challenge these assumptions. I wanted to demonstrate that, far from encouraging egoism and a privatized morality, the idea of fundamental human rights can contribute to a common ethos; it can encourage what Appeal Court Judge Stephen Sedley has called 'a common sense of equity, an ethic of kindness, a morality of feeling' which distinguishes justice from law.[25] Too often described in formal legal or constitutional terms, the potential for rights expressed as a bill of rights to provide a set of basic, ethical values for a modern, diverse society has gone largely uncharted in the UK.[26] I wanted to fill this gap.

In other countries like America and South Africa, of course, the symbolic nature of bills of rights is entirely obvious. By contrast in the UK, not only is there little experience of such an approach, but the political and legal culture is such that it is not even recognized when it arrives. Thus the respected historian Linda Colley could call for 'a new millennium charter or contract of citizens' rights' as 'indispensable' to constructing a 'new, revived, citizen nation' without apparently realizing that we were on the threshold of travelling at least partly down this road at the very moment that she made her significant appeal.[27]

The three waves of rights revisited

To justify the claim that the Human Rights Act could have symbolic as well as legal significance, I realized it was necessary to delve more deeply into what the idea of human rights is all about and the way this idea has developed over time. This is where my voyage of discovery began.

The journey I took to explore the evolution in rights thinking sent me backwards and forwards in time. It took me to earlier centuries characterized by wars, revolutions and strong states. And it propelled me forward to a brave new universe that is only just now starting to unfold. One where governments could have less power to control rights abuses than some transnational corporations, and where new technology meant that few people could shield themselves from the suffering of others around the world.

In the course of this voyage I discovered what I have chosen to describe as three waves of rights. All such typologies are to some extent personal, but for me this categorization goes beyond well-trodden distinctions between generations of rights (civil and political, social and economic, and environmental). It goes deeper, even, than an appreciation of the difference between the Enlightenment era, which popularized the idea of the 'natural rights' of citizens, and the post-war era, which sought to establish universal human rights for all humankind.

The depiction of rights as waves is intended to convey the dynamism of the quest for fundamental rights. This idea did not emerge fully clothed out of the minds of the great philosophers to be handed over to judges and legal theorists for interpretation. Its evolution has been a complex process in which large numbers of people have played a central role influenced by the major events of their day.

The passage of time has involved not only changes to the *type* of rights given universal recognition – although the more recent attention to social and economic rights suggests that this has happened to a degree – but also to the scope of their underlying values and the purposes they are intended to fulfil.

Brutal regimes and religious dogma provided the backdrop to the popularization of the idea of 'natural rights' in the late eighteenth century. Liberty and justice were the predominant values that characterized rights at that time. But in the wake of the horrors of the Second World War the focus shifted away from individual emancipation as the principal target of rights discourse.

The post-war attempt to establish a set of universal rights standards was primarily an ethical endeavour. From the point of view of the drafters of the 1948 Universal Declaration of Human Rights

(UDHR) 'the human rights they proclaimed were ... the moral cement that binds together the increasingly pluralistic societies of the modern world'.[28] Or, as UN Special Rapporteur Erica-Irene Daes has put it in her analysis of some of the underlying philosophy of the UDHR:

The world community should accept the thesis that the seat of human rights is primarily in the conscience of mankind and then in moral and positive law.[29]

Since this time, the project to create international human rights standards has in large measure been a quest to create a better world for everyone. The drafters of international human rights treaties have sought to establish a framework of values driven not just by the ideals of liberty and justice but also by such concepts as community, equality and dignity. And they have tried to grapple with the difficulties that arise when this synthesis proves problematic. Much of the recent case law of the European Court of Human Rights, which has begun to develop victims' rights out of the right to a fair trial, for example, can be understood in these terms.[30]

Increasingly, more and more people worldwide are relating to the great debates about fundamental rights, wresting control from the well-intentioned international standard setters and jurists who have monopolized this endeavour since the Second World War. Because of this participation – and because rights are increasingly presented as more than just claims against governments but also as a set of obligations that individuals owe to each other – a new value of mutuality can be said to characterize an emerging third wave of rights.[31]

The UK's new Bill of Rights as a source of common, ethical values

If the human rights project is accepted as one which has evolved from a search for individual freedom to a quest for common, ethical values, then the criticism that rights encourage egoism and selfishness is clearly way off the mark. Those who blame rights for contributing to what they perceive to be society's disintegration have missed the obvious point that rights are potentially a force for moral cohesion. This applies especially in a country of diverse communities like the UK.

Of course, the term 'rights' can be, and has been, co-opted to bolster any claim, from smoking on public transport to playing loud music unrestrained. But to exploit this phenomenon in order to make broad generalizations about the underlying philosophy of rights is to miss the point entirely. In fact, the concept of inalienable rights is aimed precisely at distinguishing those rights which are essential for the furtherance of human dignity from those which are not. Far from the idea of fundamental human rights encouraging relativism, it defines a common norm. Far from promoting individualism, it suggests what the limits to freedom might be and the obligations individuals, as well as states, owe to other individuals. Far from weakening the bonds of communities, it sets down a notion of the common good in a democratic society.

Underlying the European Convention on Human Rights (ECHR) are two types of values which are now enshrined in UK law. First, a range of substantive values, which it is beholden on everyone, including governments, to directly or indirectly observe. These include tolerance; respect for the dignity and lifestyle choices of others; allowing others to speak their mind or to protest without obstruction; and treating others fairly and without discrimination or degradation. Second, other values, some of which are procedural in nature and which it is primarily the duty of the state to secure, include justice, limitations on rights which are proportionate and necessary in a democratic society, legality, accountability, liberty and security.[32]

The structure of the Human Rights Act reinforces this ethical message by widening the range of bodies with legal responsibility for upholding fundamental rights from the traditional one of the state to private and voluntary organizations which carry out public functions and even to individuals who appear before the courts for whatever reason.[33] But, sceptics argue, while the Act establishes rights which individuals can claim, what it does not do is set down their legal responsibilities in daily life, and in that sense it cannot be described as providing a moral vision for society as a whole. The individuals get the rights and states the duties under the principles of human rights law, it is maintained.

A significant part of this book is aimed at disproving this point, not only in relation to the Human Rights Act but also to all bills of rights based on post-war international human rights standards. Besides specific references to the responsibilities of individuals, which are present, but admittedly sparse, in the ECHR,[34] the many limitations and qualifications on rights attached to most of the Articles establish that individuals must exercise their rights responsibly and with regard both to the needs of other individuals and the common good.

This is not to say that only responsible individuals have rights under the ECHR. Quite the contrary. One of the cardinal principles of international human rights law is that you lose rights only to the extent that it is necessary – and not more than that – to protect the rights of others and the broader community.[35] But the limitations on rights in the ECHR, replicated in the Human Rights Act, undoubtedly provide a guide to individuals as to where their right (for example, to free speech) must be tailored to take account of other rights or values (for example, not to be slandered or subject to racial hatred). In other words, 'the limits on the right set the boundaries within which the rights can be exercised'.[36]

If limitation clauses bestow indirect duties on individuals, so, increasingly, does the case law of the European Court of Human Rights through its doctrine of 'positive obligations'.[37] This approach mandates states to take positive actions to secure rights in certain circumstances rather than just refrain from abusing them. As a consequence, states have even been required to uphold rights between private parties; for example, to ensure that demonstrators can protest without being physically attacked by opponents[38] or that children can be reared without inhuman punishment.[39] These last illustrations, taken from the case law of the European Court of Human Rights, demonstrate the nub of the argument. If people do not take individual responsibility for upholding the values underlying human rights standards then the entire enterprise is ultimately doomed to failure.

Most people have no wish or need to go to court to protect their rights in their everyday lives. Not many individuals want recourse to privacy laws to prevent former employees writing about their families, for example. Even fewer seek to publish books about the security services and find themselves falling foul of the Official Secrets Act.

Of course, it is an essential ingredient of the human rights vision that in such circumstances people know, and can claim, their legal rights. But most of us have to rely on other individuals to protect our fundamental rights. We need our neighbours to respect our right to a private life uninterrupted by unacceptable noise levels or intrusion. We require our employers or parents to let us speak our mind and give us the opportunity to do so. No state can constantly intervene to guarantee such interactions without destroying the foundations of a remotely free society.

Even where there is state intervention this is often not enough. Despite legislation to outlaw race, sex or disability discrimination there can be little meaningful exercise of these rights if colleagues subtly degrade or undermine their fellow workers on such grounds. For that matter courts need all of us to accept that ex-prisoners must be allowed to live in peace on completing their prison sentences if the right to liberty is to be upheld. If the Human Rights Act is to be effective, in other words, it stands to reason that the values it enshrines must become part of a broad, shared ethos.

The state's responsibility to uphold the rights in the Act, even if it were to be executed impeccably, could never guarantee them in practice. Under human rights treaties every individual has an explicit duty to promote human rights observance.[40] In the last fifty years it has been increasingly clear to the international human rights community that neither the courts nor politicians nor any public authority can guarantee the values which underpin human rights – like pluralism, tolerance and broadmindedness[41] – if they are not endemic in a broader culture.

This is my reply to those who caricature the idea of rights as a product of the 'me society'. To those who are all in favour of human rights when applied to people being tortured in far-off lands but who fail to see the relevance of the idea to the UK, my response is that our new Bill of Rights is the only vehicle I am aware of which has the potential to provide in a diverse society the common set of values that they seek.

In fairness, it is true that human rights values do not speak directly to many of the sexual and social issues that concern those who are most worried about an apparent absence of shared moral values in this country. But what the Human Rights Act should do is establish a framework within which such debates can take place; one which emphasizes tolerance, privacy and autonomy on the one hand, and concern for the rights of others and the needs of the wider community on the other.

This approach, and the values which underlie it, may offend some people and incur profound disagreement. The human rights project can, of course, be dismissed as too wedded to tolerance and diversity by those concerned to promote greater uniformity and a particular worldview. But none of that can subtract from the moral vision which is at the heart of modern human rights thinking and which is a world away from the caricature of individualism and license conjured up by its critics.

Proclaiming the fundamental rights of men, women and (more recently) children is probably the only half-successful attempt there has ever been to establish a set of common values that are not intended to be exclusive to one religious group or nation. The idea of human rights, as it is understood today, does not require a belief in anything more than the dignity of each human person. Nor is the human rights approach necessarily secular in the sense of being incompatible with belief in a god. As commentators from a number of faiths have observed, concepts like the inherent dignity and essential equality of each human being can equally be said to have a religious heritage based on the conviction that every person is created in God's image.[42]

At the same time human rights discourse provides an opening for those, such as the philosopher Dr Anthony Grayling, who plead for an alternative avenue to determine 'the great moral questions of the present age' to the churches, which he considers are given 'a privileged – almost, indeed, an exclusive – position in the social debate about morality'.[43] Our new Bill of Rights, based on values which stem ultimately from the Universal Declaration of Human Rights, provides one possible alternative source to guide us in those great moral debates.

Human rights and a new progressive politics

But it is not just that human rights have the potential to provide a common set of values for those concerned about an apparent lack of a shared moral ethos in the UK. They also offer a framework for those searching beyond the failed utopias of the twentieth century to find a new approach to politics.

There have been a number of attempts to define this new politics in recent years, of which the 'third way' is only one. Some of these are unselfconsciously, but nevertheless markedly, close to a third-wave rights vision with its emphasis on rights, responsibilities and mutuality. This is not in any way to suggest that support for human rights is, or should be, allied to any particular political party. It is to point to a largely invisible congruence between the philosophical stance underlying the idea of human rights and many of the preoccupations of those searching for a new politics.

Peter Hain, for example, now a minister in the Foreign Office, has revisited what he calls the 'libertarian socialist tradition' of the Levellers and Diggers and 'the radical activists of that era',[44] who 'lost out' to the 'statist or top-down' vision of Socialism. The Left, he has suggested, should now reclaim this heritage of 'participatory democracy'. Citing devolution as a policy squarely within this tradition he appeared not to notice the significance for his thesis of Labour finally introducing a bill of rights.[45]

Geoff Mulgan, former Director of the think-tank Demos and now a 10 Downing Street adviser, argued as long as ten years ago for the importance of mutuality. He maintained that:

a sense of mutual obligations is central to why most people think of themselves as Socialists. It is the moral core of Socialism as personal credo, as opposed to the Socialism of scientific analysis and world-conquering movements. It is what carries the Left to the moral high ground. The dangers come from the fact that the Left still shies away from the implications of a strong ethos of individual responsibility[46]

More recently, the Left-leaning political commentator Peter Kellner wrote an essay subtitled: 'Forget Socialism. Dump Thatcherism. Try Mutualism'. Other than his insistence on addressing 'citizens' rather than 'individuals',[47] his description of what 'mutualism' implies has many similarities to a third-wave rights vision. It provides, he claimed:

a fresh framework within which to consider limits to personal freedom. It seeks to balance two mutual-respect objectives: the respect that governments owe individual citizens and the respect that citizens owe each other. Mutualism does not, however, go the whole libertarian hog . . . and steps in only when people cause actual harm. The mutualist approach is to test each proposed restriction on personal liberty against a clear principle: the gains to others must unambiguously outweigh the loss of freedom suffered by those whose actions are restricted[48]

None of these writers appeared to be the slightest bit aware of the relevance of modern human rights thinking to their proposals. Nor, apparently, was the Prime Minister, Tony Blair, when he argued in his 1999 Labour Party Conference speech for 'equality of worth' as one of the defining principles of the 'new politics', which should concentrate on values and goals rather than processes and structures.[49] A more apt description of the human rights approach it would be hard to find. But this connection was not made by any political commentator on a speech which attracted considerable attention. In this country, with no significant indigenous positive rights tradition (as opposed to a historic culture of unwritten liberties), the idea that human rights is about far more than just individual claims which can be made in court is almost entirely unappreciated anywhere.

In an attempt to shift this perception and explore the relevance of human rights thinking to some of the debates on a new approach to politics, I have delved into the legacy of Tom Paine and the virtual obliteration of his ideas by opponents of all political shades, from Burke to Bentham to Marx.[50] Two hundred years ago there would have been no problem in seeing how the idea of fundamental rights could inform a new progressive politics.

Nowadays this link is obscure to all but a tiny number in the UK. Few will be aware that themes like the duties owed by individuals to the community to which they belong, the link between rights and responsibilities and the appropriate balance between personal autonomy and the exigencies of the common good, have been tirelessly addressed by human rights thinkers for decades. In writing this book I wanted to put the spotlight on this neglected aspect of human rights thinking in order to correct some of the misconceptions of rights – and more particularly our new Bill of Rights – as charters for license.

This does not mean that the human rights approach that has developed over the last fifty years sits entirely comfortably with a communitarian or so-called 'third way' perspective. Quite the contrary. I have suggested some of the ways in which it challenges the relationship between rights and responsibilities promoted by some political thinkers close to New Labour as well as some government ministers.[51] But it is also entirely false to see the adoption of the Human Rights Act as an unexplained aberration – a moment of madness, even – by an otherwise anti-libertarian government. If this book has one main aim it is to suggest that the values of community and mutuality have now combined with liberty to form the defining features of human rights thinking.

The distinguished American professor of philosophy Alan Gerwith describes human rights as 'ethical individualism' with 'a strong communitarian specification' and 'some important ties to Socialism'.[52] It is worth quoting from him at some length:

what the principle of human rights justifies is . . . a whole system of equal and mutually supportive rights and duties. This system comprises a common good in the distributive sense that goods are common to . . . each of the individual members of the community; but it adds the requirement of mutuality whereby persons ... must help others to obtain these goods when they cannot obtain them by their own efforts[53]

Having defined the link between the human rights and communitarian visions, he seeks to tie these to the historic pursuits of the Left in ways which speak directly to the current debates about the direction of a new progressive politics in the UK:

The communitarianism thus developed has some important ties to Socialism. Socialism has been defined in many different ways: sometimes upholding equality above all, sometimes as advocating public ownership of the main means of production, sometimes as central planning of the economy, sometimes as class or party dictatorship ... But many of the persons who called themselves Socialists had in mind a more graphic, more distinct, and less technical conception. Above all, they were saddened, indeed revolted, by the spectacle of immense human physical suffering and economic deprivation ... and they believed it was the duty of the state to protect people from it.[54]

For Gerwith, then, the modern human rights project – what he calls 'the community of rights' – is to some degree an attempted synthesis between liberalism, communitarianism and Socialism. To substantiate this perspective, Gerwith naturally includes social and economic rights in his characterization of human rights, giving them equal weight to civil and political rights as intended by the drafters of the UDHR.

This inclusion of social and economic rights is crucial if the relevance of the human rights approach to current political debate is to become clear. While many bills of rights, our own, exclude social and economic rights on the grounds that they are not enforceable through the courts,[55] there are a number of such rights which are already effectively justiciable,[56] like rights to education,[57] housing,[58] and a whole range of social rights which emanate from the European Union.[59] International human rights treaties on social, economic and cultural rights anyway tend to be drafted largely in aspirational terms, although they are still subject to regular monitoring by the relevant supervisory committees.[60]

But the central point is that the combined values that have driven human rights thinking since the Second World War – liberty, justice, dignity, equality, community and now mutuality – inevitably lead to a concern with social and economic rights whatever means of enforcement is adopted.[61] The quest to build a 'decent society' – or 'decent world' – whose furtherance is the object of all post-war human rights thinking, is increasingly influenced by concerns like the right to development or to a healthy environment.[62] This in turn leads straight back to the terrain of those seeking a new progressive politics, distinct from the Left and Right of old.

Objections to a rights-based politics

There have, however, been a number of stumbling blocks to appreciating the relevance of human rights thinking to this search. There have been three broad historic critiques of human rights discourse which continue to haunt cross-cultural dialogues on the future direction of human rights. I have barely addressed these so far but they are worth turning to here, briefly.

The absence of collective rights

The first accusation is that there is an apparent lack of any appreciation of the group or collective, as opposed to the isolated individual, in international human rights law.[63] This criticism is partly a throwback to an Enlightenment-driven conception of rights and reflects a misunderstanding of how the idea of human rights has evolved post-war. Despite the value given to individual liberty, the collective is not neglected in modern human rights thinking, although its status is frequently misunderstood.[64]

It is true that virtually every entitlement in international human rights treaties is expressed as an individual right.[65] But there are at least three explicit ways in which recognition is given to groups or collectives in post-war human rights law. First, some rights can be meaningfully exercised only by individuals acting in conjunction with others, such as rights to assembly, protest, association, trade union membership or to marry and found a family.

Second, there are rights, or aspects of rights, which protect particular groups of people, even if they can be claimed only by the individuals who comprise such groups; for example, minorities, children, defendants in criminal trials or prisoners. When individuals from specific communities win cases, if this results in a change to the law or policy then all members of the group are set to benefit. The decriminalization of homosexuality in Northern Ireland, for example, took place following a successful case against the UK government by an individual gay man.[66]

Third, under the ECHR groups of individuals, NGOs and even companies (but not public bodies) can take cases to the European Court of Human Rights. They must, however, individually qualify as victims in the sense that a violation of the ECHR must have affected them in some way. This feature of the European Convention has been replicated in the Human Rights Act.[67] This means that bodies like churches, pressure groups, trade unions or corporations can claim rights under the new Bill of Rights if they can establish victim-status.

There is a caveat here. This is a provision which is just as likely to lead to powerful companies claiming rights as oppressed groups. It highlights the complexities of the argument that collective rights are to be preferred over individual ones as the best means of protecting the most vulnerable people.[68]

This underlines the main dilemma in giving collective rights equal status to individual rights. Not only can it be a route to powerful groups claiming rights at the expense of less powerful ones, but it can also be a smoke-screen behind which the strongest group members abuse weaker members of the same group. If the right to a family life, for example, were to be claimed by the family as a whole rather than the individuals who comprise it, then what is to prevent its notional head – traditionally the father – from using this right to impose his will on other members? This is the line of argument which takes us back to the historical grounds for opposing the enhanced autonomy of women or children whose oppression has provided one of the motors for evolving international human rights standards in recent decades.

Collective rights, in other words, if not carefully applied, can be a means by which the most powerful individuals in a group – whether a trade union, a company, a family or a nation – control the rest. For in the final analysis collectivities cannot claim rights in reality, they are always represented by living people. As Michael Freeman has argued in an article otherwise sympathetic to the idea of collective rights:

Collective identities can be manipulated and/or coercively imposed, and they can form the basis of unjust demands. Liberal individualism has often been characterized as egoistic and collectivism as altruistic. This is quite mistaken, for individualism can emphasize responsibility as well as rights and collectivism can be ruthlessly selfish.[69]

It is because history has taught us, moreover, that conferring rights on collectivities can ultimately delegitimize claims to individual rights – not least in the former Soviet Union – that the main bearers of rights in international human rights law remain individual people. But, as already pointed out in another context, this is far from saying that individualism is its creed. At the heart of post-war human rights thinking is a collectivist vision. If there was one issue that was reinforced for me in writing this book it was the strength of this vision.

The caricature of a 'rights culture' as one which requires the state to take an ethically neutral stance while upholding the autonomy of individuals, so beloved of certain communitarian commentators, could not be further from reality.[70] The worldview generated by the UDHR, and all that has flowed from it, is one in which individuals are essentially social beings who owe obligations not only to other individuals but also to the community to which they belong and from which the 'development' of their 'personality' derives.[71]

Private abuses of rights

A second major critique of the human rights approach, which continues to inform international debate, is its perceived irrelevance to abuse of power by any other body than the state. With globalization and privatization growing features of modern life, and the areas where governments have direct control continuing to shrink, an approach which is apparently predicated on protecting individuals from the state can appear increasingly outdated.[72]

Probably the major champions of this criticism in recent years have been women's NGOs and feminist writers. Their concern has been that human rights have traditionally spoken to the male domain of public life. At its most extreme, the claim is made that rights discourse can even enhance the position that men should be free to do what they wish in their private lives, which by implication includes raping their wives and beating their children.[73]

If there was undoubtedly merit in this criticism in the past its appropriateness is now receding. As this book has illustrated, the formerly rigid public/private divide in human rights thinking is on the wane. The European Court of Human Rights, for example, has condemned the lack of effective sanctions in the UK against parents or carers who severely beat their children.[74] It has also backed the English courts' removal of the common law protection against prosecution for rape in marriage, stating that:

the abandonment of the unacceptable idea of a husband being immune against prosecution for rape of his wife was in conformity not only with a civilized concept of marriage but . . . with the fundamental objectives of the Convention, the very essence of which is respect for human dignity and human freedoms[75]

There are other examples. After years of protest that the crime of rape was given insufficient weight under international humanitarian law governing war and genocide, the Statute of the Yugoslav Tribunal, established in the wake of atrocities committed in the Balkans conflicts of the early 1990s, addressed this concern. In response to evidence that tens of thousands of Muslim women had been systematically raped as part of a wartime strategy, Article 5 of the Statute included rape among the list of acts defined as 'crimes against humanity'.[76]

This shift in thinking, it should be acknowledged, is partly because of the increasing engagement of women's groups around the world in debates on human rights. This, in turn, is characteristic of the new third wave of rights with its greater emphasis on participation and its openness to NGOs – what Professor Kevin Boyle calls 'the third force in international human rights politics after states and international agencies'.[77]

As part of this increased openness, the 1995 Beijing World Conference on Women entered one of the most difficult terrains of human rights thinking with debates on which practices should be protected as private and immune from state interference or as the domain of particular cultures, and which should be open to challenge under international human rights law.[78] The statement which came out of the conference tried to achieve a balance between respect for different cultures and religions and eradication of practices which cause unequivocal harm to women, like female genital mutilation and institutional discrimination. A cursory reading of the document, however, suggests that some of the more difficult tensions caused by such an attempted reconciliation remained unresolved.[79]

Universalism and the danger of a human rights dogma

This last example highlights a third, more general, problem that threatens to undermine the current potency of the human rights message as an international force and as a major factor in a new progressive politics. It is the assertion that fundamental human rights are universal and by implication that there is one single ethical framework which we must all abide by. Behind this claim lies both the allure and potential nemesis of the idea of human rights.

It is this bid for universal recognition which gives human rights discourse its potency. The idea is as giddy a proposition in the modern world as was the cry of the deists thousands of years ago that there was only one god. There is now no government on earth which feels able to ignore this claim to universality, even if it is to deny it.

But within this achievement lies a familiar trap. If the human rights message were, through its own success, to metamorphose from an evolving framework of values into a fully fledged ideology which closes down debate rather than opens it, then the human rights project is likely to go the way of the other failed utopias of the last century.

Of course, much of the opposition to the idea of universal human rights is entirely cynical. It comes from political leaders in countries like Singapore and Malaysia who have condemned 'Western-style' human rights as a threat to economic development and social harmony in the East. A senior adviser to the Malaysian government, Tun Daim Zainuddin, for example, has argued that the Universal Declaration of Human Rights needs to be made 'relevant for present times and . . . acceptable to all nations and peoples'.[80]

While this stance is partly a smoke-screen for governments to continue to oppress their people without being held to account by the international community, the fact is that it is not without wider resonance. Human rights activists around the world demand adherence to the values in the UDHR while also pleading that 'the struggle to promote human rights is more likely to be won if it is fought in ways that speak to local cultural traditions'.[81]

Critics of this appeal argue that the danger is that 'universalism' will be 'conceived very thinly, allowing cultures considerable space in which to interpret rights in their own ways'.[82] In response the political theorist Professor Bhikhu Parekh, for example, argues for a 'non-ethnocentric universalism' which should 'arise out of an open and uncoerced cross-cultural dialogue' involving both large, international gatherings and smaller groups of informed people, perhaps encouraging 'regional arrangements for defining and enforcing universal values'.[83] What Parekh appears to be trying to find is a path between a relativism which offers no means of judging other societies' or cultures' practices and an absolutism where human rights appear to be yet another means of arguing for the superiority of Western liberal values over other beliefs.

My voyage of discovery in writing this book, however, has suggested to me the following: that this cross-cultural dialogue has already begun and is one of the hallmarks of what I call the third wave of rights;[84] that it is anyway not possible to simply equate second-wave human rights values as they have evolved since the Second World War with the classical Western liberal thought that informed the first wave of rights; that the Universal Declaration of Human Rights, although the endeavour of a select, disproportionately Western élite, was from the outset influenced by the values of most of the world's major religions as well as liberal, Socialist, communitarian and Confucian thought;[85] and that in reality human rights values are already expressed through the prism of different cultural norms.

Take the right to free expression. This is a liberty of almost mythic status in the US. It is possibly the defining value of American democracy. In Europe, however, particularly in those countries that were occupied by the Nazis little more than half a century ago, free speech has been used to undermine democracy as well as promote it. Hence the easy acceptance of the idea, as expressed in the ECHR, that this right can be limited to curb the activities of those, like fascists, who would rob all others of free speech. Africa presents yet a third cultural manifestation of the same right. There, free expression is often portrayed by human rights activists as part and parcel of the right to development.

The Salman Rushdie affair, which erupted in 1990 after the author of *The Satanic Verses* was shockingly sentenced to death by an Iranian fatwa for writing a book which deeply offended many Muslims, brought this debate about universalism and free speech to these shores. Two polarized positions quickly sprang up, barely able to hear each other. One was about liberty, the other about dignity. On the one hand, the supporters of free expression could not accept that taking offence at the views of an author – however deeply this offence was felt by virtually an entire people – should in any circumstances justify banning books. On the other hand, no amount of repeating the value of free speech in a democracy could pacify those who felt demeaned and devalued by *The Satanic Verses* in a society which many Muslims consider does not appreciate their worth anyway.[86]

This clash of views could not be wished away by simply claiming that all human rights are universal. But a lesson can be learnt from the way this incident was played out that suggests which direction human rights is likely to take in the emerging, participative third wave of rights.

Rushdie's life – threatened only because he had expressed offensive views – is obviously inviolable. Like the right to be free from torture or slavery, there are some rights under international law which are absolute in that their meaning is virtually incontestable and they can almost never be limited to meet some competing claim.[87] But the line between speech which is simply offensive yet must always be protected and which is degrading and potentially threatening to a whole group in an unequal society will always be open to debate. No amount of proclamations of universal or inalienable rights can change this. The pertinent question is what this tells us about the capacity for human rights values to flourish and grow as we enter a new era in the UK with our first modern Bill of Rights.

Democratization of rights

Incidents like the Rushdie affair suggest that human rights values as they have evolved over the last two hundred years are scarcely understood in the UK. Some of us know about common law liberties, about civil liberties, about a culture of freedom, but, if we are to be honest, we understand little about human rights in their modern incarnation.

Our perception of this phenomenon is generally stuck in an eighteenth-century mould. Our notion of bills of rights is largely drawn from American movies. We rarely distinguish between rights and liberties in popular conversation. We are almost oblivious to the degree to which latter-day human rights thinking attempts to synthesize values like liberty, justice, equality, community, dignity and mutuality. In addition, many of us freeze when we hear references to the Human Rights Act or the European Convention on Human Rights. This is the domain of lawyers and academics. To most people, its relevance to ordinary life, if any, is far from clear.

If, with our new Bill of Rights, the idea of human rights is to prosper in the years ahead, then clearly its grip on the popular imagination will need stronger roots than international law under-stood by a tiny élite. It will not be enough to say that a trial is unfair or a deportation wrong simply because the European Court of Human Rights says so. If a broader spectrum of people are to see the value in such rulings, then the basic philosophy underpinning human rights values will need to be as widely understood and debated as democratic principles now are in the UK.

This is not in any way to underplay the significance of human rights law and enforcement mechanisms in establishing the position that human rights currently occupies in the world. If human rights values were not translatable into enforceable laws then they would be no more than pipe-dreams. Jurists around the world have made an enormous contribution in fleshing out the broad statements in rights treaties and declarations. They have provided a resounding answer to Bentham's critique of rights that they are all vacuous unless defined in specific pieces of legislation. Judges and lawyers have demonstrated that rights can be more than 'nonsense upon stilts'.[88] And if rights are to go on being more than paper shields then the courts – domestic and international – must be given the power and authority to develop this project. The Human Rights Act allows British lawyers to fully engage in this process for the first time.

But on its own this can never be enough to create or sustain an environment in which human rights values flourish. And in so far as the law and legal culture contribute to mystifying the basic principles and values which are the foundations of human rights, then their role can be counter-productive. It is not possible in a democracy to attempt to create a human rights culture without involving the people in its formation. And it is simply not sustainable to pin so much on the idea of human rights, both domestically and internationally, without widespread participation in developing its meaning and scope.

What is the foundation of human rights?

Fundamental to the project of widening the appeal of human rights is the question of what underpins it. If compliance with human rights standards needs a stronger justification than obedience to the law what should this be? Broadly speaking, we have moved in two hundred years from the quasi-religious notion of 'natural rights' to concepts like dignity and our common humanity as the generally accepted foundations of fundamental rights.

But my journey in writing this book revealed a more complex debate emerging about what, if anything, can be cited to explain the prominent position given to the idea of human rights at the dawn of the twenty-first century. The concept of human dignity is widely recognized to have replaced god or nature as the main justification for claiming human rights since the Second World War. But this begs the question, why should this value be given such overriding significance in the first place?

Gaining currency is the view that it is a mistake to answer the question 'Where do rights come from?' within a traditional rights perspective. A number of communitarians claim that the idea of rights flows from the concept of duties.[89] As we have seen, they maintain that unless rights derive from responsibilities, rather than the other way round, the idea of rights fast degenerates into a one-way ticket to license. What is never explained adequately is who or what has the authority to determine the shape of these duties from which rights apparently flow? It is hard to see how this approach does not ultimately take us back in the direction of unquestioning obedience to god, family and the state which led to demands for inalienable rights in the first place.[90]

For some political theorists the foundation of rights is not duty but our need for security, survival and co-operation as a species. For others they stem from a deeper, more essentially human, need to assuage our moral conscience. So-called 'Postmodernists' like Richard Rorty, on the other hand, are opposed to any such attempts to define an objective foundation of human rights. He claims that human rights cultures are made, not given. In other words, that the capacity to empathize with others, to see that what you have in common is greater than that which separates you from your fellow human beings, is the driving force behind the idea of human rights.[91] In so far as this approach puts human action at its centre, it chimes with the thrust of this book. For, in the final analysis, the idea of human rights stems from the lessons human beings have learnt to make life liveable.

If human rights values are to influence the century ahead, with the aim of making it less bloody than the one that has just passed, then debates like these will have to come down from the bookshelf and lecture podium. If human rights defenders are not to be as irrelevant by the end of the twenty-first century as Christian missionaries became by the end of the twentieth, they are going to have to engage more fully with the rest of the population on these questions, and in terms which relate to people's lives.[92]

This is, after all, a uniquely propitious time to be having such debates, not just in the UK but in the wider world. After a century of failed utopias there is an openness to fresh ideas most of us have not seen in our lifetime. The tightly drawn ideological battles which drowned out most of the subtleties of the human rights project since its inception no longer dominate the world. Human rights arguments seem fresh and appealing in many quarters where once they sounded weak and stale.

There *is*, moreover, a way in which the universality of human rights is gradually being realized. It is through a developing conversation which is taking place on a global scale and is growing in volume and scope. Where once virtually every major national or international event was presented within the terms of a debate which pitted capital against labour, or Socialism against free enterprise, an additional discourse is taking hold.[93] Through this global conversation the values and language of human rights are becoming familiar to more and more people, who judge the merits or otherwise of political or economic decisions increasingly in human rights terms.

But the lessons of the past must be learnt. Any worldview or set of values which is presented as self-evident is ultimately doomed to failure. The case for human rights will always need to be made and remade; this is a struggle which can never be won. It is just not credible, in a world where globalization too often seems like a modernized version of old-fashioned cultural imperialism, that the claim that human rights are universal will be accepted without question. It is not enough for human rights defenders, however sincere, to claim that human rights values are absolute for them to become so. These claims will forever be contested.

It is only by keeping the quest for human rights sufficiently attuned to *both* the anguished cries *and* cultural norms of those who need rights most that the aspiration for universal acceptance can hope to be sustained long term. This is the legacy that the third wave of rights inherits, two hundred years after the first wave took the world by storm.

Text of the Human Rights Act 1998

Section 1(3) SCHEDULE 1
THE ARTICLES

PART I
THE CONVENTION

RIGHTS AND FREEDOMS

Article 2
Right to life

1. Everyone's right to life shall be protected by law. No one shall be deprived of his life intentionally save in the execution of a sentence of a court following his conviction of a crime for which this penalty is provided by law.

2. Deprivation of life shall not be regarded as inflicted in contravention of this Article when it results from the use of force which is no more than absolutely necessary:

(a) in defence of any person from unlawful violence;

(b) in order to effect a lawful arrest or to prevent the escape of a person lawfully detained;

(c) in action lawfully taken for the purpose of quelling a riot or insurrection.

Article 3
Prohibition of torture

No one shall be subjected to torture or to inhuman or degrading treatment or punishment.

Article 4
Prohibition of slavery and forced labour

1. No one shall be held in slavery or servitude.

2. No one shall be required to perform forced or compulsory labour.

3. For the purpose of this Article the term 'forced or compulsory labour' shall not include:

(a) any work required to be done in the ordinary course of detention imposed according to the provisions of Article 5 of this Convention or during conditional release from such detention;

(b) any service of a military character or, in case of conscientious objectors in countries where they are recognised, service exacted instead of compulsory military service;

(c) any service exacted in case of an emergency or calamity threatening the life or well-being of the community;

(d) any work or service which forms part of normal civic obligations.

Article 5
Right to liberty and security

1. Everyone has the right to liberty and security of person. No one shall be deprived of his liberty save in the following cases and in accordance with a procedure prescribed by law:

(a) the lawful detention of a person after conviction by a competent court;

(b) the lawful arrest or detention of a person for non-compliance with the lawful order of a court or in order to secure the fulfilment of any obligation prescribed by law;

(c)   the lawful arrest or detention of a person effected for the purpose of bringing him before the competent legal authority on reasonable suspicion of having committed an offence or when it is reasonably considered necessary to prevent his committing an offence or fleeing after having done so;

(d)   the detention of a minor by lawful order for the purpose of educational supervision or his lawful detention for the purpose of bringing him before the competent legal authority;

(e)   the lawful detention of persons for the prevention of the spreading of infectious diseases, of persons of unsound mind, alcoholics or drug addicts or vagrants;

(f)   the lawful arrest or detention of a person to prevent his effecting an unauthorised entry into the country or of a person against whom action is being taken with a view to deportation or extradition.

2.   Everyone who is arrested shall be informed promptly, in a language which he understands, of the reasons for his arrest and of any charge against him.

3.   Everyone arrested or detained in accordance with the provisions of paragraph 1(c) of this Article shall be brought promptly before a judge or other officer authorised by law to exercise judicial power and shall be entitled to trial within a reasonable time or to release pending trial. Release may be conditioned by guarantees to appear for trial.

4.   Everyone who is deprived of his liberty by arrest or detention shall be entitled to take proceedings by which the lawfulness of his detention shall be decided speedily by a court and his release ordered if the detention is not lawful.

5.   Everyone who has been the victim of arrest or detention in contravention of the provisions of this Article shall have an enforceable right to compensation.

Article 6
Right to a fair trial

1. In the determination of his civil rights and obligations or of any criminal charge against him, everyone is entitled to a fair and public hearing within a reasonable time by an independent and impartial tribunal established by law. Judgment shall be pronounced publicly but the press and public may be excluded from all or part of the trial in the interest of morals, public order or national security in a democratic society, where the interests of juveniles or the protection of the private life of the parties so require, or to the extent strictly necessary in the opinion of the court in special circumstances where publicity would prejudice the interests of justice.

2. Everyone charged with a criminal offence shall be presumed innocent until proved guilty according to law.

3. Everyone charged with a criminal offence has the following minimum rights:

(a) to be informed promptly, in a language which he understands and in detail, of the nature and cause of the accusation against him;

(b) to have adequate time and facilities for the preparation of his defence;

(c) to defend himself in person or through legal assistance of his own choosing or, if he has not sufficient means to pay for legal assistance, to be given it free when the interests of justice so require;

(d) to examine or have examined witnesses against him and to obtain the attendance and examination of witnesses on his behalf under the same conditions as witnesses against him;

(e) to have the free assistance of an interpreter if he cannot understand or speak the language used in court.

Article 7
No punishment without law

1. No one shall be held guilty of any criminal offence on account of any act or omission which did not constitute a criminal offence under national or international law at the time when it was committed. Nor shall a heavier penalty be imposed than the one that was applicable at the time the criminal offence was committed.

2. This Article shall not prejudice the trial and punishment of any person for any act or omission which, at the time when it was committed, was criminal according to the general principles of law recognised by civilised nations.

Article 8
Right to respect for private and family life

1. Everyone has the right to respect for his private and family life, his home and his correspondence.

2. There shall be no interference by a public authority with the exercise of this right except such as is in accordance with the law and is necessary in a democratic society in the interests of national security, public safety or the economic well being of the country, for the prevention of disorder or crime, for the protection of health or morals, or for the protection of the rights and freedoms of others.

Article 9
Freedom of thought, conscience and religion

1. Everyone has the right to freedom of thought, conscience and religion; this right includes freedom to change his religion or belief and freedom, either alone or in community with others and in public or private, to manifest his religion or belief, in worship, teaching, practice and observance.

2. Freedom to manifest one's religion or beliefs shall be subject only to such limitations as are prescribed by law and are necessary

in a democratic society in the interests of public safety, for the protection of public order, health or morals, or for the protection of the rights and freedoms of others.

Article 10
Freedom of expression

1.   Everyone has the right to freedom of expression. This right shall include freedom to hold opinions and to receive and impart information and ideas without interference by public authority and regardless of frontiers. This Article shall not prevent States from requiring the licensing of broadcasting, television or cinema enterprises.

2.   The exercise of these freedoms, since it carries with it duties and responsibilities, may be subject to such formalities, conditions, restrictions or penalties as are prescribed by law and are necessary in a democratic society, in the interests of national security, territorial integrity or public safety, for the prevention of disorder or crime, for the protection of health or morals, for the protection of the reputation or rights of others, for preventing the disclosure of information received in confidence, or for maintaining the authority and impartiality of the judiciary.

Article 11
Freedom of assembly and association

1.   Everyone has the right to freedom of peaceful assembly and to freedom of association with others, including the right to form and to join trade unions for the protection of his interests.

2.   No restrictions shall be placed on the exercise of these rights other than such as are prescribed by law and are necessary in a democratic society in the interests of national security or public safety, for the prevention of disorder or crime, for the protection of health or morals or for the protection of the rights and freedoms of others. This Article shall not prevent the imposition of lawful restrictions on the exercise of these rights by members of the armed forces, of the police or of the administration of the State.

Article 12
Right to marry

Men and women of marriageable age have the right to marry and to found a family, according to the national laws governing the exercise of this right.

Article 14
Prohibition of discrimination

The enjoyment of the rights and freedoms set forth in this Convention shall be secured without discrimination on any ground such as sex, race, colour, language, religion, political or other opinion, national or social origin, association with a national minority, property, birth or other status.

Article 16
Restrictions on political activity of aliens

Nothing in Articles 10, 11 and 14 shall be regarded as preventing the High Contracting Parties from imposing restrictions on the political activity of aliens.

Article 17
Prohibition of abuse of rights

Nothing in this Convention may be interpreted as implying for any State, group or person any right to engage in any activity or perform any act aimed at the destruction of any of the rights and freedoms set forth herein or at their limitation to a greater extent than is provided for in the Convention.

Article 18
Limitation on use of restrictions on rights

The restrictions permitted under this Convention to the said rights and freedoms shall not be applied for any purpose other than those for which they have been prescribed.

PART II
THE FIRST PROTOCOL

Article 1
Protection of property

Every natural or legal person is entitled to the peaceful enjoyment of his possessions. No one shall be deprived of his possessions except in the public interest and subject to the conditions provided for by law and by the general principles of international law.

The preceding provisions shall not, however, in any way impair the right of a State to enforce such laws as it deems necessary to control the use of property in accordance with the general interest or to secure the payment of taxes or other contributions or penalties.

Article 2
Right to education

No person shall be denied the right to education. In the exercise of any functions which it assumes in relation to education and to teaching, the State shall respect the right of parents to ensure such education and teaching in conformity with their own religious and philosophical convictions.

Article 3
Right to free elections

The High Contracting Parties undertake to hold free elections at reasonable intervals by secret ballot, under conditions which will ensure the free expression of the opinion of the people in the choice of the legislature.

PART III
THE SIXTH PROTOCOL

Article 1
Abolition of the death penalty

The death penalty shall be abolished. No one shall be condemned to such penalty or executed.

Article 2
Death penalty in time of war

A State may make provision in its law for the death penalty in respect of acts committed in time of war or of imminent threat of war; such penalty shall be applied only in the instances laid down in the law and in accordance with its provisions. The State shall communicate to the Secretary General of the Council of Europe the relevant provisions of that law.

Universal Declaration of Human Rights

PREAMBLE

Whereas recognition of the inherent dignity and of the equal and inalienable rights of all members of the human family is the foundation of freedom, justice and peace in the world,

Whereas disregard and contempt for human rights have resulted in barbarous acts which have outraged the conscience of mankind, and the advent of a world in which human beings shall enjoy freedom of speech and belief and freedom from fear and want has been proclaimed as the highest aspiration of the common people,

Whereas it is essential, if man is not to be compelled to have recourse, as a last resort, to rebellion against tyranny and oppression, that human rights should be protected by the rule of law,

Whereas it is essential to promote the development of friendly relations between nations,

Whereas the peoples of the United Nations have in the Charter reaffirmed their faith in fundamental human rights, in the dignity and worth of the human person and in the equal rights of men and women and have determined to promote social progress and better standards of life in larger freedom,

Whereas Member States have pledged themselves to achieve, in cooperation with the United Nations, the promotion of universal respect for and observance of human rights and fundamental freedoms,

Whereas a common understanding of these rights and freedoms is of the greatest importance for the full realization of this pledge,

Now, therefore The General Assembly proclaims This Universal Declaration of Human Rights as a common standard of achievement for all peoples and all nations, to the end that every individual and every organ of society, keeping this Declaration constantly in mind, shall strive by teaching and education to promote respect for these rights and freedoms and by progressive measures, national and international, to secure their universal and effective recognition and observance, both among the peoples of Member States themselves and among the peoples of territories under their jurisdiction.

ARTICLE 1.

All human beings are born free and equal in dignity and rights. They are endowed with reason and conscience and should act towards one another in a spirit of brotherhood.

ARTICLE 2.

Everyone is entitled to all the rights and freedoms set forth in this Declaration, without distinction of any kind, such as race, colour, sex, language, religion, political or other opinion, national or social origin, property, birth or other status. Furthermore, no distinction shall be made on the basis of the political, jurisdictional or international status of the country or territory to which a person belongs, whether it be independent, trust, non-self-governing or under any other limitation of sovereignty.

ARTICLE 3.

Everyone has the right to life, liberty and security of person.

ARTICLE 4.

No one shall be held in slavery or servitude; slavery and the slave trade shall be prohibited in all their forms.

ARTICLE 5.

No one shall be subjected to torture or to cruel, inhuman or degrading treatment or punishment.

ARTICLE 6.

Everyone has the right to recognition everywhere as a person before the law.

ARTICLE 7.

All are equal before the law and are entitled without any discrimination to equal protection of the law. All are entitled to equal protection against any discrimination in violation of this Declaration and against any incitement to such discrimination.

ARTICLE 8.

Everyone has the right to an effective remedy by the competent national tribunals for acts violating the fundamental rights granted him by the constitution or by law.

ARTICLE 9.

No one shall be subjected to arbitrary arrest, detention or exile.

ARTICLE 10.

Everyone is entitled in full equality to a fair and public hearing by an independent and impartial tribunal, in the determination of his rights and obligations and of any criminal charge against him.

ARTICLE 11.

(1) Everyone charged with a penal offence has the right to be presumed innocent until proved guilty according to law in a public trial at which he has had all the guarantees necessary for his defence.

(2) No one shall be held guilty of any penal offence on account of any act or omission which did not constitute a penal offence, under national or international law, at the time when it was committed. Nor shall a heavier penalty be imposed than the one that was applicable at the time the penal offence was committed.

ARTICLE 12.

No one shall be subjected to arbitrary interference with his privacy, family, home or correspondence, nor to attacks upon his honour and reputation. Everyone has the right to the protection of the law against such interference or attacks.

ARTICLE 13.

(1) Everyone has the right to freedom of movement and residence within the borders of each state.

(2) Everyone has the right to leave any country, including his own, and to return to his country.

ARTICLE 14.

(1) Everyone has the right to seek and to enjoy in other countries asylum from persecution.

(2) This right may not be invoked in the case of prosecutions genuinely arising from non-political crimes or from acts contrary to the purposes and principles of the United Nations.

ARTICLE 15.

(1) Everyone has the right to a nationality.

(2) No one shall be arbitrarily deprived of his nationality nor denied the right to change his nationality.

ARTICLE 16.

(1) Men and women of full age, without any limitation due to race, nationality or religion, have the right to marry and to found a family. They are entitled to equal rights as to marriage, during marriage and at its dissolution.

(2) Marriage shall be entered into only with the free and full consent of the intending spouses.

(3) The family is the natural and fundamental group unit of society and is entitled to protection by society and the State.

ARTICLE 17.

(1) Everyone has the right to own property alone as well as in association with others.

(2) No one shall be arbitrarily deprived of his property.

ARTICLE 18.

Everyone has the right to freedom of thought, conscience and religion; this right includes freedom to change his religion or belief, and freedom, either alone or in community with others and in public or private, to manifest his religion or belief in teaching, practice, worship and observance.

ARTICLE 19.

Everyone has the right to freedom of opinion and expression; this right includes freedom to hold opinions without interference and to seek, receive and impart information and ideas through any media and regardless of frontiers.

ARTICLE 20.

(1) Everyone has the right to freedom of peaceful assembly and association.

(2) No one may be compelled to belong to an association.

ARTICLE 21.

(1) Everyone has the right to take part in the government of his country, directly or through freely chosen representatives.

(2) Everyone has the right of equal access to public service in his country.

(3) The will of the people shall be the basis of the authority of government; this will shall be expressed in periodic and genuine elections which shall be by universal and equal suffrage and shall be held by secret vote or by equivalent free voting procedures.

ARTICLE 22.

Everyone, as a member of society, has the right to social security and is entitled to realization, through national effort and international cooperation and in accordance with the organization and resources of each State, of the economic, social and cultural rights indispensable for his dignity and the free development of his personality.

ARTICLE 23.

(1) Everyone has the right to work, to free choice of employment, to just and favourable conditions of work and to protection against unemployment.

(2) Everyone, without any discrimination, has the right to equal pay for equal work.

(3) Everyone who works has the right to just and favourable remuneration ensuring for himself and his family an existence worthy of human

dignity, and supplemented, if necessary, by other means of social protection.

(4) Everyone has the right to form and to join trade unions for the protection of his interests.

ARTICLE 24.

Everyone has the right to rest and leisure, including reasonable limitation of working hours and periodic holidays with pay.

ARTICLE 25.

(1) Everyone has the right to a standard of living adequate for the health and well-being of himself and of his family, including food, clothing, housing and medical care and necessary social services, and the right to security in the event of unemployment, sickness, disability, widowhood, old age or other lack of livelihood in circumstances beyond his control.

(2) Motherhood and childhood are entitled to special care and assistance. All children, whether born in or out of wedlock, shall enjoy the same social protection.

ARTICLE 26.

(1) Everyone has the right to education. Education shall be free, at least in the elementary and fundamental stages. Elementary education shall be compulsory. Technical and professional education shall be made generally available and higher education shall be equally accessible to all on the basis of merit.

(2) Education shall be directed to the full development of the human personality and to the strengthening of respect for human rights and fundamental freedoms. It shall promote understanding, tolerance and friendship among all nations, racial or religious groups, and shall further the activities of the United Nations for the maintenance of peace.

(3) Parents have a prior right to choose the kind of education that shall be given to their children.

ARTICLE 27.

(1) Everyone has the right freely to participate in the cultural life of the community, to enjoy the arts and to share in scientific advancement and its benefits.

(2) Everyone has the right to the protection of the moral and material interests resulting from any scientific, literary or artistic production of which he is the author.

ARTICLE 28.

Everyone is entitled to a social and international order in which the rights and freedoms set forth in this Declaration can be fully realized.

ARTICLE 29.

(1) Everyone has duties to the community in which alone the free and full development of his personality is possible.

(2) In the exercise of his rights and freedoms, everyone shall be subject only to such limitations as are determined by law solely for the purpose of securing due recognition and respect for the rights and freedoms of others and of meeting the just requirements of morality, public order and the general welfare in a democratic society.

(3) These rights and freedoms may in no case be exercised contrary to the purposes and principles of the United Nations.

ARTICLE 30.

Nothing in this Declaration may be interpreted as implying for any State, group or person any right to engage in any activity or to perform any act aimed at the destruction of any of the rights and freedoms set forth herein.

Notes

INTRODUCTION Human Rights: An Idea Whose Time Has
Come

1. See Anthony Giddens, *The Third Way: The Renewal of Social Democracy* (Polity Press, 1998).
2. Education Act 1996, Section 351. See, for example, Dr Nicholas Tate, the then Chief Curriculum Adviser of the School Curriculum and Assessment Authority (now the Qualifications and Curriculum Authority), in a speech to an SCAA Conference on Education for Adult Life (January 1996).
3. For example, Neal Ascherson has expressed the view that after 1989 'the US version of human rights culture spread across the world' in his article 'The Truth on Trial', *Observer* (5 March 2000).
4. See Geoffrey Robertson, *Crimes Against Humanity: The Struggle for Global Justice* (Allen Lane/The Penguin Press, 1999), on current developments in international human rights.
5. Andrew Marr, 'Chilling Intimacy of the Killers', *Observer* (20 June 1999).
6. Paul Oestreicher, 'Military Victories are Not Always Moral', *Observer* (27 June 1999).
7. *R. v. Bow Street Metropolitan Stipendiary Magistrates ex p. Pinochet Ugarte (no. 3)* [1999], 2 WLR 827.
8. In particular the 1987 UN Convention against Torture and Other Cruel, Inhuman or Degrading Treatment or Punishment.
9. See Geoffrey Robertson who described extradition in the circumstances where a defendant is too 'senile' to instruct his lawyers as 'oppressive' in his article 'Taking Liberties', *Guardian* (18 January 2000). Whether this medical assessment of Pinochet proves to have been correct in the long term is another question.
10. Jack Straw, House of Commons *Hansard*, cols. 574 and 577 (2 March 2000).
11. One of the anomalies of international human rights law is that sitting heads

of state still enjoy immunity before the *national* courts of other countries.

12. These *ad hoc* UN tribunals set up to try perpetrators of alleged 'crimes against humanity' should eventually be replaced by a permanent International Criminal Court. A Statute to establish this Court was signed in Rome in 1988 by 120 states (with the US 1 of only 7 countries opposed). The Rome Statute will not come into effect until ratified by 60 states, which may take several years.

13. *Guardian* (2 February 2000).

14. The European Convention on Human Rights, enforced by the European Court of Human Rights in Strasbourg, was adopted by the member states of the Council of Europe, including the UK, in 1950 and came into force in 1953. See Chapter 1.

15. For example, the Shadow Home Secretary, Ann Widdecombe. She made comments to this effect in television interviews on 13 March 2000 after the Home Secretary, Jack Straw, announced that he would abide by the European Court of Human Rights' judgment on the sentencing procedures governing child murders in the case of Thompson and Venables, who were convicted of murdering the toddler James Bulger. See Chapter 6.

16. Marcel Berlins, 'The Radical Lawyers', *New Statesman* (5 March 1999).

17. Formerly known as the National Council for Civil Liberties, the organization relaunched itself as Liberty in January 1989, just before the current 'human rights phase' took off.

18. See Liz Parratt, 'Unfinished Business: Liberty's Campaign for a Bill of Rights', in A. Hegarty and S. Leonard (eds.), *Human Rights: An Agenda for the Twenty-First Century* (Cavendish, 1999), Chapter 16.

19. *Guardian* (24 June 1999).

20. See Chapter 1 for further clarification of this point.

21. House of Commons Press Release (18 May 1999).

22. At the time of writing the future of the Agreement is unclear, but the provisions on human rights and equalities stand.

23. See Northern Ireland Act 1998, Section 6 (2)(c).

24. Section 107.

25. Section 29.

26. That is, the Scottish courts can overturn Acts of the Scottish Parliament only. The difference between the Scottish and English courts on this derives from the principles of devolution. See Chapter 1.

27. Section 57 (2).

28. For example, Chris Brown, 'Universal Human Rights: A Critique', in Tim Dunne and Nicholas Wheeler (eds.), *Human Rights in Global Politics*

(Cambridge University Press, 1999), p. 115. See also Peter Cumper, 'Human Rights: History, Development and Classification', in Hegarty and Leonard (eds.), n. 18 above, pp. 6–9 for a critical analysis.

29. See Rabinder Singh, *Human Rights in the United Kingdom* (Hart, 1997), pp. 51–8 for a discussion on 'the myth of negative rights'.

30. Tom Paine, 'Ways and Means', *Rights of Man* [1791] (Penguin, 1984).

31. See, for example, Elizabeth Sarah, 'Reassessments of "First Wave" Feminism', *Women's Studies International Forum* 5, no. 6 (Pergamon Press, 1982).

32. For an explanation of how this applies both under international law and through the Human Rights Act see Chapters 1 and 6.

33. The best introduction to the subject is probably still Paul Sieghart's *The Lawful Rights of Mankind* (Oxford University Press, 1986). See also Henry Steiner and Philip Alston, *International Human Rights in Context: Law, Politics, Morals* (Clarendon Press, 1996).

34. The best of which is Keir Starmer's *European Human Rights Law, the Human Rights Act 1988 and the European Convention on Human Rights* (Legal Action Group, 1999). See also John Wadham and Helen Mountfield, *Blackstone's Guide to the Human Rights Act 1998* (Blackstone, 1999), and David Leckie and David Pickersgill, *The 1998 Human Rights Act Explained* (Stationery Office, 1999).

35. Which is another way of saying: that the Council of Europe, which begat the ECHR, is a separate body to the European Union (EU); that the European Court of Human Rights and the EU's European Court of Justice (ECJ) are unrelated; and that the ECHR is a descendant of the UN's Universal Declaration of Human Rights rather than a species of European Union law. Other than Article 119 concerning equality between men and women, there were, in fact, no human rights provisions included in the foundation treaties of the European Economic Community, as it was then called, but the ECJ has increasingly interpreted Community Law in conformity with the ECHR. For an analysis of further recent developments in that direction brought about by the 1997 Treaty of Amsterdam – which is beyond the scope of this book – see Philip Alston (ed.), *The EU and Human Rights* (Oxford University Press, 1999).

36. See Chapter 2, generally, for illustrations.

37. See, for example, David Selbourne, *The Principle of Duty* (Sinclair-Stevenson, 1994).

38. See some of these debates explained in, for example, Joanne Bauer and Daniel Bell (eds.), *The East Asian Challenge for Human Rights* (Cambridge University Press, 1999); Carrie Gustafson and Peter Juviler (eds.), *Religion and Human Rights, Competing Claims?* (M. E. Sharp, 1999); Eva Brems,

'Enemies or Allies? Feminism and Cultural Relativism as Dissident Voices in Human Rights Discourse', *Human Rights Quarterly* 19 (1997), pp. 136–64.

39. Leonard Hand, Speech, New York City (21 May 1944).

40. See Francesca Klug, 'A Bill of Rights as Secular Ethics?', in Richard Gordon and Richard Wilmot-Smith (eds.), *Human Rights in the United Kingdom* (Oxford University Press, 1996), pp. 37–56.

41. See Robertson, n. 4 above.

42. This phrase will be clarified further in Chapter 5 but it is not meant to imply that human rights are any less relevant to those who have a particular religious faith than to those who do not.

CHAPTER 1   The Quiet Revolution: The UK's New Bill of Rights

1. As we have already seen, under the devolution legislation the Scottish Parliament and executive and the Welsh Assembly are already required to act compatibly with ECHR rights. The same duty applies to the Northern Ireland Assembly. See Introduction and Chapter 6.

2. For the extent to which the ECHR itself imposes a duty on the state to provide free legal assistance see Starmer, Introduction, n. 34, p. 205.

3. See Appendix II.

4. The Council of Europe is completely separate from the European Union, although the two are frequently confused. The European Economic Community, as it was called then, came into existence in 1958 and is currently composed of only fifteen member states, all in Western Europe. The UK did not become a member of the EU until 1973.

5. The European Court of Human Rights, based in Strasbourg, was set up by the Council of Europe to enforce the European Convention on Human Rights. In the past individuals were required to petition the European Commission on Human Rights, also based in Strasbourg, which could refer cases to the Court, but the Commission has recently been abolished, providing direct access to the Court. The new procedures were set out in Protocol 11 to the ECHR, which came into force in November 1998.

6. These figures are until the end of 1999.

7. The Human Rights Act incorporates only the substantive rights in the ECHR, that is: Articles 2–12, 14–18 and Protocols 1 and 6. Two substantive Articles, 1 and 3, are excluded along with Protocols 4 and 7, which have not been ratified by the UK. Chapter 6 explains the provisions of the Act in greater detail and Appendix I contains all the rights in the ECHR which are included in the Act.

8. *Reynolds* v. *Times Newspapers Ltd* [1999], 3 WLR 1030.

9. Keith Ewing, 'The Human Rights Act and Parliamentary Democracy', *Modern Law Review* 62 (1999), p. 86. See also Professor Conor Gearty, 'The Human Rights Act 1998 and the Role of the Strasbourg Organs: Some Preliminary Reflections', in Gavin W. Anderson (ed.), *Rights and Democracy in Canada and the UK* (Blackstone, 1999).

10. Jack Straw, Speech at IPPR Criminal Justice Forum Launch, Design Centre, Covent Garden (13 January 2000).

11. See Chapter 3. This first Bill of Rights was apparently introduced in 1688 and approved in 1689. Hence it is variously referred to as the 1688 and 1689 Bill of Rights in different texts.

12. The application of the Bill of Rights to individual states took place through an expansive interpretation of the XIVth Amendment, which was originally passed in 1868, in the wake of the Civil War. See Charles R. Epp, *The Rights Revolution: Lawyers, Activists and Supreme Courts in Comparative Perspective* (University of Chicago Press, 1998), pp. 26–43.

13. *Brown* v. *Board of Education* (1954), 347 US 483.

14. The Inter-American Commission on Human Rights, a regional human rights supervisory body, concluded in 1987 that the US Government violated Article 1, the right to life, of the Organization of American States' 1948 American Declaration of the Rights and Duties of Man by executing two men who were juveniles at the time of their crimes. Resolution 3/87; Case 9647.

15. The VIIIth Amendment. In 1972, however, the Supreme Court found that unlimited discretion on the part of the courts led to arbitrary use of the death penalty in violation of the VIIIth Amendment, leading to the effective suspension of capital punishment for four years. *Furman* v. *Georgia* (1972), 408 US 238.

16. The XIVth Amendment requires that 'No State shall ... deny to any person within its jurisdiction the equal protection of the laws.'

17. *McCleskey* v. *Kemp* (1987), 107 S.Ct at 1781.

18. For a general overview from a legal perspective see Philip Alston, *Promoting Human Rights through Bills of Rights: Comparative Perspectives* (Oxford University Press, 1999).

19. See, for example, Constitution Unit, *The Impact of the Human Rights Act: Lessons from Canada and New Zealand* (University College London, 1999).

20. The Charter of Rights was introduced as part of the 'repatriation' of the Constitution to Canada from the UK.

21. See Robert J. Sharpe, 'The Judiciary: A Canadian Perspective', in Alston, n. 18 above, p. 451.

22. Constitution of the Republic of South Africa, 1996.

23. See Chapter 6 for a discussion of the campaign that preceded the introduction of the Human Rights Act.

24. *The New York Times* (3 October 1999).

25. See Chapter 2.

26. See Sarah Spencer and Ian Bynoe, *A Human Rights Commission: The Options for Britain and Northern Ireland* (IPPR, 1998).

27. See, for example, a statement to this effect by Mike O'Brien, Home Office minister, House of Commons *Hansard*, vol. 314, col. 1087 (24 June 1998).

28. See Introduction. See also *Human Rights in Scotland* (Scottish Office, 1998).

29. 'Human Rights Task Force Terms of Reference', HRTF (99) 4, unpublished Home Office paper (1999).

30. *Conventional Behaviour: Questions about the Human Rights Act, an Introduction for Public Authorities* (Home Office, 1999).

31. Linda Colley, 'Blueprint for Britain', *Observer* (12 December 1999).

32. Obviously the Welsh, Scottish and (both traditions of) Irish versions of history would dispute many parts of this narrative.

33. See Introduction, n. 15.

34. Ronald Dworkin, 'The Moral Reading of the Constitution', *New York Review* (21 March 1996).

35. See Appendix I.

36. *Kjeldsen Busk Madson and Peterson* v. *Belgium* (1979–80), 1 EHRR 711, para. 53.

37. *Handyside* v. *UK* (1979–80), 1 EHRR 737.

38. *Young, James & Webster* v. *UK* (1982), 4 EHRR 38, para. 63.

39. Articles 17 and 10 respectively.

40. This point is discussed in greater detail in Chapter 4.

41. See Chapter 3.

42. See, for example, the case of *Soering* v. *UK* (1989), 11 EHRR 439, para. 89.

43. 'The Development of Human Rights in Britain under an Incorporated Convention on Human Rights', Tom Sargant Memorial Lecture, *Public Law* (Summer 1998), p. 236.

44. What follows applies to the approach to law in England and Wales, and generally in Northern Ireland. Scotland has a different system of law but many of the general comments about legal culture are still applicable.

45. *R.* v. *DPP ex p. Kebeline* 3 WLR [1999] 972 at 988.

46. Jack Straw, 'Building a Human Rights Culture', Address to Civil Service College Seminar (9 December 1999). The implications of the Human Rights Act for legal culture are discussed further in Chapter 6.

47. Judges appointed to the House of Lords, the Law Lords, act as the final Court of Appeal (but not for criminal cases in Scotland) in the UK.

48. Lord Browne-Wilkinson, Speech at Law Society (15 October 1997).

49. Lord Browne-Wilkinson, 'The Impact on Judicial Reasoning', in Basil Markesinis (ed.), *The Impact of the Human Rights Bill on English Law* (Clarendon Press, 1998), pp. 22–3.

50. *AG* v. *Guardian Newspapers (No. 2)* [1990], IAC 109.

51. A. V. Dicey, *The Law of the Constitution* [1885], 10th edn. (Macmillan, [1959]), pp. 186–8, 197–200, 202–3. See Chapter 3 for a fuller account of this thesis.

52. For an explanation of the use of the term 'interests' rather than 'rights' in this context see Francesca Klug, Keir Starmer and Stuart Weir, *The Three Pillars of Liberty, Political Rights and Freedoms in the UK*, Democratic Audit, Essex University Human Rights Centre (Routledge, 1996), p. 91.

53. See Lord Bingham, 'Should There be a Law to Protect Rights of Personal Privacy?', *European Human Rights Law Review* 5 (1996). This question will be discussed further in Chapter 6.

54. *McLeod* v. *UK* (1998), 27 EHRR 493.

55. *Constantine* v. *Imperial Hotels Ltd* [1944], KB 693.

56. At the time of writing this is due to be remedied with regard to race discrimination by the Race Relations (Amendment) Bill 1999.

57. See Chapter 4 for an analysis of the inadequacies of Article 14, the anti-discrimination provision of the ECHR.

58. CCPR/C/I/Add. 17:108 [1977]. The Human Rights Committee is the supervisory body for the UN's International Covenant on Civil and Political Rights.

59. *DPP* v. *Jones and Lloyd* [1999], 2 All ER 257.

60. Most of what follows also applies to magistrates and tribunal members as the rights in the Human Rights Act can be claimed in any court or tribunal in the land.

61. *MOT* v. *Noort, Police* v. *Curran* [1992], 3 NZLR.

62. The model for incorporating the ECHR contained in the Human Rights Act will be explained in greater detail in Chapter 6.

63. *R.* v. *Secretary of State for the Home Department ex p. Bugdaycay* [1987], AC 514.

64. *Associated Provincial Picture Houses Ltd* v. *Wednesbury Corporation* [1948], 1 KB 223.

65. *R.* v. *Ministry of Defence ex p. Smith* [1996], QB 517 at 554.

66. Ibid. at 558.

67. Rabinder Singh, *The Future of Human Rights in the United Kingdom: Essays on Law and Practice* (Hart, 1997), pp. 39–40.

68. *Smith & Grady* v. *UK* (1999), Applications 33985/96 and 33986/96 at 138.

69. *R.* v. *Ministry of Defence ex p. Smith* [1996], 1 All ER 257.

70. Ibid. at 266.

71. *The Stephen Lawrence Inquiry*, Report of an Inquiry by Sir William Macpherson of Cluny CM-4262-1 (Stationery Office, 1999), p. 312.

72. Reported in 'Criminal Behaviour', Navnit Dholakia, *Guardian* (16 December 1999) and 'Stop and Think', Denis O'Conner, Assistant Commissioner of the Metropolitan Police, *Guardian* (19 January 2000).

73. Police and Criminal Evidence Act 1984, Section 1.

74. Through the Race Relations (Amendment) Bill going through Parliament at the time of writing.

75. A report commissioned by the Metropolitan Police, *Searches in London* by Dr Marian FitzGerald, published in December 1999, suggested a correlation between a reduction in searches and an increase in some reported crime. The National Association for the Care and Resettlement of Offenders challenged this interpretation of the statistics. *Guardian* (16 December 1999).

76. Reported in the *Guardian* (14 October 1999).

77. There has been no jurisprudence under the European Court of Human Rights directly on this issue to date but the UK courts will anyway be free to develop their own case law under the Human Rights Act.

78. See *Engel* v. *Netherlands* (1979–80), 1 EHRR 647 at para. 69.

79. *Competence Standards on the Human Rights Act*, National Police Training (2000).

80. See O'Conner, n. 72 above.

81. Human Rights Act, Section 6. This is explained further in Chapter 6.

82. *Osman and another* v. *Ferguson and another* [1993], 4 All ER 344.

83. *Osman* v. *UK* (1999), 1 FLR 198, para. 151.

84. Ibid., para. 115 (my emphasis).

85. It is worth noting that in Northern Ireland the anti-religious discrimination legislation is widely recognized as having real teeth as well as helping to bring about a cultural shift.

86. House of Lords *Hansard*, vol. 582, col. 1227, para. 1308 (3 November 1997). See Francesca Klug, 'The Human Rights Act 1998, *Pepper* v. *Hart* and All That', *Public Law* (Summer 1999), pp. 247–74.

87. *Whiteside* v. *UK* (1994), 76-A DR 80; *Osman* v. *UK*, see n. 83 above.

88. *Lopez Ostra* v. *Spain* (1999), 20 EHRR, para. 277.

89. *Platform Arzte für das leben* v. *Austria* (1991), 12 EHRR.

90. House of Commons *Hansard*, vol. 317, col. 1358 (21 October 1998).

91. For those who want to remember them see, for example, Peter Osborne, *Alastair Campbell, New Labour and the Rise of the Media Class* (Aurum Press, 1999).

CHAPTER 2 A Curious Mixture: Rights, Responsibilities and the Third Way?

1. The Blair administration's style of government is discussed by Peter Hennessy, in *The Blair Revolution in Goverment?* (Polis, 2000).

2. Hugo Young, 'The Strange Fruit of a Thousand Days in Office', *Guardian* (27 January 2000).

3. However, a 'State of the Nation' survey conducted by MORI in 1995 found 79 per cent of people polled supported a bill of rights for Britain.

4. Lord Habgood, The Sydney Bailey Memorial Lecture, Westminster Abbey, London (April 1998).

5. *The Politics of Thatcherism*, edited by Stuart Hall and Martin Jacques (Lawrence & Wishart, 1983), provides insights into the policies of the era, as does Roger Scruton in *The Meaning of Conservatism* (Penguin, 1980), from a very different perspective.

6. The Home Secretary made this point in a speech in January 2000. See Straw, Chapter 1, n. 10.

7. Peter Mandelson and Roger Liddle, *The Blair Revolution: Can New Labour Deliver?* (Faber & Faber, 1996), p. 17.

8. The sentiments behind this debate appear timeless. It was Socrates who wrote in 500 BC: 'Our youth today love luxury. They have bad manners, contempt for authority, disrespect for older people,' and so forth.

9. Debate on 'society's moral and spiritual well-being', House of Lords *Hansard*, vol. 573, col. 1772 (5 July 1996).

10. Ibid., col. 1751.

11. Ibid., col. 1717.

12. See Selbourne, Introduction, n. 37, p. 277.

13. Melanie Phillips, 'Why I am Really a Progressive', *New Statesman* (14 February 2000).

14. *Observer* (7 July 1996).

15. Baroness O'Neill, Lecture, 'Is Universalism in Ethics Dead?' King's College, London (19 January 2000).

16. Jonathan Sacks, *The Politics of Hope* (Jonathan Cape, 1997), p. 233.

17. Quoted in Erica-Irene Daes, *Freedom of the Individual under Law: A*

Study of the Individual's Duties to the Community and the Limitations on Human Rights and Freedoms under Article 29 of the UDHR (UN, 1990), p. 40.

18. Quoted in I. Szabo and others, *Socialist Concept of Human Rights* (Budapest: Akademiai Kiado, 1966), pp. 52–61.

19. 'The Evaluation of the Guidance Materials for Schools' Promotion of Pupils' Spiritual, Moral, Social and Cultural Development', *Final Summary Report* (QCA, May 1999).

20. Nicholas Tate, Speech at IPPR Citizenship and Education Conference (16 June 1999).

21. See Giddens, Introduction, n. 1.

22. It is a term that originated at the turn of the century and has been used by both social democrats and the far Right to distinguish themselves from Capitalists and Communists.

23. Transcript, 'Presidential Seminar on the Third Way', Washington (April 1999); published in *New Statesman* (24 May 1999).

24. Ibid.

25. See, for example, Shlomo Avineri and Avner de-Shalit (eds.), *Communitarianism and Individualism* (Oxford University Press, 1992).

26. John Rawls, *A Theory of Justice* (Clarendon Press, 1972).

27. Robert Nozick, *Anarchy, State and Utopia* (Blackwell, 1974).

28. See, for example, Michael Sandel, *Liberalism and the Limits of Justice* (Cambridge University Press, 1982); Charles Taylor, *The Ethics of Authenticity* (Harvard University Press, 1991).

29. Amitai Etzioni, *The Spirit of Community: Rights, Responsibilities and the Communitarian Agenda* (Crown, 1993), p. 247.

30. *Economist* (18 March 1995).

31. For an early, interesting example, see Geoff Mulgan, 'The Buck Stops Here', *Marxism Today* (September 1990).

32. Respectively: Dick Atkinson, *The Common Sense of Community* (Demos, 1994); John Gray, *After Social Democracy* (Demos, 1996); Damien Green, *Communities in the Countryside* (Social Market Foundation, 1996); and John Marenbon, *Answering the Challenge of Communitarianism* (Politeia, 1996).

33. See Etzioni, n. 29 above, p. 4.

34. Amitai Etzioni, *The New Golden Rule: Community and Morality in a Democratic Society* (Profile Books, 1997), p. 12.

35. Ibid., p. 139.

36. Ibid., p. 13 (his emphasis).

37. Ibid., p. 42.

38. Ibid., p. 43.

39. Ibid., p. 44.

40. Tony Blair, Speech, 'Faith in the City – Ten Years On', Southwark Cathedral (29 January 1996).

41. Ibid.

42. Tony Blair, Speech, Cape Town, South Africa (14 October 1996).

43. Tony Blair, *The Third Way: New Politics for the New Century* (Fabian Society, 1998), pp. 4 and 12.

44. See Mandelson and Liddle, n. 7 above, p. 20.

45. See Blair, n. 43 above, p. 4.

46. Jack Straw, Speech, 'Building Social Cohesion, Order and Inclusion in a Market Economy', Nexus Conference, King's College, London (3 July 1998).

47. Tony Blair, Speech at Labour Party Conference, Brighton (30 September 1997).

48. Robin Cook, Speech at Lord Mayor's Easter Banquet, Mansion House (23 April, 1998). The presentation of foreign policy as 'ethical' has now effectively been dropped. See interview with government minister Peter Hain, *New Statesman* (3 April 2000).

49. Tony Blair, John Smith Memorial Lecture (February 1996).

50. Jack Straw and Paul Boateng, *Bringing Rights Home: Labour's Plan to Incorporate the European Convention on Human Rights into United Kingdom Law* (Labour Party, 1996).

51. See Blair, n. 49 above.

52. House of Commons *Hansard*, vol. 306, cols. 782–3 (16 February 1998).

53. House of Lords *Hansard*, vol. 582, col. 1227 (3 November 1997).

54. 'Jack Straw Announces Implementation Date for the Human Rights Act', Press Release (Home Office, 18 May 1999).

55. Jack Straw, Charter 88 Lecture, Church House, London (26 June 1996).

56. House of Commons *Hansard*, vol. 317, col. 1358 (21 October 1998) (my emphasis).

57. See Chapter 1.

58. Mike O'Brien, Speech at Local Government Association (21 May 1999) (my emphasis).

59. 'Because Britain Deserves Better', *Labour Party Manifesto* (1997), p. 35.

60. See *Hansard*, n. 53 above, col. 1308.

61. See Press Release, n. 54 above.

62. Reported in the *Guardian* (14 September 1999).

63. Tony Blair, Speech at Labour Party Conference, Bournemouth (28 September 1999).

64. Jack Straw, 'Building a Human Rights Culture', Address to Civil Service College (9 December 1999). Because of shortage of time Straw was unable to deliver the speech in full.

CHAPTER 3 The Quest for Freedom: First-Wave Rights

1. National Archive and Records Administration, *A More Perfect Union: The Creation of the US Constitution*, www.nara/gov/exhall/charters/constitutions/conhist.html.

2. The precise terms used depend on the translation. Tom Paine, for example, writing in 1791, used 'imprescriptible' rather than 'sacred'.

3. See, for example, Epp, Chapter 1, n. 12, p. 32. Interestingly, there has never been a Socialist movement in America on the scale of Europe's.

4. This is the term generally used to mark the passage of time between the late seventeenth century and the great upheavals at the end of the eighteenth century.

5. Immanuel Kant, 'What is Enlightenment?' [1784], in Isaac Kramnick (ed.), *The Portable Enlightenment Reader* (Penguin US, 1995), p. 1.

6. See Richard Tuck, *Natural Rights Theories, Their Origin and Development* (Cambridge University Press, 1995).

7. Although there is speculation that this may be more down to marketing hype than anything else. *Guardian* (3 November 1999).

8. Jonathan Freedland, *Bring Home the Revolution: How Britain Can Live the American Dream* (Fourth Estate, 1998), p. 204.

9. See Michael Freeman, 'The Philosophical Foundations of Human Rights', *Human Rights Quarterly* 16 (1994). I return to this theme, briefly, in the Conclusion.

10. See Carlos Santiago Nino, *The Ethics of Human Rights* (Clarendon Press, 1991).

11. Alasdair MacIntyre, *After Virtue* (University of Notre Dame Press, 1981), p. 67.

12. See, for example, John Hart Ely, *Democracy and Distrust: A Theory of Judicial Review* (Harvard University Press, 1980).

13. For example, *Cossey* v. *UK* (1981), 13 EHRR 35; and *Sheffield & Horsham* v. *UK* (1999), 27 EHRR 163.

14. See National Archive and Records Administration, n. 1 above.

15. Ibid. Both Jefferson and Madison went on to become presidents of the US.

16. Amendments III and II respectively. The original Bill of Rights was binding only on the federal government and it was not until after the XIVth

Amendment was passed in 1868 that it began to be applied to the individual states.

17. Jean-Jacques Rousseau, *The Social Contract* (1762).

18. See Paine, Introduction, n. 30, p. 114.

19. Clause 4.

20. Clauses 10 and 11 respectively.

21. Henry Shue, 'Mediating Duties', *Ethics* 98 (July 1998), p. 690.

22. Quoted in Epp, Chapter 1, n. 12, p. 12.

23. Although *Marbury* v. *Madison* established that the Supreme Court could review the constitutionality of Acts of Congress, this was a case about the Constitution generally, not specifically about the Bill of Rights.

24. See Ely, n. 12 above, and William J. Quirk and R. Randall Bridwell, *Judicial Dictatorship* (Transaction Publications, 1997), for two different views on this debate.

25. This was a specific provision in the Constitution and was aimed at deciding the relative electoral strength of the various states. Slaves were not granted any rights at all under the original Bill of Rights.

26. *Dred Scott* v. *Sandford* (1857).

27. By the XIIIth Amendment, passed in the wake of the American Civil War.

28. *See Brown* v. *Board of Education*, Chapter 1, n. 13.

29. See Daes, Chapter 2, n. 17, p. 5.

30. For example, Article 6 of the ECHR.

31. James Madison, Alexander Hamilton and John Jay, *The Federalist Papers* [1788] (Penguin, 1987), p. 475.

32. A more radical group, known as the 'True Levellers' or 'Diggers', often described as early communists, set up a commune in Surrey in 1649. Their pamphleteer, Gerrard Winstanley, equated private property with original sin and saw the spread of his 'agrarian communism' as heralding a new era of egalitarianism.

33. John Locke, 'Of Political or Civil Society', in Peter Lasleffs (ed.), *Two Treatises of Government* [1689] (Cambridge University Press, 1967).

34. 'Of the Beginning of Political Societies', ibid.

35. Notably the late Renaissance Dutch scholar Hugo Grotius and the German philosopher and contemporary of Locke's Samuel Pufendorf.

36. Thomas Hobbes, *Leviathan* [1651], ed. C. B. Macpherson (Penguin, 1968).

37. Quoted by D. D. Raphael, 'Enlightenment and Revolution', in Neil MacCormick and Zenon Bankowski (eds.), *Enlightenment, Rights and Revolution: Essays in Legal and Social Philosophy* (Aberdeen University Press, 1989), p. 5.

38. E. P. Thompson, *The Making of the English Working Class* (Pelican, 1968), p. 34. The other, he maintains, is John Bunyan's *Pilgrim's Progress* [1678–84].

39. The emphasis given to the right to property among Enlightenment thinkers must be viewed in the context of an era where the seizure of possessions by the state was not uncommon and the levying of taxes, often to fund foreign conquests, could be highly arbitrary and unjust.

40. Eric Foner, Introduction to *Rights of Man*; see Paine, Introduction, n. 30.

41. John Keane, *Tom Paine: A Political Life* (Bloomsbury, 1995), p. 331.

42. Quoted in Thompson; see n. 38 above, p. 118.

43. Quoted in Keane; see n. 41 above, p. 335.

44. Mary Wollstonecraft, *A Vindication of the Rights of Woman* [1792] (Pelican, 1975).

45. Edmund Burke, *Reflections on the Revolution in France and on the Proceedings in Certain Societies in London Relative to that Event* (1790).

46. Miriam Brody, Introduction to Wollstonecraft, see n. 44 above.

47. Paget Toynbee (ed.), *The Letters of Horace Walpole* (Oxford, 1905), pp. 131–2 and 337–8.

48. See Chapter 2.

49. See Keane, n. 41 above, p. 365.

50. Quoted in J. Bowring (ed.), *The Works of Jeremy Bentham* (William Tait, 1838–43), Vol. II, p. 501.

51. See John Dinwiddy, *Bentham* (Oxford University Press, 1989), pp. 77–8.

52. See Dicey, Chapter 1, n. 51.

53. Letter to Baroness Ewart-Biggs (26 May 1989).

54. Tom Paine wrote a powerful essay attacking slavery in 1775. See Keane, n. 41 above, pp. 99–100.

55. See Thompson, n. 38 above, p. 254. The Chartists' People's Charter of 1838 is sometimes mistaken for a bill of rights when it was really a set of demands for the democratization of Parliament.

56. See Jeremy Walden (ed.), *Nonsense upon Stilts – Bentham, Burke and Marx on the Rights of Man* (Methuen, 1987).

57. Karl Marx, *On the Jewish Question* (1843).

58. Friedrich Engels, *The Anti-Duhring* (1878).

59. V. I. Lenin, *Report to the First Congress of the Third International* (1919).

60. Tom Campbell, 'Marx and the Socialist Critique of Justice', in *Justice* (Macmillan, 1988), p. 187.

61. It is impossible here to do more than skirt over the history of the Left's relationship to the rights movement over time. Most books that touch on it are highly partisan. It would benefit from dispassionate and detailed historical research.

62. Including H. G. Wells, Clement Attlee, Vera Brittain, Winifred Holtby, Edith Summerskill and Harold Laski.

63. For example over the miners' strike in the mid-1980s. See Brian Dyson, *Liberty in Britain: A Diamond Jubilee History of the NCCL* (Civil Liberties Trust, 1994), pp. 54–6. See also Chapter 6.

64. Interestingly, modern-day feminists have been more inclined to 'own' the heritage of Mary Wollstonecraft than Socialists have tended to 'own' Tom Paine.

CHAPTER 4 From Liberty to Community: Second-Wave Rights

1. *The Times* (20 October 1939).

2. H. G. Wells, *The Rights of Man, or What are We Fighting For?* (Penguin, 1940), p. 79.

3. Ibid., p. 82.

4. Quoted in Jan Burgess, 'The Road to San Francisco: The Revival of the Human Rights Idea in the Twentieth Century', *Human Rights Quarterly* 14 (1992), p. 448.

5. Ibid.

6. The only exceptions were references to 'fair and humane conditions of labour' and the 'just treatment' of the inhabitants of dependent (Trust) territories in Article 23. See Robertson, Introduction, n. 4, pp. 15–19.

7. See Burgess, n. 4 above, pp. 455–9.

8. Preamble, UDHR.

9. Harry S. Truman, *Years of Decision* (Doubleday, 1995), p. 292.

10. It is said that Roosevelt was appointed to this post because President Truman wanted to keep the widow of the late president away from domestic affairs. At the time of her appointment the Commission was not seen as very significant.

11. The International Covenant on Civil and Political Rights and the International Covenant on Economic, Social and Cultural Rights, were both adopted on 16 December 1966 and ratified ten years later.

12. See Sieghart, Introduction, n. 33, pp. 32–3.

13. Ibid., p. 64.

14. See, for example, Jack Donnelly, 'Social Construction of International Human Rights', in Dunne and Wheeler (eds.), Introduction, n. 28, p. 72.

15. Johannes Morsink, *The Universal Declaration of Human Rights: Origins, Drafting and Intent* (University of Pennsylvania Press, 1999), p. xiv.

16. All quoted in Morsink; see n. 15 above, pp. 36–7.

17. David Feldman, 'Human Dignity as a Legal Value – Part 1', *Public Law* (Winter 1999), p. 685.

18. As we saw, the term 'dignity' was also used in the Preamble to the UN Charter.

19. See Feldman, n. 17 above, p. 687.

20. Bishop Belo, 'The Dignity of the Individual', in B. van der Heijden and B. Tahzib-Lie (eds.), *Reflections on the Universal Declaration of Human Rights: A Fiftieth Anniversary Anthology* (Kluwer, 1998), p. 59.

21. See M. Glen Johnson and Janusz Simonides, *The Universal Declaration of Human Rights: A History of its Creation and Implementation, 1948–1998* (UNESCO, 1998), pp. 42–8.

22. Quoted in Morsink; see n. 15 above, p. 316.

23. Ibid., p. 318.

24. See Thomas Hammarberg, 'The Principles and Politics of Human Rights', The Dorah Patel Lecture, LSE (18 February 1999).

25. See Bikhu Parekh, 'Non-ethnocentric Universalism', in Dunne and Wheeler (eds.), Introduction, n. 28; Mahmood Monshipouri, 'The Muslim World Half a Century after the Universal Declaration of Human Rights: Progress and Obstacles', *Netherlands Quarterly of Human Rights* 16, no. 3 (September 1998); and Michael J. Perry, 'Are Human Rights Universal? The Relativist Challenge and Related Matters', *Human Rights Quarterly* 19 (1997), pp. 461–509.

26. Hossein Mehrpour, 'Human Rights in the Universal Declaration and the Religious Perspective', in Heijden and Tahzib-Lie (eds.), n. 20 above.

27. Mary Robinson, 'The Universal Declaration of Human Rights: The International Keystone of Human Dignity', ibid.

28. Quoted in Morsink; see n. 15 above, p. 33.

29. See Chapter 3.

30. See Donnelly, n. 14 above, p. 78.

31. This was explicitly recognized in the French Declaration of Rights, which stated in Clause 13 that: 'For the maintenance of the public force and for the expenses of administration a common tax is indispensable.'

32. See Morsink, n. 15 above, p. 131.

33. In France the Conseil Constitutionnel (Constitutional Council) decided in 1995 that, in view of the importance attached to protecting the dignity of the individual in the Preamble to the 1946 Constitution, it was open to the legislature to make appropriate provisions for the state to provide decent housing for the homeless and for travellers. See Feldman, n. 17 above, p. 700.

34. See Robinson, n. 27 above; and Mary Robinson, Transcript, 'Meeting the Challenge of Human Rights', Sounding the Century Lecture, London (23 September 1999).

35. Rabinder Singh, *Human Rights in the UK: Essays on Law and Practice* (Hart, 1997), p. 54.

36. See Chapter 1.

37. *Dred Scott* v. *Sandford* (1857).

38. Quoted in Bernard Schwartz, *A History of the Supreme Court* (Oxford University Press, 1993), p. 119.

39. Declaration of Independence (4 July 1776).

40. Another explanation was the more pragmatic concern to find a compromise between the North and the slave-owning South.

41. Adolph Hitler, *Mein Kampf* (1925), p. 150.

42. Quoted in Morsink; see n. 15 above, p. 38.

43. See Morsink, n. 15 above, pp. 28–33.

44. See Morsink, n. 15 above, p. 93.

45. The second sentence of Clause 6 of the French Declaration reads: 'All citizens, being equal before [the law] are equally admissible to all public offices, positions and employments according to their capacity, and without other distinction than that of virtues and talents.' The IVth Amendment to the American Bill of Rights, passed in 1868, goes so far as to refer to the 'equal protection of the laws', which was subsequently used successfully in anti-segregation cases in the 1950s and 1960s.

46. John Stuart Mill, *On Liberty* [1859] (Penguin, 1974), p. 62.

47. For example, *Brown* v. *Board of Education* (1954); *Johnson* v. *Virginia* (1963); *Watson* v. *Memphis* (1963). See also Schwartz, n. 38 above and Chapter 1.

48. Kevin Boyle, 'Invisibility of Human Rights, Social Justice and Article 18 of the Universal Declaration', in Peter Baehr et al. (eds.), *Innovation and Inspiration: Fifty Years of the UDHR* (Royal Netherlands Academy of Arts and Sciences, 1999).

49. Quoted in Mary Robertson; see Heijden and Tahzib-Lie (eds.), n. 20 above, p. 256.

50. International Convention on the Elimination of All Forms of Racial Discrimination (1979) and Convention on the Elimination of All Forms of Discrimination against Women (1979).

51. See Chapter 1; and Klug, Starmer and Weir, Chapter 1, n. 52, pp. 112–15.

52. UN Declaration on the Granting of Independence to Colonial Countries and Peoples (1960).

53. UN Declaration on the Elimination of All Forms of Intolerance and of Discrimination Based on Religion or Belief (1981).

54. UN Convention on the Suppression and Punishment of the Crime of Apartheid (1973), Article 1.

55. Declaration on the Rights of Persons Belonging to National or Ethnic, Religious and Linguistic Minorities (1992).

56. Judgment, International Military Tribunal, Transcript of Proceedings, p. 16878 (1 October 1946).

57. Quoted in Morsink; see n. 15 above, p. 240.

58. Ibid., p. 242.

59. Ibid., p. 248.

60. Ibid.

61. See Daes, Chapter 2, n. 17, p. 17.

62. Ibid., p. 19.

63. Ibid.

64. See Morsink, n. 15 above, p. 241.

65. Ibid., p. 245.

66. See Dinwiddy, Chapter 3, n. 51, p. 78.

67. See Morsink, n. 15 above, pp. 97 and 343; and Hammarberg, n. 24 above.

68. See Chapter 2.

69. Torkel Opsahl, *Law and Equality: Selected Articles on Human Rights* (Ad Notam Gyldendal, 1996), p. 431.

70. See *Taking Duties Seriously: Individual Duties in International Human Rights Law, A Commentary* (International Council on Human Rights Policy, 1999), p. 14.

71. See Morsink, n. 15 above, p. 250.

72. Articles 4, 5 and 10 respectively.

73. See Paine, Introduction, n. 30, p. 67 and Mill, n. 46 above, p. 70.

74. A similar sentiment in Article 26, the right to education, requires that education be directed at 'strengthening . . . respect for human rights and fundamental freedoms'.

75. James Nickel distinguishes between primary duties on individuals and institutions to refrain from violating rights along with duties on governments to uphold them and secondary duties on everyone to maintain and support institutions that themselves have a secondary duty to uphold rights and discourage rights violations in 'How Human Rights Generate Duties to Protect and Provide', *Human Rights Quarterly* 15 (1993), pp. 77–86.

76. Geoffrey Robertson, QC, estimates that over 100 international human rights treaties, conventions and declarations have been promulgated since 1948, in *Crimes Against Humanity*, see Introduction, n. 4, p. 32.

77. See Daes, n. 61 above, p. 41.

78. See Chapter 1. See also Starmer, Introduction, n. 34, Chapter 5.

79. The ICCPR and ICESCR have both been ratified by the UK but successive governments have refused to ratify the Optional Protocol to the ICCPR, which would allow individuals to take complaints to the Covenant's supervisory body, the Human Rights Committee.

80. See Daes, Chapter 2, n. 17, p. 50.

81. See Chapter 1.

82. See Shue, Chapter 3, n. 21.

83. See International Council on Human Rights Policy, n.70 above, p. 48.

84. See Geoffrey Marston, 'The United Kingdom's Part in the Preparation of the ECHR, 1950', *International and Comparative Law Quarterly* 42 (October 1993).

85. FO 371/88756 (18 October 1950).

86. See A. H. Robertson, *Human Rights in Europe: Being an Account of the European Convention for the Protection of Human Rights and Fundamental Freedoms Signed in Rome on 4 November 1950* (Manchester University Press, 1961), p. 7.

87. The Council of Europe's European Social Charter was adopted in 1961. It is a weaker document than its UN equivalent, the International Covenant on Economic Social and Cultural Rights (ICESCR), and has had far less impact on the growth of social and economic rights in Europe than has the European Union and its charters.

88. 'Teitgen Report' – Report of the Committee of Legal and Administrative Questions, quoted in *Consultative Assembly Official Report* (7 September 1949), p. 127 and *Documents of the Assembly*, Document 77, paras. 4–5.

89. Quoted by Roy Jenkins in The Eileen Illtyd David Memorial Lecture, Swansea (17 November 1986).

90. Ibid.

91. LCO 2/5570 [3363/22, part 2].

92. For an insight into the 'difficulties' ratification did indeed cause to the running of the Empire see Brian Simpson, 'The Exile of Archbishop Makarios III', *EHRLR* (1996), pp. 391–403.

93. See, among many examples, *Muller* v. *Switzerland* (1991), 13 EHRR 212, where the European Court of Human Rights used the ICCPR to interpret free expression under the ECHR. See Starmer, Introduction, n. 34, pp. 162–4 for further illustrations.

94. See *Jersild* v. *Denmark* (1995), 19 EHRR 1, which examined the hate speech provisions of The International Convention on the Elimination of All Forms of Racial Discrimination; and *A.* v. *UK* (1999), 27 EHRR 611, which was one of a number of recent cases to refer to the 1989 UN Convention on the Rights of the Child.

95. *Niemietz* v. *Germany* (1993), 16 EHRR 97.

96. *D.* v. *UK* (1997), 24 EHRR 423. See Starmer, Introduction, n. 34, pp. 407–8 for an interesting analysis of this point.

97. This was the body that individuals had to petition if they wished to take a case to the European Court of Human Rights until it was abolished by new Protocol 11 to the ECHR on 1 November 1998.

98. *East African Asians Case* (1981), 3 EHRR 76.

99. The UK has ratified Protocols 1 and 6 of those protocols which cover substantive rights. Protocol 6, on the death penalty, was ratified as the result of a vote to include it in the Human Rights Act during the parliamentary debate on the Bill.

100. Draft Protocol No. 12 to the ECHR and Draft Explanatory Report, CDDH (99) (10, 22 June 1999).

101. *A.* v. *UK* (1998), 2 FLR 959.

102. *Whiteside* v. *UK* (1994), 76-A DR 80.

103. *Paton* v. *UK* [1980], 19 DR 244.

104. See *A.* v. *UK*, n. 101 above.

105. See Chapter 1.

106. See *Paton* v. *UK*, n. 103 above.

107. The way that restrictions on rights are formulated is similar in both the ECHR and ICCPR, another example of the swapping of ideas during the drafting processes. Work on the various drafts of the instruments began at similar times and there was considerable cross-fertilization of ideas.

108. Article 5.1(c).

109. Articles 8 and 11. Again, governments are also limited in how far they can legitimately curtail fundamental rights. Under both treaties restrictions must be 'prescribed by law' and be 'necessary in a democratic society'. In other words, they must be foreseeable, proportionate and aimed at meeting a 'pressing social need' in a democracy. See Chapter 1.

110. Article 5 (1)(e).

111. Article 10 (2).

112. Article 8 (2).

113. *Doorson* v. *Netherlands* (1996), 22 EHRR 330.

114. *Baegen* v. *Netherlands* (1995), European Commission on Human Rights (unreported), A327-B.

115. *McCourt* v. *UK* (1993), 15 EHRR CD 110. See Starmer, Introduction, n. 34, p. 314.

116. For example, see *Tyrer* v. *UK* (1981), 2 EHRR 1; *Sigurjonsson* v. *Iceland*

(1993), 16 EHRR 462; and *Sheffield & Horsham* v. *UK* (1999), 27 EHRR 163.

117. See, for example, *Rees* v. *UK* (1987), 9 EHRR 56; and *Mathieu-Mohin & Cerfayt* v. *Belgium* (1998), 10 EHRR 1.

118. See Chapter 2.

119. Mary Ann Glendon, *Rights Talk: Impoverishment of Political Discourse* (Free Press US, 1993), p. 10.

120. Stephen Holmes and Cass R. Sunstein, *The Cost of Rights: Why Liberty Depends on Taxes* (W. W. Norton, 1999), p. 159.

121. See Glendon, n. 119 above.

122. Or at least this is how his latest views were portrayed in Ben Roger's 'Portrait of John Rawls', *Prospect* (June 1999).

123. Ronald Dworkin, 'The Moral Reading of the Constitution', *New York Review* (21 March 1996).

124. *Glimmerveen and Hagenbeek* v. *Netherlands* (1997), 18 DR 187; and *Kuhnen* v. *Germany* (1998), 56 DR 205. These cases in fact involved a breach of Article 17, which, as we have seen, applies to individuals and groups as well as states.

125. Article 20 (2).

126. David Feldman, 'Content Neutrality', in Ian Loveland (ed.), *Importing the First Amendment: Freedom of Expression in American, English and European Law* (Hart, 1998), p. 143.

127. See Chapter 1.

128. Amitai Etzioni, *The Limits of Privacy* (Basic Books, 1999), p. 15.

129. See Brown, Introduction, n. 28, p. 110.

130. The situation is not dissimilar in Canada, which, as a North American country, has been strongly influenced by the Enlightenment conception of the state and fundamental rights. See the famous case of *Dolfin Delivery*, 2 SCR 573 [1986], and also *Manning* v. *Hill*, 126 DLR (4th) 129 [1995].

131. *DeShaney* v. *Winnebago Department of Social Services* (1989), 489 US 189. Although it is an accepted principle of US constitutional law that the Bill of Rights can be enforced only against state action, in an early case the Supreme Court held that as the courts constituted state action they could strike down a racist, restrictive covenant on property which breached the XIVth Amendment. *Shelley* v. *Kramer*, 334 US 1 (1948). See Jonathan Cooper, 'The Horizontal Application of Human Rights Standards' (JUSTICE, 1999).

132. See *A.* v. *UK*, n. 101 above.

133. See, generally, Lawrence Tribe, *American Constitutional Law* (3rd edn.) (Foundation Press, 1999).

134. As was stated in Chapter 1, this point refers to the broad grounds on which the Bill of Rights is supported, not to the debate about whether the Articles within it can be interpreted in the light of changing circumstances.

135. Sir John Law, 'The Constitution, Morals and Rights', *Public Law* (Winter 1996).

136. See Robinson Transcript, n. 34 above.

137. *Roe* v. *Wade* (1973).

138. *Dudgeon* v. *UK* [1982], 4 EHRR 149; *Sutherland* v. *UK* [1998], EHRLR 117; see also *Smith & Grady* v. *UK*, Chapter 1, n. 65 above.

139. *B.* v. *France* (1994), 16 EHRR 1; *Sheffield and Horsham* v. *UK* (1999), 27 EHRR 163.

140. Quoted in the *Guardian* (23 July 1999).

141. There are still many other international human rights treaties the US government refuses to ratify, including the American Convention on Human Rights, the regional equivalent to the ECHR, which is enforced by the Inter-American Court of Human Rights.

142. See Daes, n. 61 above, pp. 51–2.

CHAPTER 5 Globalization and Third-Wave Rights

1. This chapter cannot begin to do justice to the myriad new developments in human rights thinking under the impact of globalization; a few random examples are presented here to advance the thesis that a new wave of rights thinking may be emerging which is more than the sum of its parts.

2. See Mary Kaldor, 'Transnational Civil Society', in Dunne and Wheeler (eds.), Introduction, n. 28, pp. 195–213.

3. Otherwise known as the Final Act of the Conference on Security and Co-operation in Europe (CSCE).

4. See Chapter 4.

5. See Tony Evans, *US Hegemony and the Project of Universal Human Rights* (Macmillan, 1996).

6. See Paul Hirst and Graham Thompson, *Globalization in Question* (Polity Press, 1996).

7. See Introduction.

8. According to newspaper reports at the time.

9. Preamble, UDHR 1948, para. 2.

10. See Chapter 2, generally. See also Will Hutton, 'Up and a Way', *Observer* (21 November 1999); and Polly Toynbee, 'Take a Stab at Change', *Guardian* (23 November 1999).

11. Quoted in 'Teenage Culture Harming Pupils', *Observer* (13 February 2000). See also Conclusion.

12. See survey for the BBC's 'Soul of Britain' by Opinion Research Business, reported in the *Guardian* (29 May 2000). See also James Meek, 'Free Fall', *Guardian* Society Section (2 February 2000). There is some evidence, however, that the decline in 'organized religion' has seen a growth in 'alternative' religious or spiritual movements.

13. House of Lords *Hansard*, vol. 573, col. 1692 (15 July 1996).

14. See Chapter 2.

15. For many devout followers of any religion this characterization of rights as a set of values can be even more threatening than their presentation as a set of legal rules in that it appears to challenge many sacred beliefs from an apparently secular Western perspective. It is not possible to do justice to this argument here without deviating too far, but it will be returned to briefly in the Conclusion.

16. See Chapters 1 and 4.

17. The European Court has never, in fact, developed a working theory of 'positive obligation'. See Andrew Clapham's ground-breaking *Human Rights in the Private Sphere* (Clarendon Press, 1993).

18. *Velasquez Rodriguez* v. *Honduras* (29 July 1988).

19. *Platform Arzte für das Leben* v. *Austria* (1991), 13 EHRR 204.

20. *Stubbings* v. *UK* (1996), 23 EHRR 213.

21. *Costello-Roberts* v. *UK* (1993), 19 EHRR 112.

22. The European Convention for the Prevention of Torture and Inhuman or Degrading Treatment or Punishment (1987), Article 2.

23. Andrew Puddephatt, Director of Article 19, 'Human Rights and Globalization', Speech at the Institute for Foreign Affairs, Stockholm (21 April 1999).

24. Andrew Clapham, 'Globalization and the Rule of Law', in Adama Dieng (ed.), *Globalization, Human Rights and the Rule of Law* (ICJ, 1999).

25. See Introduction.

26. See Spencer and Bynoe, Chapter 1, n. 26, pp. 62–3.

27. *Principles Relating to the Status of National Institutions*, General Assembly Resolution 28/134 (20 December 1993).

28. See Robinson Transcript, Chapter 4, n. 34.

29. For the most comprehensive analysis of this failure see Robertson, Introduction, n. 4.

30. *Human Rights: Quarterly Review of the Office of the United Nations High Commission for Human Rights*, no. 1 (1999), p. 13.

31. See Robinson Transcript, Chapter 4, n. 34.

32. See n. 30 above, p. 6.

33. See Laurence Dubin, 'The Direct Appliance of Human Rights Standards To, and By, Transnational Corporations', in Dieng (ed.), n. 24 above.

34. Bennett Freeman, Deputy Assistant Secretary of State, US State Department, Speech at Conference on Corporate Citizenship, Royal Institute of International Affairs (8 November 1999).

35. Sir Geoffrey Chandler, 'People and Profits', *Guardian* (14 November 1996).

36. For example, Sir Geoffrey Chandler, former senior executive at Shell, became Chair of Amnesty International's UK Business Group.

37. See Robinson Transcript, Chapter 4, n. 34.

38. See Clapham, n. 24 above, p. 21.

39. Of course, this raises different issues when it is Third World companies rather than transnational corporations that are held responsible for human rights violations, particularly if it is suspected that human rights standards are being required of them in order to reduce the competition to Western businesses. This was an issue that surfaced at the 1999 World Trade Organization in Seattle, bringing a new generation of protesters on different sides of the debate into an awareness of the difficult issues aired by this third wave of human rights. Not dissimilar questions are raised when the EU and other regional or international bodies tie aid or debt relief to human rights performance, another growing issue for debate between development NGOs and governments.

40. Ulrich Beck, 'Beyond the Nation State', *New Statesman* (6 December 1999).

41. See Clapham, n. 24 above, p. 20.

42. UDHR, Article 26, and ICESCR, Article 13.

43. The Permanent Arab Regional Commission on Human Rights came into existence in 1968 but has not yet produced a promised charter of rights.

44. Article 29, clauses 6 and 1 respectively.

45. The American Declaration of the Rights and Duties of Man adopted by the OAS in 1948 also includes a separate list of individuals' duties. The Inter-American Court of Human Rights has claimed jurisdiction over the Declaration but has not, it seems, given an opinion on the duties articles. See Chapter 4.

46. For example, in Article 3 (2).

47. UN Declaration on the Rights and Responsibilities of Individuals, Groups and Organs of Society to Promote and Protect Universally Recognized Human Rights and Fundamental Freedoms, adopted 9 December 1998.

48. Justice Goldstone is also a judge at the South African Constitutional Court.

49. Preamble, Declaration of Human Duties and Responsibilities, UNESCO (January 1999). The Liberal Democrat Peer Shirley Williams was an active member of the UK delegation.

50. Articles 18 and 10 respectively. Quoted in International Council on Human Rights Policy, see Chapter 4, n. 70, pp. 55–7.

51. Note from Justice Goldstone to Andrew Clapham, quoted in Clapham, n. 24 above, p. 24.

52. But see Introduction, n. 38, for some of the literature that discusses both the potential for and difficulties of reconciling human rights with other worldviews.

53. See Chapters 1 and 6.

54. See Chapter 3.

55. See Hammarberg, Chapter 4, n. 24.

56. See Robinson Transcript, Chapter 4, n. 34.

57. ECHR, Article 15.

58. See Chapter 4.

59. See Conclusion for further reflections on the implications of cross-cultural dialogues for the claim that human rights are universal.

60. Alan Gerwith, *The Community of Rights* (University of Chicago Press, 1996), p. 6.

CHAPTER 6 **The Human Rights Act:** A Third-Wave or Third-Way Bill of Rights?

1. Qualification and Curriculum Authority, *Developing the School Curriculum* (1999).

2. See David Steel, *No Entry: The Background and Implications of the Commonwealth Immigrants Act 1968* (C. Hurst & Co., 1969).

3. Anthony Lester, *Democracy and Individual Rights* (Fabian Society, 1968); John Macdonald, *Bill of Rights* (Liberal Party, 1969).

4. Lord Scarman, 'English Law: The New Dimension', Hamlyn Lecture (1974).

5. An exception to this was provided by the English lawyer, Sir Edward Coke, who in *Dr Bonham's Case* in 1610 claimed that: 'When an Act of Parliament is against common right and reason, or repugnant, or impossible to be performed, the common law will control it and adjudge such Act to be void.' However, no statute was ever overturned on the basis of this rhetoric.

6. See Dicey, Chapter 1, n. 51, pp. 39–41, 87–91. The first significant dent to the durability of the doctrine of parliamentary sovereignty in modern times has, of course, come from the EU (*Factortame Ltd* v. *Secretary of State for Transport* ZAC 85 HL [1990]). Some would argue that the UK government's decision to allow individuals to petition the European Commission on Human Rights in Strasbourg in 1966 was an equally significant landmark in what continues to be the dilution of the doctrine.

7. *Young, James and Webster* v. *UK* (1981), 4 EHRR 38.

8. See A. G. Griffith, *The Politics of the Judiciary* (4th edn.) (Fontana, 1991).

9. See Keith Ewing and Conor Gearty, *Freedom under Thatcher, Civil Liberties in Modern Britain* (Oxford University Press, 1990); and *Democracy of a Bill of Rights* (Society of Labour Lawyers, 1991).

10. Professor John Griffiths has criticized the Human Rights Act for this reason. See John Griffiths, 'Human Rights, Legal Wrongs', *New Statesman* (31 July 1998).

11. See Epp, Chapter 1, n. 12, p. 12.

12. At one time an adviser to the then Labour Home Secretary, Roy Jenkins, Anthony Lester, QC, was later to defect from the Labour Party, eventually becoming one of the founder members of the Social Democratic Party (SDP).

13. *Law Society Gazette* 73 (29 September 1976), p. 774.

14. *UK Charter of Human Rights*, Discussion Document for the Labour Movement (Labour Party, 1976). The sub-committee included Lord Gardiner and MPs Peter Archer and Sam Silkin. Shirley Williams was later to defect to the SDP.

15. Home Office Discussion Paper, *Legislation on Human Rights: With Particular Reference to the European Convention* (June 1976).

16. SACHR, *The Protection of Human Rights by Law in Northern Ireland* (HMSO, 1977), Cmnd., 7009.

17. *Report of the Select Committee on a Bill of Rights*, House of Lords Paper, 176 (June 1978).

18. For a further exposition of the Bill of Rights campaign in this period see Robert Blackburn, *Towards a Constitutional Bill of Rights* (Pinter, 1999), pp. 5–15; and Michael Zander, *A Bill of Rights?* (Sweet & Maxwell, 1997), pp. 1–27.

19. House of Commons *Hansard*, cols. 251–2 (6 July 1989).

20. See, for example, 'Wrong of a Bill of Rights', *Agenda* (Liberty, 20 July 1990).

21. In the later years this tardiness was largely because of opposition to becoming an avowedly human rights organization by a split executive; most of the NCCL staff wanted to embrace this change long before it happened.

22. There were periodic exceptions to this in NCCL's history. For example, in 1947 it hosted an international conference on human rights in London, and it has long been affiliated to the International League for Human Rights.

23. The most notable of the Right-wing libertarian organizations was the Freedom Association, but there were also a number of maverick Tory MPs with a strong reputation for supporting civil liberties.

24. See two publications from the Democratic Audit, Essex University Human Rights Centre: Klug, Starmer and Weir, Chapter 1, n. 52; and Stuart Weir and David Beetham, *Political Power and Democratic Control in Britain* (Routledge, 1999).

25. See Murray Hunt, *Using Human Rights Law in English Courts* (Hart, 1997), for a detailed analysis of how some judges started to develop human rights principles in UK law in that period.

26. Who have gone on to become a Labour peer and MP respectively.

27. For an insightful analysis of this journey see Parratt, Introduction, n. 18.

28. See Chapter 4.

29. Francesca Klug, *A People's Charter: Liberty's Bill of Rights* (Liberty, 1991).

30. Anthony Lester et al., *A British Bill of Rights* (IPPR, 1991).

31. For a discussion of these various drafts see Klug, Foreword, n. 29 above (2nd edn., 1996).

32. See Interview with Roy Hattersley, 'Hattersley the Radical?', *New Statesman* (26 July 1991).

33. House of Commons *Hansard*, col. 1029 (27 May 1993).

34. See Francesca Klug and John Wadham, 'The Democratic Entrenchment of a Bill of Rights, Liberty's Proposals', *Public Law* (Winter 1993).

35. Unpublished papers of the Policy Commission on Constitutional Reform (17 February 1993).

36. John Smith, Lecture to Charter 88, 'A Citizen's Democracy', London (1 March 1993).

37. This was also the line agreed between the Liberal Democrats and Labour in their Joint Consultative Committee on constitutional reform, which reported prior to the 1997 general election.

38. Other participants included the British Institute of Human Rights, Charter 88, the Constitution Unit, the Human Rights Incorporation Project at King's College, London, IPPR and the Public Law Project. The black human rights group, the 1990 Trust, became involved once its human rights programme was established under the direction of Veena Vasista. A number of these groups are represented on the government's Human Rights Task Force, discussed in Chapter 1.

39. Nicole Smith, *Human Rights Legislation* (Constitution Unit, 1996).

40. 'A New Agenda for Democracy: Labour's Proposals for Constitutional Reform', NEC statement (April, 1993).

41. See Mandelson and Liddle, Chapter 2, n. 7, p. 196.

42. Anthony Barnett addresses this question in *This Time, Our Constitutional Revolution* (Vintage, 1997).

43. See Straw and Boateng, Chapter 2, n. 50.

44. *Rights Brought Home: The Human Rights Bill*, Cmnd. 3782 (Stationery Office, 1997).

45. Jack Straw, Foreword to Wadham and Mountfield, Introduction, n. 34.

46. Section 4. This approach, along with a number of other aspects of the adopted model, was recommended by the Human Rights Incorporation Project, Kings College, London, in Francesca Klug, 'Briefing on Incorporation of the ECHR into UK Law: The "British Model" ', unpublished Home Office briefing (June 1997). See also Francesca Klug, 'A Bill of Rights for the UK: A Comparative Summary', *European Human Rights Law Review* 5 (1997), p. 501; and Andrew Puddephatt, 'Incorporating the European Convention on Human Rights', in Hegarty and Leonard (eds.), Introduction, n. 18, pp. 325–37.

47. Section 10. Where there are no such 'compelling reasons' to rush through legislation parliamentary time will have to be found or a suitable bill in which to insert the proposed amendment.

48. The European Communities Act 1972, which brought the UK into the EU (then the EEC), was the first statute to make the UK subject to the 'higher law' of the EU but its writ runs only where the EU has 'competence'; an expanding, but still limited, area. The Human Rights Act is the first 'higher law' to apply to the whole of UK law.

49. See also Chapter 1.

50. See Spencer and Bynoe, Chapter 1, n. 26. See also Chapter 1.

51. For example, by a Law Lord, Lord Steyn, giving the keynote speech at Liberty's 1999 Human Rights Awards.

52. See Chapter 4.

53. Articles 14 and 26 respectively. See Chapter 4, p. 00.

54. Article 1 requires states to 'secure to everyone within their jurisdiction the rights and freedoms' in the ECHR, and Article 13 provides for the right to 'an effective remedy' for anyone whose Convention rights have been breached.

55. See Starmer, Introduction, n. 34, pp. 11–13; and Klug, Chapter 1, n. 86.

56. See, for example, John Wadham, 'Bringing Rights Half-way Home', *European Human Rights Law Review* 2 (1997), pp. 141–5.

57. For a balanced critique of the Act see Jonathan Cooper, 'The Human Rights Act of 1988: Modernizing the Constitutional Framework for the Protection of Rights', *Amicus Curiae* (1998).

58. See Francesca Klug, 'The Role of a Bill of Rights in a Democratic Constitution', in Anthony Barnett et al. (eds.), *Debating the Constitution: New Perspectives on Constitutional Reform* (Charter 88 and Polity, 1993), pp. 44–54. The 'notwithstanding clause' has been used by the Quebec National Assembly five times and it was largely with the situation in French-speaking Quebec in mind that the clause was included in the Charter. See Aisling Reisling, *The Impact of the Human Rights Act: Lessons from Canada and New Zealand* (Constitution Unit, 1999).

59. See Ewing, Chapter 1, n. 9, pp. 98–9.

60. See Chapter 4. Under the Irish Constitution, in contrast, individuals can sue each other directly for breaches of fundamental rights.

61. Section 6 (1). This applies unless a public authority is mandated to do otherwise by an Act that the courts cannot interpret to comply with the ECHR. See Section 6 (2).

62. Section 6 (3)(b).

63. See Human Rights Unit, *Private Sector, Public Service: Human Rights for All, The Human Rights Act 1998* (Home Office, 2000).

64. Section 6 (3)(a).

65. House of Lords *Hansard*, col. 783 (24 November 1997).

66. See Chapter 1.

67. *Kaye* v. *Robertson* [1991], FSR 62. Kaye was granted relief only on the separate ground of 'malicious falsehood' by the newspaper.

68. See Rabinder Singh, 'Privacy and the Media after the Human Rights Act', *European Human Rights Law Review* 6 (1998).

69. Section 3. The rationale for this is that all legislation is a creature of the state and therefore should be made to comply with the new 'higher law'.

70. See Chapters 1 and 5.

71. Under Section 6 (6). Of concern is the fact that Parliament is excluded from this provision, which means that the failure to legislate to prevent or outlaw breaches of Convention rights is excluded from the terms of the Act.

72. See above and Chapter 1.

73. *R.* v. *Human Fertilization and Embryology Authority ex p. Blood* [1997] 2 WLR 806 (CA).

74. *Brindt* v. *Secretary of State for the Home Department* [1991], All ER 735.

75. See Chapter 5.

76. Section 10.

77. 'Reducing the Risk of Legal Challenge', Cabinet Office circular (1987).

The second circular, issued the same year, was not specifically about the ECHR but about judicial review generally and was titled 'The Judge over your Shoulder'.

78. House of Lords *Hansard*, vol. 583, col. 1163 (27 November 1997).

79. Some of what follows is explained in greater detail in Chapter 1.

80. For example: *Human Rights Comes to Life, The Human Rights Act 1998, Guidance for Departments*; *A New Era of Rights and Responsibilities, Core Guidance for Public Authorities*; and *Putting Rights into Public Service, an Introduction to the Human Rights Act 1998 for Public Authorities*. All of these were published by the Home Office in 1999.

81. See n. 63 above.

82. Northern Ireland Office, *Policy Appraisal and Fair Treatment Guidelines* (Northern Ireland Office, 1993).

83. See Sarah Spencer and Ian Bynoe, *Mainstreaming Human Rights in Whitehall and Westminster* (IPPR, 1999).

84. See Straw, Chapter 1, n. 46.

85. See, for example, Citizen Foundation, *Human Rights Impact* (2000) and human rights material published by the 1990 Trust aimed at the black community.

86. Quoted in John Grace, 'The New Citizens', *Guardian Education* (15 February 2000).

87. *Education for Citizenship and the Teaching of Democracy in Schools* (QCA, 1998). See also Francesca Klug and Sarah Spencer, 'Education for Citizenship, Joint Response to the Interim Report of the Advisory Group on Education for Citizenship' (1998), unpublished IPPR paper.

88. DFEE, *The Review of the National Curriculum in England, The Secretary of State's Proposals* (DFEE, 1999).

89. See Chapter 1.

90. Conversely, it would greatly assist an appreciation of human rights values if governments were to acknowledge when legislation or policy is being amended to comply with the ECHR, rather than disguise it or let it pass unnoticed.

91. This is called the doctrine of 'a margin of appreciation'. See Rabinder Singh, Murray Hunt and Marie Demetriou, 'Is There a Role for the "Margin of Appreciation" in National Law after the Human Rights Act?', *European Human Rights Law Review* 1 (1999), pp. 15–22, on why it is not appropriate for the domestic courts simply to replicate this doctrine here.

92. See Chapter 4.

93. See, for example, *McCann* v. *UK* (1995), 21 EHRR 97; *Osman* v. *UK*, Chapter 1, n. 83.

94. David Feldman, 'The Human Rights Act 1998 and Constitutional Principles', *Legal Studies* 19 (2) (1999), pp. 165–206.

95. Article 6 (2). See *R* v. *DPP ex p. Kebeline*, Chapter 1, n. 45.

96. However, because the Human Rights Act has incorporated Article 16 of the HRA, which allows states to restrict the political rights of 'aliens', the outcome of a challenge on such grounds cannot be predicted.

97. Which reads: 'No one shall be subjected to torture or to inhuman or degrading treatment.' See *Soering* v. *UK*, Chapter 1, n. 42.

98. Immigration and Asylum Bill, Human Rights Compliance (JUSTICE, 1999).

99. See Puddephatt, n. 46 above, p. 335.

100. Obviously this does not apply to human rights lawyers whose pioneering work helped to create the climate that led the Labour government to introduce the Human Rights Act. See also Chapter 1.

101. *Pepper* v. *Hart* [1993], AC 593.

102. See, for example, *Tryer* v. *UK* (1981), 2 EHRR 1; and *Marckx* v. *Belgium* (1979–80), 2 EHRR 330.

103. Murray Hunt, 'The Human Rights Act and Legal Culture: The Judiciary and the Legal Profession', *Journal of Law and Society* 26 (1) (March 1999).

104. *Daily Mail* (17 December 1999).

105. *T.* v. *UK*; Applications no. 24724/94 [1999], para. 97.

106. See Hunt, n. 103 above, p. 89.

107. Ibid., pp. 89–90.

108. Donald W. Shriver, Foreword to Gustafson and Juviler (eds.), Introduction, n. 38, p. xi.

109. See Straw and Boateng, Chapter 2, n. 50. As the Welsh Assembly can make only subordinate legislation this is covered by the same provisions governing subordinate legislation in England; that is, it can be quashed by the courts.

110. See Robertson, Introduction, n. 4.

111. This distinction was proposed in Liberty's *A People's Charter* (see Klug, n. 29 above). Deliberately excluded from judicial entrenchment are rights that are limited on broad, general grounds and which inevitably collide with other ECHR rights like free expression, privacy and assembly.

112. See Chapter 5.

113. Section 28 banned the 'intentional promotion of homosexuality' by local authorities and the promotion of teaching in maintained schools of 'the acceptability of homosexuality as a pretended family relationship'.

114. *Daily Telegraph* (5 February 2000).

115. *Roe* v. *Wade* (1973).

116. See Lord Scarman, n. 4 above.

117. At the time of writing the 'warm-up' for such headlines had already begun. As a taste of things to come the liberal broadsheet the *Observer* headed an article on 13 February 2000 'Rights Act Will Put British Way of Life on Trial'. Five days later the *Daily Telegraph* ran a piece titled 'The Judges – our New Oppressors' on how 'the Human Rights Act will turn the judiciary into unaccountable legislators'. A feature in the *Daily Mail* on 30 March 2000 by Edward Heathcote Amory was headed 'A Euro Law Time Bomb'. It was about the HRA.

118. See Straw, Chapter 1, n. 46. He made the same point in his speech to the Constitution Unit, Church House, London (27 October 1999).

119. See Alun Michael, Helena Kennedy, QC, and Francesca Klug, 'Labour's "Rights and Responsibilities" Debate', *Political Quarterly* 68 (2) (April– June 1997), pp. 153–62.

120. See Chapter 2. The Home Secretary repeated this point in his speech to the Civil Service College in December 1999. See Straw, Chapter 1, n. 46.

121. One of the traditional arguments for a bill of rights, of course, is the need to establish a set of values which are not prey to every populist cause.

122. For example, the Declaration of Human Duties and Responsibilities (1998) and the Universal Declaration of Human Responsibilities (1997). See Chapter 5.

123. See Conclusion for a fuller discussion of this point.

124. See Chapter 2.

125. See Chapter 4.

126. See Straw, Chapter 2, n. 54.

CONCLUSION Human Rights in an Era of Failed Utopias

1. See Chapter 3 for an analysis of how the 1689 Bill of Rights was more concerned with establishing the doctrine of parliamentary sovereignty than individuals' rights.

2. See Chapter 3.

3. *Observer* (13 February 2000); *Daily Telegraph* (18 February 2000).

4. As was made clear by Diane Blood in a letter to the *Guardian* on 15 February 2000. She battled against the Human Fertilization and Embryology Authority for four years before being allowed to become pregnant using her dead husband's sperm. See Chapter 6, n. 73.

5. In breach of Articles 3 and 8 of the ECHR.

6. This was the subject of a government Inquiry, *Lost in Care*, chaired by Sir

Ronald Waterhouse, published by the Stationery Office in February 2000. Although there were criminal prosecutions of some of the worst abusers, the CPS has not proceeded with any charges involving 'malfeasance in public office' (neglect of duty). Had the Human Rights Act been in force, any civil case of negligence brought against the local authorities by the children themselves would have been significantly strengthened. In effect, the onus would have been on the authorities to demonstrate that they had taken sufficient action to protect the 'physical integrity' of the children rather than the children having to prove that the authorities were negligent.

7. See Chapters 1 and 6 in particular.

8. See Chapters 3 and 6.

9. See Chapter 6.

10. *Daily Mail* (30 March 2000).

11. Nick Cohen, 'Don't Leave Justice to the Judges', *New Statesman* (13 December 1999).

12. See Chapters 1 and 6.

13. As we have seen, the model adopted for the devolved assemblies means that they have powers to strike down their own legislation along the lines of the more traditional bill of rights approach. All subordinate legislation, regardless of where it emanates, can also be overturned by the courts under the Human Rights Act 1998. See Introduction and Chapter 6.

14. The squeeze on legal aid for some types of cases ushered in by the same government that has introduced the Human Rights Act mitigates against this increased access to justice.

15. See Chapter 1 for an explanation of this claim.

16. See Chapter 2, generally.

17. The former Marriage Guidance Council. Ed Straw is also the brother of the current Home Secretary.

18. 'Politicians Should Not Tell Us How To Live Our Lives', *Guardian* (8 September 1999).

19. Illustrations of this stance are provided in Chapter 2.

20. Mary Warnock, 'Consoled by Faith, Prodded by Reason', Book Reviews, *Times Higher Educational Supplement* (5 November 1999).

21. These ideas are explained in Chapter 2.

22. Charles Leadbeater, 'Crisis, What Crisis?', *New Statesman* (28 June 1996).

23. These assertions are extensively documented in Chapter 2.

24. Mary Warnock, 'Human Rights and Moral Imperatives', *Independent* (14 June 1999).

25. Stephen Sedley, 'How Laws Discriminate', *London Review of Books* (29 April 1999); although this is not about bills of rights, as such.

26. This depiction of human rights, although increasingly common in rights literature, is not undisputed. See Rolf Kunnermann, 'A Coherent Approach to Human Rights', *Human Rights Quarterly* 17 (1995), p. 339.

27. See Colley, Chapter 1, n. 31.

28. See Morsink, Chapter 4, n. 15, p. 327.

29. See Daes, Chapter 2, n. 17, p. 172. See also 'President's Message', Ford Foundation Annual Report (1998).

30. See Chapter 4.

31. This idea is explained in detail in Chapter 5.

32. For a legal analysis of this distinction see David Feldman, 'The Human Rights Act 1998 and Constitutional Principles', *Legal Studies* 19 (2) (1999). See also Chapters 1 and 6.

33. See Chapter 6.

34. In Articles 10 and 17 of the ECHR. See Chapter 4 for more explicit references to individual responsibilities in other human rights instruments.

35. This point is expanded upon in Chapter 6.

36. See International Council on Human Rights Policy, Chapter 4, n. 70.

37. For further clarification of this doctrine see Chapters 1 and 4.

38. See *Platform Artze für das Leben* v. *Austria*, Chapter 5, n. 19.

39. See *A.* v. *UK*, Chapter 4, n. 101.

40. The Preamble to the UN's International Covenant on Civil and Political rights, for example, includes the following exhortation: 'Realizing that the individual, having duties to other individuals and to the community to which he belongs, is under a responsibility to strive for the promotion and observance of the rights recognized in the present Covenant . . .' See Chapters 4 and 6.

41. As famously expressed by the European Court of Human Rights in *Handyside* v. *UK*, see Chapter 1, n. 37.

42. See, for example, S. Bailey (ed.), *Human Rights and Responsibilities in Britain and Ireland: A Christian Perspective* (Macmillan, 1998).

43. A. C. Grayling, 'Don't Leave Morals to the Madmen', *Guardian* (22 March 2000).

44. See Chapter 3.

45. Peter Hain, 'Meet Blair, the Libertarian Socialist', *New Statesman* (12 March 1999).

46. See Mulgan, Chapter 2, n. 31.

47. One of the principles of international human rights thinking is that they can be claimed by all individuals within a given jurisdiction, regardless of their citizenship status.

48. Peter Kellner, 'A New "ism" for Our Times', *New Statesman* (22 May 1998).

49. Tony Blair, Speech at Labour Party Conference, Bournemouth (September 1999). See also Mathew Taylor and Jim Godfrey (eds.), *Forces of Conservatism* (IPPR, 1999).

50. See Chapter 3.

51. See Chapter 6 in particular.

52. See Gerwith, Chapter 5, n. 60, pp. 97–8.

53. Ibid.

54. Ibid., p. 98.

55. See Chapter 6.

56. See Richard Burchill et al. (eds.), *Economic, Social and Cultural Rights: Their Implementation in the United Kingdom Law* (University of Nottingham Human Rights Law Centre, 1999).

57. Ibid., Chapter 4.

58. Under the Housing Act 1996 Part VII, for the homeless in priority need.

59. For example, in the 'Social Chapter' Protocol to the Maastricht Treaty, 1992, which is now incorporated into the Amsterdam Treaty, 1997 Title XI.

60. Article 2 of the UN's International Covenant on Economic, Social and Cultural Rights (ICESCR), for example, requires each 'State Party' to 'undertake to take steps . . . to the maximum of its available resources with a view to achieving progressively the full realization of the rights' in the Covenant. See Chapter 4.

61. This can include an indirect route to social and economic rights through internationally recognized civil and political rights like rights to life, to respect for 'home' and to welfare benefits as property rights in the ECHR, Articles 2 (1), 8 (1) and Protocol One, Article 1, respectively. See Starmer, Introduction, n. 34, Chapters 14, pp. 22–3; and see also Chapter 28 on workplace rights under the ECHR.

62. See Kevin Boyle, 'Stock-Taking on Human Rights: The World Conference on Human Rights, Vienna 1993', in David Beetham (ed.), *Politics and Human Rights* (Blackwell, 1995).

63. This relates to a number of the criticisms hurled at rights by communitarians and others discussed above but is more specifically about collective rights, as such.

64. See Michael Freeman, 'Are There Collective Human Rights?', in Beetham (ed.), n. 62 above, pp. 25–40.

65. Exceptions to this broad approach include 'the right to self-determination' in the two UN International Covenants (Article 1), which is an entitlement belonging to 'all peoples' and has to be understood in the context of colonialism, which was still extensive at the time the Covenants were drafted; a section on 'peoples' rights' in the African Charter on Human Rights covering similar grounds; and Article 25 of the UN's ICESCR, which recognizes the rights of 'peoples' to enjoy 'their natural wealth and resources'. However, even the reference to 'minority rights' in Article 27 of the UN's ICCPR is phrased so that 'persons belonging to such minorities' are the recipients of this protection. See Patrick Thornberry, *International Law and the Rights of Minorities* (Clarendon Press, 1991), pp. 173–7.

66. See *Dudgeon* v. *UK*, Chapter 4, n. 138. The decriminalization covered homosexual acts between consenting gay adult men in private.

67. Section 7 (7).

68. In Canada, for example, laws restricting tobacco advertising have been overturned by the Supreme Court in *RJR MacDonald Inc.* v. *Canada* [1995], 3 SCR 199.

69. See Freeman, n. 64 above, p. 39.

70. See Chapter 2.

71. UDHR Article 29. See Chapter 4 for a fuller discussion of this Article and its consequences.

72. See Chapter 5, generally.

73. For a discussion of these issues see, for example, Hilary Charlesworth, 'Worlds Apart: Public/Private Distinctions in International Law', in Margaret Thornton (ed.), *Public and Private: Feminist Legal Debate* (Oxford University Press, 1995); Rebecca Cook, *Human Rights of Women, National and International Perspectives* (University of Pennsylvania Press, 1994); and Elizabeth Fraser and Nicola Lacey, *The Politics of Community: A Feminist Critique of the Liberal-Communitarian Debate* (Harvester Wheatsheaf, 1993).

74. See *A.* v. *UK*, Chapter 4, n. 101.

75. *SW & CR* v. *UK* [1995], 21 EHRR 363 para. 44.

76. See Doris E. Buss, 'Women at the Borders: Rape and Nationalism in International Law', *Feminist Legal Studies* VI, no. 2 (1998).

77. See Boyle, n. 62 above, p. 81.

78. For fuller treatment of these issues see Brems, Introduction, n. 38.

79. 'Beijing Declaration and Platform for Action', Fourth UN World Conference on Women (1995). See also Brems, Introduction, n. 38, p. 153.

80. Quoted in Clapham, Chapter 5, n. 24, p. 23.

81. See Bauer and Bell (eds.), Introduction, n. 38, p. 12. See also, for further discussion about the claims of the UDHR to universality, Chapter 4.

82. Ken Booth, 'Three Tyrannies', in Dunne and Wheeler (eds.), Introduction, n. 28, p. 58.

83. Bhikhu Parekh, 'Non-ethnocentric Universalism', in Dunne and Wheeler (eds.), Introduction, n. 28, pp. 139 and 154.

84. See Chapter 6.

85. See Chapter 4.

86. See Bhikhu Parekh, 'Group Libel and Freedom of Expression: Thoughts on the Rushdie Affair' in Sandra Coliver (ed.), *Striking a Balance, Hate Speech, Freedom of Expression and Non-discrimination* (Article 19, 1992), p. 358.

87. This distinction between types of rights in international human rights law is explained in Chapters 4 and 6.

88. See Chapter 3.

89. This semi-Kantian concept is strongly supported by the writer David Selbourne (see Introduction, n. 37) and a number of other commentators. See Chapter 2.

90. This argument is expanded upon in Chapter 6.

91. For an overview of these different theories see 'Human Rights and the Fifty Years' Crisis', in Dunne and Wheeler (eds.), Introduction, n. 28, p. 5.

92. The social commentator Polly Toynbee has recently argued more or less the opposite view-point when she wrote: 'Even if we don't like to admit it, we are all missionaries and believers that our own way is best when it comes to the things that really matter ... Our culture is the culture of universal human rights and there is no compromise possible.' 'The West Really is the Best', *Observer* (5 March 2000).

93. Following the recent elections in Iran, for example, there is evidence of an emerging Iranian democracy that respects human rights, drawing on values that are Islamic and Iranian as well as international human rights norms.

Index